EXPERIENCING ALICE COOPER

The Listener's Companion
Kenneth LaFave, Series Editor

Titles in **The Listener's Companion** provide readers with a deeper understanding of key musical genres and the work of major artists and composers. Aimed at nonspecialists, each volume explains in clear and accessible language how to *listen* to works from particular artists, composers, and genres. Looking at both the context in which the music first appeared and has since been heard, authors explore with readers the environments in which key musical works were written and performed.

EXPERIENCING ALICE COOPER

A Listener's Companion

Ian Chapman

ROWMAN & LITTLEFIELD
Lanham • Boulder • New York • London

Published by Rowman & Littlefield
An imprint of The Rowman & Littlefield Publishing Group, Inc.
4501 Forbes Boulevard, Suite 200, Lanham, Maryland 20706
www.rowman.com

Unit A, Whitacre Mews, 26-34 Stannary Street, London SE11 4AB

British Library Cataloguing in Publication Information Available

Library of Congress Cataloging-in-Publication Data

Names: Chapman, Ian, 1960– author.
Title: Experiencing Alice Cooper : a listener's companion / Ian Chapman.
Description: Lanham : Rowman & Littlefield, [2018] | Series: Listener's companion | Includes bibliographical references and index.
Identifiers: LCCN 2017043902 (print) | LCCN 2017044478 (ebook) | ISBN 9781442257719 (electronic) | ISBN 9781442257702 (cloth : alk. paper)
Subjects: LCSH: Cooper, Alice, 1948– —Criticism and interpretation. | Rock music—United States—History and criticism.
Classification: LCC ML420.C67 (ebook) | LCC ML420.C67 C53 2018 (print) | DDC 782.42166092—dc23 LC record available at https://lccn.loc.gov/2017043902

For Ben, Mia, and Arlo

CONTENTS

SERIES EDITOR'S FOREWORD

The goal of the Listener's Companion series is to give readers a deeper understanding of pivotal musical genres and the creative work of its iconic composers and performers. This is accomplished in an inclusive manner that does not require extensive musical training or elitist shoulder rubbing. Authors of the series place the reader in specific listening experiences in which the music is examined in its historical context with regard to both compositional and societal parameters. By positioning the reader in the real or supposed environment of the music's creation, the author provides for a deeper enjoyment and appreciation of the art form. Series authors, often drawing on their own expertise as both performers and scholars, deliver to readers a broad understanding of major musical genres and the achievements of artists within those genres as lived listening experiences.

Among the great traditions of Western art is the assault on tradition. As Ian Chapman demonstrates in his energetic look at the music and career of the godfather of shock rock, Alice Cooper led an assault so successful that the brand has become a tradition itself. Chapman takes us from the origins of Alice-Cooper-the-band in the late 1960s, to the emergence of singer Vincent Furnier as Alice-Cooper-the-solo-project. The musical origins of both, as Chapman puts it, amounted to "a musical love child of Frank Zappa and Syd Barrett . . . with a sprinkling of Beatles thrown in. Or, one could simply employ the word *bizarre*."

That last word does not so much apply to Alice Cooper's music, which is more melodic than one might guess from marketing impressions, but to a striking, horror-show theatricality in the music's presentation. This posed a special challenge for Chapman: Alice Cooper's theatrics are as vital as the music to the totality of his art. How to include them in a book that focuses on the track-by-track musical experience of every recording? Chapman does this by discussing the theatrics alongside the music, relating one to the other. The author also writes of seeing Alice in concert, and the impact the encounter had on him.

Chapman rightly places Alice Cooper in the tradition of "Grand Guignol," a phrase that has come down to us meaning, roughly, a graphic horror show—but one with the subterranean purpose of criticizing the very culture that would permit such a thing. The Theater of the Grand Guignol was an actual venue in the sordid Pigalle neighborhood of Paris from 1897 to 1962. "Guignol" was the name of a traditional French puppet character whose adventures were intended to parody the political figures of the day. As a latter-day Grand Guignol, Alice Cooper skewered the political foibles of a more complicated time.

Each chapter in this book is prefaced by press quotes appropriate to the period discussed. This provides an unfolding context that traces the cultural history of which Alice Cooper has been a part. Alice Cooper entered the world of music at precisely the moment when everything changed. Despite the historical looking-over-the-shoulder while the decade of the 1950s gave birth to rock 'n' roll, it was not until the 1960s, and really not until after the Beatles' historic *Ed Sullivan Show* appearance in February 1964, that rock came into its own as a cultural powerhouse. As late as 1960, the best-selling album of the year was not a rock album at all, but a Broadway cast recording: *Camelot*. But that changed at the speed of light after 1964. The years from about 1966 to 1970 were key. That period saw the maturation of the first wave of the British invasion—the Beatles, the Rolling Stones, the Who—and the emergence of new, seminal bands such as Led Zeppelin, Pink Floyd, the Doors, and the Grateful Dead. Each had its own unique profile and sociopolitical perspective. Alice Cooper arrived almost as the fulfillment of an unstated need for social satire in which Eros and death, wrapped in a carnival atmosphere that mirrored the mainstream of war, greed, and mindless sex, looked at society "through a glass, darkly." That Alice Cooper continues to thrive today is, in some way, a tragic reminder that nothing much has really changed.

Alice Cooper helped define a musical age that lasted essentially for his entire adult life. From a radical youth in the late 1960s to a golf-loving Christian half a century later, his music and its message have stayed more or less the same. Chapman notes the fluctuations of style, the modifications of attitude, the shift of focus here and there. But the overall progress of the music from decade to decade was always in the same direction: that of cultural criticism by way of cultural appropriation. Paraphrasing a 1990s critic quoted by Chapman, Alice Cooper grew gray and old, but at least he did so disgracefully.

Kenneth LaFave

ACKNOWLEDGMENTS

To the Coop: I've been a fan since the early seventies when I totally wore out my copies of *Schools Out* and *Welcome to My Nightmare.* You and the Alice Cooper band cared not for convention and instead wrote your own rock 'n' roll rulebook. In the process you provided for an international legion of misfit kids a permission-to-be-different lifeline, and we've all been much the better for it. Thank you.

Thanks to Lisa Marr for her assistance with compiling the index, and to the Department of Music, Theatre and Performing Arts at the University of Otago for funding Lisa's involvement. Special thanks to the sparkly Elsa May for helping me through the hard times and enhancing the good times.

INTRODUCTION

Alice Cooper, born Vincent Furnier and known affectionately as "the Coop" among his legions of fans located all over the globe, is a one-off performer, a mold-breaker, an innovator, and a rock 'n' roll pioneer. He's also an enigma in that he is not only a rock star like no other, but also a fanatical (and talented) golfer and, in more recent decades, a proud and committed Christian, philanthropist, tireless youth worker, and very popular radio host with his own internationally syndicated radio show, *Nights with Alice Cooper*. Once the villain extraordinaire of rock music, feared by parents across the world as they muttered under their breath about the subversion of the nation's youth while confiscating their son's or daughter's black mascara and hiding the family's pet snake, now Alice Cooper is a revered elder statesman of rock, with longevity and continued popularity equal to only a handful of other performers.

Prior to his controversial emergence in the late 1960s and subsequent elevation to unlikely and unprecedented stardom in the early 1970s, rock 'n' roll had seen nothing like him. Or, more accurately, like *them*, because at this stage Alice Cooper was a band consisting of five musicians and not just a single performer, even though, confusingly at times, he alone bore the name within the group as well. During the 1970s "glam rock" era (known as "glitter rock" in the United States), erroneous comparisons were often made to the United Kingdom's most outrageous performer, David Bowie, while KISS famously modeled themselves on the notion that if one Alice Cooper was bringing such success for its architect, what could a team of four similarly attired Alice Cooper semi-clones accomplish? In later years Marilyn Manson was deemed by some to have taken up the Cooper shock rock mantle. But none of these comparisons really work because of Cooper's inherent uniqueness. David Bowie, while clearly a superbly theatrical performer in his own right, was cut from a very different performative cloth than Cooper. Whereas Cooper's theatricality can be seen as a rock 'n' roll bastardization of vaudeville and Grand Guignol (the Parisian theater of horror), run through with the pop cultural influence of trash TV, movies, and comics, Bowie was a mashup of Brecht and Warhol mixed with music hall and cabaret.[1] KISS certainly invested in a similarly nightmare-inspired look—most especially in the form of the world's most famous tongue-waggling fire-breather, Gene Simmons—and a similarly evident and admirable sweat-for-our-audience ethos. But, frankly, the quality of their music seldom touched the heights of Cooper's. And as for Marilyn Manson, certainly he had the shock factor going on, but try to find any trace of Cooper's famous endearing humour and knowing wink, and one is left totally bereft. Cooper's awareness of the absurdity of what he was doing then—and today, and his sheer exuberant enjoyment in doing so, sets him apart from his contemporaries. As far back as 1978, on America's iconic *The Muppet Show*, Sam the Eagle, who represented hand-on-heart America and was often pictured in front of the stars and stripes and charged with upholding the values and morals of the nation, confronted Alice Cooper in his dressing room, charging the rock star thus: "Mr. Cooper, let me come right to the point. You, sir, are a demented, sick, degenerate, barbaric, naughty, freako!" To this obvious affront, Alice simply smiled and replied, "Why, thank you!"

Other evidence of his self-awareness abounds in interviews and self-penned critiques of his own work, as Cooper is a highly intelligent and well-learned artist, able to articulate with ease his motivations and performative methodologies alike. For instance, when reminiscing about the cover of his best-selling album ever, *Billion Dollar Babies*, which was recorded with the Alice Cooper group prior to his becoming a solo act:

> That was us making total fun of ourselves. We're billion dollar babies, a bunch of "babies" from Phoenix that large multinational corporations (starting with our record company) were now throwing money at. The same guys who couldn't get a gig because we were too

weird . . . and now everybody wanted a piece of us. The cover was fashioned as a giant wallet with cash strewn, and babies with eye makeup. We were laughing at our audience and at ourselves and at the circus spectacle and absurdity of our success.[2]

Yes, Alice Cooper, the knowing, lovable archvillain of rock, is unique. The archvillain component of his act is a vital one, and a very large part of the reason why he has been both revered and reviled for five decades. In his own words,

The good thing about Alice being a villain is he shows the audience the evil in the world, then he gets executed. Evil never wins in my show, even though I'm the one who gets nailed in the end. Like in this show, I get my head cut off, and I get put into a giant vice . . . they have to kill me twice this time. I think it's a morality play. No matter what Alice does up there, he always ends up paying for it. I think it's kind of a classical Shakespearean bad guy/good guy thing. I think I need to be the villain; I'm so good at being the villain that in the end—when Alice comes out at the very end, after they execute me—he always comes out in a white top-hat and tails. And it's balloons, and confetti, and everything's okay. I never leave the audience with a bad taste in their mouth. I always want them to leave saying, "Man, that was the greatest party I was ever at." They have confetti in their hair, and streamers . . . it's like, "Were you just at a New Year's party?" "No, I was at an Alice concert!" Whereas I think a lot of bands forget to do that. It's a show, and it's fun, and my stuff is totally choreographed.[3]

New Zealanders, aka Kiwis, are a pretty laid-back bunch of people. Some say we are a little reserved or undemonstrative, and others might use the term laconic. It's fair to generalize and say that Kiwi kids and teenagers exist on an even keel for the most part. So how was it that, as a seventeen-year-old boy in 1977, Alice Cooper had me hollering at the top of my lungs to witness his bloody execution as I stood shoulder to shoulder with thousands of my similarly baying countrymen and women and watched him performing his unique brand of theatrical rock 'n' roll live onstage at Auckland's Western Springs Stadium? Actually, we were doing much more than watching him; we were part of the show—part of the unique rock experience of *Welcome to My Nightmare*. We weren't observing Alice's nightmare; we were *in* it with him. Alice Cooper is an inclusive performer who welcomes his fans in, never excluding them. That's just one of his qualities.

Just what *is* Alice Cooper? In an industry that strives to always categorize artists, there are few more difficult subjects to align to a single descriptor than Alice Cooper. As he himself asks, "Am I Classic Rock? Progressive Rock? Heavy metal? I don't know."[4] Delving through the multitude of reviews that have accumulated over the years, in addition to those terms that Cooper mentions, one will inevitably come across a myriad of others including glam rock, garage rock, acid rock, freak rock, punk rock, theater rock, glitter rock, shock rock, hard rock, arena rock, visual rock, and art rock. In all likelihood, all of these attempts at categorization are true to a lesser or greater extent. Simply, it is a rather pointless exercise to try to come up with a single hold-all descriptor, and I have therefore refrained from doing so. Nevertheless, Cooper remains a preeminent template for the successful blending of rock music and theater; one that many have attempted to emulate, but with very few achieving anything like as much success. Alice Cooper is the ultimate showman. Perhaps not the first to bring a top hat and cane to the rock stage (Screaming Lord Sutch, anyone?), he is most definitely the one who made it fit.

What did it mean to be an Alice Cooper fan back in the early 1970s when the band came to international attention? Well, if you went to a party with any one of the albums *Love It to Death, Killer, School's Out, Billion Dollar Babies,* or *Muscle of Love* under your arm, you were making a big statement about yourself without even having to open your mouth. It meant that you saw right through the whitewashed facade of polite everyday society, and could instead see both the beauty and the ugliness of modern living. Why deny society's ugly underbelly? Wasn't the Vietnam War still happening? Sexism, racism, religious tension, horrors of multiple manifestations—were they not part of modern living too? Life wasn't all pretty and fair, especially for those who felt disenfranchised, alienated, marginalized or in some other way made "other" for any one—or more—of a plethora of reasons. Much like David Bowie in the United Kingdom around the same time, Alice Cooper was a rallying point for the disaffected. Carrying that Alice Cooper album under your arm told people that you were not a clone; that you were smart and couldn't be fooled easily. Maybe you were shy and felt inadequate or awkward during social occasions? If so, that Alice

Cooper album introduced you to others without you even having to open your mouth. You were rebelling, but it wasn't the mindless every-one-in-the-pool kind of standard off-the-shelf youth rebellion based solely upon generational difference. Alice Cooper–style rebellion went deeper. It was a taking-the-scab-off-the-wound kind of exposure of societal hypocrisy. No wonder the Alice Cooper band was hated by those with much to lose and celebrated by those with everything to gain.

It is highly unlikely that any rock band or artist could achieve through music today what the likes of Alice Cooper did back in their/his heyday. In the early 1970s, as it had been in the preceding decade, rock music was *the* form of youth expression. Today there are the multiple distractions and options offered by the Internet; gaming, for one, and therefore no single rallying point exists any more. There's no flag-bearer behind whom columns of like-minded individuals might rally. Alice Cooper remains one of those rare figures, and a lot of fans owe him a debt of gratitude for that. In addition, and unlike most artists from that era whose flames waned, flickered, and then died as the years passed, through careful musical reinvention and the reflection through his art of his own journey through life—something so many fans continue to identify with—Alice Cooper has maintained his high-profile presence at the forefront of rock 'n' roll, achieving what one might term godfather status. The band's induction into the Rock & Roll Hall of Fame in 2011 is deserved proof of that.

This book is not a biography. Dave Thompson's *Alice Cooper: Welcome to My Nightmare* fills that slot admirably, while Cooper's own autobiographical *Alice Cooper: Golf Monster* offers fans the most personal of insights into the man behind the makeup. Instead, this book considers the music of Alice Cooper—both the band and the solo artist—from the perspective of a fan. As is the case in the best fan experiences, in Alice Cooper I found a champion for my own wants, needs, desires, emotions, morals, dreams, fears, and tribulations. Alice Cooper helped me make sense of my world and establish for myself a place in it, at a time when I was struggling to do so through what one might term commonly available and more acceptable (in a societal sense) means. If there is one thing this book attempts more than anything else, it is to try to understand how that was possible. In this, though, there lies an obvious problem in that so much of the appeal of Alice Cooper lies in non-musical factors. The visual aspects of Cooper's performance methodology are of great importance, and this factor goes hand in hand with the celebrated theatricality with which the artist delivered his message in the live concert situation, a setting that was, in many ways, the most complete and ideal means for such an interdisciplinary artist to communicate with his audience. Nevertheless, first and foremost, Alice Cooper—both group and solo artist—are musicians. Without music, they would not have existed in the first place. Thus, it is the studio-recorded music that remains the focus of the book, especially apt given that it is part of a listener's guide series. All twenty-seven studio albums that have been released to date are considered in chronological order, while live albums, compilations, and other releases are omitted. Each and every song released on these studio albums is considered individually— the hits, the (relatively rare) misses, and the many hidden gems; however, bonus tracks are excluded.

Members of the original Alice Cooper group, Michael Bruce and Dennis Dunaway, to date have written their own memoirs and, in the process, filled in much detail on the genesis of the band and its recordings, a formative period that saw the five young men from Detroit go from rags to riches in a tumultuous time that remains for many fans their favorite Cooper era. Both memoirs are must-haves for anyone wanting to gain a fuller picture of what transpired in the early days. That said, the views of Cooper, Bruce, and Dunaway don't always gel with each other when it comes to recalling certain events, times, and other details that are susceptible to individual points of view. Certainly, the point in the story where Alice Cooper ceased being a band and became a solo artist is, er, somewhat fluid, to say the least. Such differing views are part and parcel of any such retrospective endeavor involving multiple individuals. Still, these works bring to light different and very important aspects of the story. Just two examples: Bruce sheds light on the song-writing process(es) within the band, most particularly in terms of the collaborations between himself and Alice, while Dunaway speaks with wonderful firsthand insight into the theatrical development of the band and the growing investment in the visual aspects of performance.[5] Accordingly, all of these books in combination tell the real story.

There are several websites managed by avid fans that do a magnificent job in collating historical material, and in this regard special mention must be made of alicecooperechive.com; the best of the lot, and a site I visited frequently during the writing of this book in order to locate rare press reviews, interviews, and more. Then there is the rather wonderful sickthingsuk.co.uk. And, of course, one should also pay a visit to ground control, Alice's own excellent website, alicecooper.com.

For me, one of the highlights of the writing of this book has been discovering recorded gems that had previously somehow passed me by. Like many other fans of acts that have achieved significant longevity, there are periods within their overall output that one appreciates or relates to more than others. By undertaking the methodical, chronological critique of Cooper's albums as required for the task at hand, I discovered some works that did not garner my attention as much as they should have at the time of their release, so experiencing them once again many years later has been a real pleasure. I never stopped being a fan, and in preparing these pages I have come to understand why Alice Cooper meant so much to me as a youth, and how it is that I still hold him in such high regard. How music speaks to us is a personal and subjective form of communication, and at times my analysis might well miss the mark for some listeners. With that caveat put on the table from the outset, I sincerely hope that readers and co-Coop fans will find commonalities and kindred thoughts within these pages.

TIMELINE

February 4, 1948	Vincent Damon Furnier born in Detroit, Michigan.
March 1964	Formation of the Earwigs—the first incarnation of what would become the Alice Cooper band—at Cortez High School, Phoenix.
September 1965	The Earwigs change their name to the Spiders and release their debut single—cover versions of "Why Don't You Love Me"/"Hitch Hike."
June/July 1966	The Spiders release the single "Don't Blow Your Mind"/"No Price Tag," both songs written by the band.
Early 1967	The Spiders rename themselves the Nazz and begin playing in Los Angeles.
Mid 1967	Release of the single "Wonder Who's Loving Her Now"/"Lay Down and Die, Goodbye"; the latter track would later appear on

	the Alice Cooper band's second album, *Easy Action*.
March 1968	The Nazz rename themselves Alice Cooper.
June 30, 1969	Debut studio album *Pretties for You* is released.
March 27, 1970	Second studio album *Easy Action* is released.
November 1970	Breakthrough single "I'm Eighteen" is released, reaching #21 on the Billboard Hot 100 chart.
March 8, 1971	Third studio album *Love It to Death* is released and reaches #35 on the Billboard album chart, marking the beginning of the band's halcyon period.
November 27, 1971	Fourth studio album *Killer* is released.
April 26, 1972	"School's Out" single is released and reaches #1 in the United Kingdom and #7 in the United States, as well as charting in numerous other locations around the world.
June 13, 1972	Fifth studio album *School's Out* is released, its success establishing the band as one of the world's top-ranking rock acts.
February 25, 1973	Sixth studio album *Billion Dollar Babies* is released and tops both the UK and US album charts, becoming the most successful Alice Cooper release ever.

November 20, 1973	Seventh studio album *Muscle of Love* is released, failing to match the success of its immediate predecessors.
1974	Band tensions, disappointments and disillusionment come to a head, with talk of band members going their own way. While the group did not officially disband, Alice recorded his own solo album, *Welcome to My Nightmare*.
March 11, 1975	Eighth studio album, and Alice's first solo album, *Welcome to My Nightmare* is released and extensively toured internationally.
June 25, 1976	Ninth studio album *Alice Cooper Goes to Hell* is released.
April 29, 1977	Tenth studio album *Lace and Whiskey* is released.
October 1977	Alice is admitted to Cornell Medical Center, New York, for treatment for alcoholism.
November 17, 1978	Eleventh studio album *From the Inside* is released
April 28, 1980	Twelfth studio album *Flush the Fashion* is released.
September 1981	Thirteenth studio album *Special Forces* is released.
August 25, 1982	Fourteenth studio album *Zipper Catches Skin* is released.
September 28, 1983	Fifteenth studio album *DaDa* is released.
September 22, 1986	Sixteenth studio album *Constrictor* is released.

September 28, 1987	Seventeenth studio album *Raise Your Fist and Yell* is released.
July 7, 1989	"Poison" single is released and emphatically restores Alice Cooper's fortunes, reaching #2 in the United Kingdom and #7 in the United States.
July 25, 1989	Cooper's most successful album in many years, eighteenth studio album *Trash* is released, reaching #2 on the UK album chart and #20 on the US chart.
July 2, 1991	Nineteenth studio album *Hey Stoopid* is released.
July 12, 1994	Twentieth studio album *The Last Temptation* is released.
October 19, 1997	Original band member Glen Buxton (born November 10, 1947) passes away.
June 6, 2000	Twenty-first studio album *Brutal Planet* is released
September 18, 2001	Twenty-second studio album *Dragontown* is released.
September 23, 2003	Twenty-third studio album *The Eyes of Alice Cooper* is released.
July 4, 2005	Twenty-fourth studio album *Dirty Diamonds* is released.
July 29, 2008	Twenty-fifth studio album *Along Came a Spider* is released.
September 13, 2011	Twenty-sixth studio album *Welcome 2 My Nightmare* is released.
May 14, 2017	Alice Cooper is joined onstage by the surviving members of the

original Alice Cooper band—
Michael Bruce, Dennis Dunaway,
and Neal Smith—in a reunion
cameo performance of five songs
during his show at the Tennessee
Performing Arts Center,
Nashville.

July 28, 2017   Twenty-seventh studio album
Paranormal is released, featuring
original band members Michael
Bruce, Dennis Dunaway, and
Neal Smith.

1

NEW FREAKS ON THE BLOCK

Pretties for You and *Easy Action*, 1969 and 1970

PRETTIES FOR YOU, 1969 [US CHART #193, UK —]

Alice Cooper is a West Coast Zappa-sponsored group: two guitars, bass, drums and a vocalist who doubles on harmonica. Echoes of 1967 psychedelia in the oscillators and distorted guitars. Showing here the influence of the Mothers, here the first-wave San Francisco sound, there and almost everywhere the Beatles. But their overall texture and the flow of randomly-selected runs interspersed by electronic gimmicks place them closer to a certain rivulet in that deluge of pre-packaged groups which can be defined as marginal acid rock. . . . Everything falls where it should, there are none of the gross, ugly, idiotic juxtapositions of the totally incongruous found in much other studio-assembled art-rock. But neither is there any hint of life, spontaneity, joy, rage, or any kind of authentic passion or conviction. As such, Alice Cooper's music is, for this reviewer at any rate, totally dispensable.—Lester Bangs, *Rolling Stone*, July 1969

We identified with Frank. We were of course influenced—when everybody hears Zappa, they're influenced by him, just like The Beatles. But we were more affected by him than influenced. . . . You can't get the visual thing on the record as much as you'd like to. We produced this album, and we'd never done that before, except when we produced singles for ourselves. What happened was Frank wanted to produce us, and with Frank we didn't get the same feeling.

He didn't get the feeling that we wanted—nothing on him, but he wasn't on the same trip.—Alice Cooper, interview with Mike Quigley, *Poppin*, September 1969

Side One

1. Titanic Overture (Bruce/Buxton/Cooper/Dunaway/Smith)
2. 10 Minutes before the Worm (Bruce/Buxton/Cooper/Dunaway/Smith)
3. Sing Low, Sweet Cheerio (Bruce/Buxton/Cooper/Dunaway/Smith)
4. Today Mueller (Bruce/Buxton/Cooper/Dunaway/Smith)
5. Living (Bruce/Buxton/Cooper/Dunaway/Smith)
6. Fields of Regret (Bruce/Buxton/Cooper/Dunaway/Smith)

Side Two

1. No Longer Umpire (Bruce/Buxton/Cooper/Dunaway/Smith)
2. Levity Ball (Live at the Cheetah) (Bruce/Buxton/Cooper/Dunaway/Smith)
3. B.B. on Mars (Bruce/Buxton/Cooper/Dunaway/Smith)
4. Reflected (Bruce/Buxton/Cooper/Dunaway/Smith)
5. Apple Bush (Bruce/Buxton/Cooper/Dunaway/Smith)
6. Earwigs to Eternity (Bruce/Buxton/Cooper/Dunaway/Smith)
7. Changing Arranging (Bruce/Buxton/Cooper/Dunaway/Smith)

Avant-garde is the simplest and most accurate description of the Alice Cooper band's first offering. Or, perhaps avant-garde with psychedelic overtones might get one closer to an adequate description of an album that actively defies being described in any common terms. Something about being the musical love child of Frank Zappa and Syd Barrett might also work, with a sprinkling of Beatles thrown in. Or, one could simply employ the word *bizarre*. And, in an admirable marriage of musical content to album cover art (or sound and vision), the inherent bizarreness of *Pretties for You* begins even before a note of music has been heard; indeed, it starts the moment one lays eyes on the cover. A friend of Zappa's, artist Edward Beardsley, created the work, which had been purchased by Zappa with the intention of using it for the Cooper album cover, the band having recently been signed to his ironically titled Straight record label. The painting, already titled *Pretties for You* at the time of its purchase, features a mustachioed middle-aged man, well dressed in a black suit with matching brimmed hat, starched white shirt, and striped tie, clutching a mug of beer. His eyes stare pointedly to the left, where a much younger brunette woman stands looking at him while lifting the front of her bright blue dress provocatively to expose her thighs and starched white underwear. On a picnic table behind the man sits a cake with strawberries, and behind this, in the center of the image, is a kind of tent with two vacant chairs set out at its rear. Completing the picture at the viewer's top left is a row of four sleek black automobiles arranged in what appears to be a funeral procession, the lead car resembling a hearse. It is a disturbing image, hard to fathom, but highly disquieting.

With the considerable luxury of almost fifty years of hindsight, there's a great deal to be gleaned from re-experiencing the one-minute-and-nine-second entirety of the first track of the very first Alice Cooper album. If the song's grandiose title, "Titanic Overture," implies that the listener is about to hear the opening orchestral salvo of a Wagnerian-weight opera, then that's not far from the truth. But this virtual "Ta Dah: Ladies and Gentlemen, the Alice Cooper Band Has Arrived!" statement comes laced with more than one Cooper-esque twist. Lesson one: expect the unexpected. The first sounds foisted upon an unsuspecting public are not those of a hard rock band at all, but instead consists of a swirling, seething mass of synthesizers and strings. After a three-note ascending fanfare ushers in the track—below which the harmonic accompaniment descends, creating contrary motion between the parts and thereby providing an eons-old classical gravitas that Bach himself would have applauded—a sweeping, monolithic, unchanging chordal landscape quickly establishes itself, dense, brooding, and dark. The electric guitars, bass, and drums of rock are nowhere to be heard, and neither is there any hint of vocals. After this austere beginning, an organ melody enters the fray, and with it the first knowing wink, or elbow in the ribs, of the yet-to-be-established Cooper modus operandi. The organ borrows note for note the melody from the opening line of "Goin' Out of My Head," Teddy Randazzo and Bobby Weinstein's 1964 hit, later to be covered by a multitude of other performers including Gladys Knight & the Pips, Ella Fitzgerald, Shirley Bassey, Frank Sinatra, and Dionne Warwick, to name but a few. The employment of this melody, instantly bringing to the listener's mind the lyrics of this well-known song, can be seen as a musical joke—the Cooper freaks implying they are literally going out of their anti-establishment heads. The purloined melody is repeated a second time before a series of variations on the theme begins. At thirty-six seconds, the borrowed melody repeats twice more before a recapitulation of the variations. Then at the one-minute, four-second mark, what has thus far appeared to be a song's introduction gives way to two declamatory piano chords that usher in a new melody, and what the listener assumes to be the main body of the song about to unfold. The dense mix of strings and synths drops away, enhancing this notion of the conclusion to an opening and of a journey about to begin. But then, inexplicably, before the new melody can begin to establish itself, *everything* quickly fades away to nothingness. The opening track is over. That was it, folks. Ladies and gentlemen: welcome to the world of Alice Cooper.

Cooper biographer Dave Thompson describes "Titanic Overture" as "infuriatingly unfinished." He's correct, but in this all-too-brief Cooper debut fans have nevertheless been privy to a wonderful glimpse into what would become established over time as the Cooper bag of tricks: humor, shades of light and dark, and the unexpected. Simply, in the first track of this debut album, the blueprint has been laid out for all to see, right from the word go. Stylistically, it is a crudely perfect beginning and a telling portent of things to come.

The following "10 Minutes before the Worm," almost as short as its brief predecessor at just over a minute and a half, does not in any way ease up on the bizarreness. Weird random effects introduce the track, leading into a free-form guitar and hi-hat freak-out, before vocals and band proper finally begin after forty seconds. Beatles-esque harmonies do little to imbue the track with any semblance of coherence, with nonsense lyrics and random musical episodes leading to a stuttered vocal ending that paints the closing lyric line, "Everything is standing still." The song does not so much end as peter out.

It is only with the entry of track three, "Sing Low, Sweet Cheerio," that any sense of musical normality ensues. While the title is an obvious word play on the traditional spiritual gospel song "Swing Low, Sweet Chariot," and as such is one of the earliest portents on record of the Cooper sense of humor that would come to be a hallmark, the title remains the only allusion to that much earlier song. Stylistically far more orthodox and consistent with the American acid rock of the day, mixed with a British Invasion quality more reminiscent of the Pretty Things than were the opening tracks, any meaning is hard to prise from the work, with lyrics that provide little central theme but perhaps might be regarded as vaguely addressing an unnamed protagonist's self-development or "journey to be one." The song is lengthy at over five-and-a-half minutes, and is effectively divided into two parts: the first three minutes consisting of orthodox verse chorus form, but then offering a succession of solos between guitar and harmonica that end in a veritable freak-out followed by a breakdown.

"Today Mueller" features vocal harmonies that are at times almost Beatles-esque early in the song, but the rest of the time are more a bizarre collection of group falsettos, most especially on the title word "Today." Another hard-to-penetrate track, just what it is about is anyone's guess; however, there are some charming moments such as the opening lines of the closing section with the pleasing-to-the-ear perfect rhymes of "Red Rover Red Rover, pass under pass over." With the rhyming scheme then completed by a closing reference to England's "White Cliffs of Dover," "Today Mueller" is quite simply a minute and three-quarters of kookiness.

Very loud in the mix, heavily distorted fuzz-box guitar dominates the fifth track of the album, the fast-paced, hard-rocking "Living." Shades of Grand Funk Railroad abound in this self-reflective, introspective, psychedelic rush. Alice opines personal enlightenment lyrics such as "Living is only one part of being—believing is to know just what you're feeling," before the circular saw of Glen Buxton's guitar returns and sweeps away all in its path.

Side one of *Pretties for You* ends in another unrelenting onslaught in "Fields of Regret," where the fuzz-tone attack of the electric guitar continues, and interplay between guitar and harmonica once again features. The subject matter is inordinately and consistently heavy: "What horror must invade the mind when the approaching judge shall find sinful deeds from all mankind?" At over five-and-a-half minutes long, "Fields of Regret" is another slice of hippy-trippy acid rock that would undoubtedly have been enhanced by the consumption of any one or more of the mind-altering substances of the day.

Turning the record over, the second side of the Alice Cooper band's debut album kicks off with the inexplicably titled "No Longer Umpire," which is led in by childlike chanting. Beatles-styled vocal harmonies lend the track a degree of charm, but the track never settles and is gone within just two minutes' duration. Unfathomable lyrics—none evidently relating to an umpire—leave the listener scratching his head once again when reading meaning into the song's central protagonist, who persists in "Painting a picture to show everyone in the world."

"Levity Ball (Live at the Cheetah)" captures, as the title suggests, the Cooper band in live action, although whether it was actually recorded at the Cheetah Club is a point of some debate. The Pretty Things sound of garage, psychedelia, and hippy freak-out is at the fore while, once again, following three-and-a-bit minutes of orthodox song form, a lengthy free-form/breakdown section occurs before a slowed-down version of the first verse carries the song to its conclusion. Obtuse like many of the previous tracks in terms of making lyrical sense, the Cooper humor nevertheless shines through in the perfectly rhyming couplet that describes the protagonist writing non-rhyming lines: "I sat down at the stairway seven hours at a time, writing all of this poetry that I knew would never rhyme." Bassist Dennis Dunaway provides valuable insight to the song's meaning: "The song 'Levity Ball' was inspired by the movie *Carnival of Souls*, so we imagined the stage was a big ballroom with ghosts dancing."[1]

At just over a minute, the following "B.B. on Mars" is a frenetic invitation to "See what's going on—see inside," a perfect late-sixties slice of psychedelic introspection that conjures up comparisons to the bands already mentioned, along with Pink Floyd and others of that ilk. Buxton's guitar is again at the fore, a fuzz-laden rallying cry to hippy culture.

The tenth song, "Reflected," is of particular interest to Alice Cooper fans listening retrospectively to *Pretties for You*, as it is a clear blueprint for the 1972 hit single, "Elected" (number four on the UK chart, twenty-sixth on the US chart), that was shortly afterwards included on the 1973 album *Billion Dollar Babies*. Even in this primitive form, one can instantly see why it was revisited and reworked, with its primary melody retained unaltered once the band was successful, because it is the most complete and coherent track on the debut album. Even the subject matter addressed in the lyrics, albeit completely changed for "Elected," can be seen with the benefit of hindsight as highly relevant to the yet-to-be-nailed-down Cooper shtick, with its pre-emptive glimpse into masking and performative alter-egos: "You look outstanding with your eyes in disguise—just beyond your masks."

Swing-waltz time surprises the listener in the subsequent "Apple Bush," the 3/4 meter carrying the song's lyric message of getting back to nature with style and ease: "Well they found a way to live with ease, by eating from the bush instead of the trees." The acoustic/natural inferences of the harmonica feature over tom-tom drum rhythms in an escape from the fuzzed electric guitar freak-out vibe of much of the rest of the album.

In addition to paying tongue-in-cheek homage to the band's earliest incarnation when they were called the Earwigs, the penultimate track (and one of the best on the album), "Earwigs to Eternity," serves as a biographical, this-is-where-we-are-at-now statement for the Alice Cooper band, name-dropping themselves and acknowledging their journey thus far: "Four long years now we stop to hear a whisper, Alice Cooper." Word painting at its best, the last three words of the line are whispered, as if the band is the next big secret. The song also serves to acknowledge their fans with gratitude, with the repeated lines: "All of the time we have—all of the time we have—all of the time we have you." The vocal line is mirrored note for note by lead guitar, and the effect is humorous.

Tasked with closing the Cooper debut, "Changing Arranging" brings together many of the threads visited on the album in three minutes of full-on rock interspersed with the by now very familiar breakdowns and freak-outs. Buxton's guitar again fuzzes and sizzles like an angry bee, providing a sort of continuity over the song's stops and starts. Lyrically the song is a revisitation of psychedelic introspection, with observations including "I've got a never-ending battle inside, just trying to rectify my personal pride," and the overall message remains vague and hard to pin down.

A better album than it is often acknowledged as, *Pretties for You* contains several strong songs (most notably "Reflected") and provides many glimpses into the future for Cooper fans, perhaps most obviously in the work's self-referential humor. Nevertheless, it also struggles to stamp much claim to true originality with its stylistic borrowings from the acid rock, psychedelia, freak-out, and British Invasion sound of the day. Frank Zappa, the Beatles, Pink Floyd, Pretty Things, Grand Funk Railroad, and others are all in the mix to greater or lesser degrees over the course of the record, and the album comes across as that of a band yet to find their own voice. Promising, to be sure, but overall somewhat directionless. In addition, Alice's voice on this album differs markedly from the voice that he would employ once the band had hit its stride in the early 1970s and throughout his solo career. He sings the songs in mostly straight fashion, avoiding the intrinsic trademark growl and menace that would become his trademark, and in a manner that made him largely indistinguishable from numerous other singers of the day.

EASY ACTION, 1970 [US CHART —, UK —]

> One of the most unusual live groups, Alice Cooper, in their second straight album, convey much of the power they possess. The extended "Lay Down and Die, Goodbye" with its many changes is among the many interesting cuts as is the powerful "Return of the Spiders" and "Refrigerator Heaven." "Below Your Means" is another good longer number, sharp instrumentally. This album can go even higher than Alice Cooper's first set, which was a chart item.—Anonymous, *Billboard*, April 1970

> We all felt that it was a big improvement on *Pretties for You* in both the song-writing and production departments.—Michael Bruce, *No More Mr Nice Guy*, 1996

> On stage they may flay dead chickens, but there's nothing nearly that interesting here. The freaky music is sort of freaky, but the pretty stuff sounds like something Walt Disney had the good sense to leave in the can.—Anonymous, *Rolling Stone*, April 1970

Side One

1. Mr. & Misdemeanor (Bruce/Buxton/Cooper/Dunaway/Smith)
2. Shoe Salesman (Bruce/Buxton/Cooper/Dunaway/Smith)
3. Still No Air (Bruce/Buxton/Cooper/Dunaway/Smith)
4. Below Your Means (Bruce/Buxton/Cooper/Dunaway/Smith)

Side Two

1. Return of the Spiders (Bruce/Buxton/Cooper/Dunaway/Smith)

2. Laughing at Me (Bruce/Buxton/Cooper/Dunaway/Smith)
3. Refrigerator Heaven (Bruce/Buxton/Cooper/Dunaway/Smith)
4. Beautiful Flyaway (Bruce/Buxton/Cooper/Dunaway/Smith)
5. Lay Down and Die, Goodbye (Bruce/Buxton/Cooper/Dunaway/ Smith)

The album cover of *Easy Action* instantly broke the rules, perversely reversing the normal state of affairs whereby a front cover will habitually show a band's faces. Happy, sad, angry, posed, natural—it didn't matter; long-established convention decreed that in all cases where a band photo was used on an album cover, the musicians would be featured showing their faces to the viewer. It is not so, however, on *Easy Action*. Here, located in the center of the attention-getting bright-red cover sat a photograph of the Alice Cooper band shot from the waist up, standing in a line with their backs to the camera, their hands nonchalantly on their hips, their heads facing directly away from the viewer, and their long, immaculately groomed hair reaching halfway down their naked backs. It is only when the viewer turns the album cover over to the rear side that the band appear front-on. Here they are shown full length and fully clothed, posed and serious, dressed in beautiful, flamboyant satin, lurex, and silk pants and jackets in an image that pre-dates by years English glam rock à la Gary Glitter, Sweet, and other performers.

The opening track, "Mr. & Misdemeanor," is a clear foretaste of what would come, finding Alice abandoning the straight vocal style of *Pretties for You* and instead employing, temporarily at least, the style that he would soon make his own—menacing, growling, and consciously affected. Lyrically too this song stands as the clearest clue thus far recorded of the band's future direction, with the musicians cast as marginalized figures positioned on the periphery of mainstream society, and name-dropping their first album in the process: "I sit beside Misdemeanor, here's new pretties for you—nobody likes me but we adore you." The song's clearly humorous title remains the only humor in the otherwise seriously themed song in which societal lines are drawn, the song's subjects finding themselves cast as "middle of the roaders" guilty of creating the divisions. It is a fine beginning to *Easy Action*, more straightforward, more concise and focused, and comparatively devoid of the indulgent acid rock and psychedelia instrumental and compositional excesses.

However, on the second song of the album, "Shoe Salesman," Alice reverts once again to the straight singing style of the band's debut in what is, on the surface at least, a curiously light and breezy song set to an equally light musical accompaniment. The lyrics contain layers, however, that act against the jaunty happiness of the surface vibe and introduce a darker side to proceedings. Of his shoe salesman acquaintance Alice sings, "One day he showed me some marks on his arms in a line." Later, he meets a girl who offers him a "special," after which, "Winking, she pokes me in the side—well we could go for a ride." Thematically and stylistically, although the Cooper song is more upbeat, there are similarities here with Lou Reed's 1972 hit, "Walk on the Wild Side," where the seedy, alluring dangers of heroin and prostitution are presented in a light pop style without the any sense of rock threat. It's an effective, well-written song, albeit somewhat incongruous with the album's opener.

The short song that follows, "Still No Air," borrows wholesale a couplet from *West Side Story*: "When you're a Jet you're a Jet all the way, from your first cigarette to your last dyin' day." Remarkably, this homage to the musical theater of Leonard Bernstein and Stephen Sondheim will be repeated in three years' time in the stylistically aligned youth warfare song, "Gutter Cat vs. the Jets," on the *School's Out* album of 1972. Here, the couplet features in a much less sure setting, and it is hard to discern the central tenet of what transpires in the song. Perhaps the most interesting feature is that here Alice shifts between his two voices within the one song, using his straight voice in the early sections and then adopting the sneer/growl during the borrowed lines.

"Below Your Means" completes side one and is a vaguely innuendo-driven song of desire: "I'll sing you my all night song . . . under the cover of a midnight scene I got the sheets below your means." A lengthy track at almost seven minutes, it follows the format of many of the earlier *Pretties for You* songs in its orthodox vocal verse/chorus form early on, that then gives way to virtuosic instrumental soloing and rhythmic experimentation for the remaining minutes of the track, thereby lacking the newly acquired concise, focused quality displayed in the preceding songs.

Side two begins with "Return of the Spiders," another self-referential title given that the band had briefly sported the Spiders as their name during their nascent days, and mirroring the band's tipping of their hat to the past in "Earwigs to Eternity" on *Pretties for You*. Alice is back to his soon-to-be signature voice for this four-and-a-half-minute track, which follows standard rock formula songwriting conventions for the first three minutes before an extended solo takes over for the duration. "I'm coming after you," jeers Alice in a critique of societal ignorance, because "You all won't hear—we all won't hear."

"Laughing at Me" follows, and it's a throwaway track that, frankly, makes little sense. "It's laughing at me—yes it's laughing at me," sings Alice, but with no situational context within which to frame the lyric. The subsequent line, "So I started to end the beginning to end" offers the listener little help, and the track passes, having made little impact.

The next track, "Refrigerator Heaven," is of real interest to Cooper fans, retrospectively speaking, because the term would resurface on Alice's 1975 solo debut, *Welcome to My Nightmare* during the song "Cold Ethyl." While it would take on quite a different meaning in the latter context, here it refers to a man who is cryogenically frozen for reasons laid out with absolute clarity: "I've been admitted to refrigerator heaven until they discover a cure for cancer." Although lyrically sparse, the theme remains clear, and "Refrigerator Heaven" can be seen as one of Alice Cooper's first forays into true Grand Guignol–style medical horror territory.

"Beautiful Flyaway" comes as a complete surprise. A piano-led journey into fantasy, the subject matter is Dali-esque and oblique, typified by lines such as "Later I think I'll disappear into another womb and take a look inside the men's room." Vocally understated, the song has a wacky charm, but contributes little to the album overall, bar stylistic diversity.

Finally comes the lengthy "Lay Down and Die, Goodbye" to end the album. Featuring another lyric that is almost impossible to penetrate, the seven-and-a-half-minute track sees a return to the self-indulgent psychedelia/acid rock terrain of *Pretties for You*. Beginning with the spoken caveat, "You are the only censor—if you don't like what I say, you have a choice. You can turn me off," the track is a disappointing end to the album.

All in all, *Easy Action* has sparkled briefly in parts, has certainly promised much to come, but in itself proved to be an uneven amalgam of stylistic experimentation. The best moments are provided by the songs that are honed and concise, and follow more standard songwriting conventions instead of being experimental and verbose. In the same way that "Reflected" had stood above the others on *Pretties for You*, here too "Mr. and Misdemeanor," "Shoe Salesman," and "Refrigerator Heaven" are not only the most notable tracks, but are also those that most clearly signal the band's future.

2

THE HALCYON YEARS OF THE ALICE COOPER BAND

Love It to Death, Killer, School's Out, Billion Dollar Babies, Muscle of Love, 1971–1973

LOVE IT TO DEATH, 1971 [US CHART #35, UK #28]

Somehow Alice has got past the gimmickry and turned his band into musicians—nothing fancy, y'understand, just hard, dirty rock. They're still weird alright, but the bizarre attitudes and lyrics are an adjunct to the music rather than an end in themselves. And it's fucking good.—Steve Mann, *Frendz*, June 1971

Now that they're making quite good records, incidentally, it is to be hoped that the Coopers will apply themselves to dreaming up a new image, that of the psychedelic drag-queen group having long since been exhausted—witness how they've had to get into gruesome (and thus inconsistent with their stated intentions of testing our sexual insecurities by being ambiguously attractive) stuff like tarantula eye makeup in order to stay ahead of their audience in terms of outrageousness.—John Mendelsohn, *Rolling Stone*, April 1971

Side One

1. Caught in a Dream (Bruce)
2. I'm Eighteen (Bruce/Buxton/Cooper/Dunaway/Smith)

3. Long Way to Go (Bruce)
4. Black Juju (Dunaway)

Side Two

1. Is It My Body? (Bruce/Buxton/Cooper/Dunaway/Smith)
2. Hallowed Be My Name (Smith)
3. Second Coming (Cooper)
4. Ballad of Dwight Fry (Bruce/Cooper)
5. Sun Arise (Butler/Harris)

Love It to Death is regarded by many fans as the first essential and, indeed, quintessential, Alice Cooper album. It is the point where the band strips things back, avoids the excesses of their earlier recordings and, while it may sound like a cliché but is meant as a compliment, simply rock out hard and dirty. The album cover even gives a portent of this change, featuring a stark black-and-white image of the band caught in a spotlight, thus abandoning the highly colorful, arty and/or clever images of the first two covers. The band here looks freakish and threatening, androgynous and dangerous, while the album title and band name are rendered simply and effectively in personal handwriting at the top right corner. With schoolboyish toilet humor, Cooper sticks his finger at groin height through the unusual cloak-like garment he is wearing, giving the impression that it is his penis and requiring a double-take from the viewer to confirm that it is not. The rear cover features the band in a more relaxed photograph with their respective instruments, while the inside of the gatefold sleeve is notable for being the band's first foray into horror. Here, the viewer finds a super closeup photograph of Alice's eyes, positioned one on each side of the gatefold with his trademark tarantula eye makeup, mascara lines stretching out like spider's legs. Gazing into Alice's shiny black pupils, one sees the rest of the band reflected.

The songs on *Love It to Death* are uniformly well written, far shorter and more succinct than on their previous recordings, and captured in the studio with newfound clarity by coproducers Jack Richardson of Guess Who fame and, more importantly given the relationship he would go on to form with all things Cooper, a young up-and-comer named Bob Ezrin. The newly honed and streamlined approach from both sides of the mixing desk is evident from the first three minutes when the album's mood-setting opener, "Caught in a Dream"—released as a single and scraping into the Billboard Top 100 at number 94—captures in a shade over three minutes not only the newly unencumbered Cooper sound, but also provides a crystal-clear critique of American life. Cooper has often said—as have numerous critics—that he reflects the truths of American life back on his audience; that he is a mirror to the society that spawned him and within which he lives. In the Michael Bruce–penned "Caught in a Dream," for the first time Cooper does exactly that with a telling exposé of the famed, revered, and reviled, American Dream. The pursuit of wealth and material goods is captured in lines such as "You know I need a houseboat and I need a plane—I need a butler and a trip to Spain." With tongue firmly in cheek, want is framed as need throughout, and the notion that the world owes the singer everything is wonderfully cast as the joke that it is. The arrow truly and surely hits the target when he opines later in the song, "When you see me with a smile on my face—then you'll know I'm a mental case." Unlike on the earlier albums, the message here is delivered clean-cut and with precision, uncluttered by lyrical, instrumental, or compositional excess or pretension. It is a fine beginning to the band's third album.

The second track reveals for the first time the band's potential talent for writing hit singles. "I'm Eighteen" would prove to be their breakthrough song, released as a single before the album was out, and reaching number twenty-one on the Billboard chart in April 1971. Tellingly, it took the commercial nose of Ezrin to carefully craft "I'm Eighteen" for commercial success. Judiciously taking an axe to what had been an eight-minute-plus song, Ezrin pulled it back to a three-minute pop format and, with appropriate rewriting of lyrics, the result was the band's first, crucial, hit single. As Cooper later related, "'I'm Eighteen' was stripped back to the bone—simple and direct, right down to the guitar and chorus hooks."[1]

In the grand tradition of youth anthems, the lyrics spoke of alienation, estrangement, and awkwardness in a direct, easily understood, and empathetic way; caught between boyhood and manhood, "I'm eighteen, I get confused every day—Eighteen, I just don't know what to say." But in addition to cleverly summating the otherness that is the universal experience of teenage-hood, in the hands of the Cooper band the youth turmoil had a twist: "And the teenage angst. Simple and raw. Like the

Stooges. Tough. Arrogant. But also *funny*—the difference between us and everyone else was that we weren't taking it completely seriously. 'I'm eighteen and I LIIIKE it!'"[2]

What is also importantly evident about "I'm Eighteen" is that the song that would bring Alice Cooper to widespread acclaim featured Alice singing in his highly recognizable, growling, guttural voice, another component for which Bob Ezrin is deservedly given credit. Alice recalls Ezrin "setting his sights on my vocals. 'Look Alice . . . people may like the live show, but you have no defining handle on your voice and the music.' Bob Ezrin taught me how to sing in a signature voice . . . an Alice sound."[3]

The third song of *Love It to Death* is the Bruce-penned "Long Way to Go." An up-tempo rocker in the best possible manner, the song's bridge gives the album its title, when Alice screams, "I guess I love it—I love it to death!" While the central theme of the lyric is hard to pin down, the song can most easily be read as a critique of both personal development and humankind's development. A particularly fine, insightful couplet begins the first verse: "What's keeping us apart isn't selfishness. What's holding us together isn't love."

The final song on the first side is Dunaway's "Back Juju," a dark, highly visual, and lengthy song tailor-made for creating theatrical opportunities in live performance but arguably more difficult to sustain on vinyl. And yet, in the hands of the Cooper band and Bob Ezrin, it works. Alternating between sparse, atmospheric sections and full-on rock, the subject matter is Grand Guignol–style horror: "Under the soil now waiting for worms . . . dead feelings are cool, down lower I sink." The best moment comes when, after the long ushering in of sleep, Alice suddenly brings the song—and the listener—back to life with a blood-curdling "Wake Up! Wake Up! Wake Up! Wake Up!" At over nine minutes long, "Back Juju" might initially appear to be a return to the lengthy meanderings of the earliest Alice Cooper offerings, but the song has structure and a theatrical narrative that ensures listener interest is maintained throughout.

Turning the record over, side two begins strongly with "Is It My Body," the song chosen as the B side to the "I'm Eighteen" single. "What have I got that makes you want to love me?" sings Alice in this critique of groupie motivation, "Now is it my body, or someone I might be?" The song seems wistful in its sentiment and goes against the time-honored rock 'n' roll fringe benefit of casual, fleeting sex with anonymous, infatuated groupies. Pondering how to get inside their minds to discover what drives them, Alice challenges them to "take the time to find out who I really am."

Neal Smith wrote the following track, intriguingly titled "Hallowed Be My Name," and it is an odd song indeed. The shortest on the album at two minutes, twenty-five seconds, it starts with a brief excerpt of studio banter after which four drumstick clicks count in an exposed, solo, funereal organ that sets up over the course of two bars a suitable religiosity that is in keeping with the song's title and lyric content. When the band enters, the sound is pure gothic rock, long before such a descriptor existed. With a nod perhaps to Black Sabbath in terms of vibe and subject matter, Alice's newly established signature voice is at its growliest yet. The song's recurring pre-chorus couplet, "Cursing their lovers—cursing the Bible," is indicative of the song's theme of religious hypocrisy and the many temptations that challenge faith in God, as the "Sluts and the hookers have taken your money."

"Second Coming" strongly continues the just-established religious theme, and Cooper's oft-cited son-of-a-preacher origins seem to permeate lyrics that—from a first-person perspective—tell of God contemplating his return, an event announced by street-corner prophets: "I just come back to show you all my words are golden. So have no gods before me, I'm the light." With no obvious evidence of tongue being held in cheek, the message seems unexpectedly honest in its evangelical zest. In a return to the oft-used song form of the first two albums, the vocals are completed by the midpoint of the track and an extended instrumental section completes the song. However, with Ezrin's message of succinctness and brevity, the track is still only three minutes in length and never at risk of outstaying its welcome.

From a seamless and beautifully florid piano segue, "Second Coming" then turns into what is for many fans of the Alice Cooper band one of their all-time favorite tracks, the image-laden emotional roller-coaster of "Ballad of Dwight Fry." A powerful critique of insanity, the song is the second longest on the album at six-and-a-half minutes, and due to its inherent theatricality was a staple of the band's live shows. Beginning with the downright creepy child's voice asking "Mommy, where's Daddy?" (a portent of similar passages that would appear in Alice's solo debut, *Welcome to My Nightmare*, four years later in 1975), the song runs the full gamut of emotions, intensities, and musical landscapes. With its central protagonist incarcerated in a mental institution, in order to help Alice portray the situation with as much realism as possible, in the recording studio he was "caged in a structure of folding chairs so as to give him the feeling of claustrophobia."[4] Certainly, a sense of desperation and panic is plainly evident in the extended breakdown middle section when one hears the repeated, increasingly intense, plea by Alice-as-Dwight-Fry, "I gotta get out of here!" The song is given extra potency in that it was written about the real-life Hollywood actor of the same name who, during the 1920s to 1940s, specialized in horror roles; Frye most famously played the character of Dracula's insane acolyte, Renfield, in the iconic 1931 version of *Dracula*, starring Bela Lugosi. In the live shows of the *Love It to Death* period and beyond, Alice would be led onto the stage in a straitjacket to perform "Ballad of Dwight Fry" before being executed in an electric chair in the following "Black Juju," clear evidence of the superb theatrical qualities that both of these *Love It to Death* songs afforded the band. Neal Smith offers excellent insight to the genesis of "Ballad of Dwight Fry":

> Most bands are influenced by other bands. But in Alice Cooper's case, we were also influenced by old Hollywood movies, horror movies in particular. The original 1931 *Dracula* with Bela Lugosi, one of my favourites, featuring the insect-eating character Renfield, a lost soul and disciple of Dracula's.[5]

A further segue ushers in the final track and the only cover version on the album. "Sun Arise," by the Australian music-comic and middle-of-the-road (MOR) entertainer Rolf Harris, on the surface seems to be an unlikely choice. Yet the band had been using it as a set opener in the live shows, and in giving it the Alice Cooper treatment, had taken the song a very long way away from the bearded antipodean's far more insipid version and made it their own. In light of the nature of the band's own lyrics earlier on the album—most particularly in the graveyard/voodoo/burial imagery of "Black Juju"—the lines of "Sun Arise" became imbued with resonances far beyond any that Harris could have ever intended: "She drive away your darkness every day—bringing back the warmth to the ground."

Love It to Death is deservedly seen as a watershed album in the career of Alice Cooper, and the fact that so many fans regard it as the true start of things is fully justifiable. The difference between this third album and the first two is marked and revelatory. Much praise has been given to the introduction of Bob Ezrin to the mix, and this is well deserved. His sense of theatricality—and more importantly, his ability to bring this to life in the recording studio—was an excellent match for the band's own investment in, and love for, this extra-musical component in their work, and Ezrin's commercial sense was exactly what the group required at the time. No more self-indulgent, psychedelic/acid rock trips for the Alice Cooper band. In Ezrin's hands, the band's creativity and unique thematic strengths were honed and packaged into highly palatable three-minute songs ripe for a popular marketplace far greater than hippy stoners. In league with Ezrin, Alice Cooper became a champion of youth capable of channeling universal angst. *Love It to Death* is the moment when the Alice Cooper band arrived. The album also set in place a blueprint for the future on which the band would build and further develop. In addition, Alice Cooper's future prowess as an instantly identifiable solo act can be traced back to this critical point.

KILLER, 1971 [US CHART #21, UK #27]

Alice Cooper has risen from relative obscurity to international prominence. They are the Peck's bad boys of rock; their onstage antics leave many cold but their music is powerful gut-level rock & roll. "Killer" is most likely the group's best effort to date exhibiting some very potent lyrics.—Anonymous, *Billboard*, November 1971

Alice Cooper has come a long way and used up a lot of gimmicks and poses to get to this stunner of an album, but it was all worth it and at this point I can hardly wait for the next one. . . . One thing is for sure: This is a strong band, a vital band, and they are going to be around for a long, long time.—Lester Bangs, *Rolling Stone*, January 1972

Side One

1. Under My Wheels (Bruce/Dunaway/Ezrin)
2. Be My Lover (Bruce)
3. Halo of Flies (Bruce/Buxton/Cooper/Dunaway/Smith)
4. Desperado (Bruce/Cooper)

Side Two

1. You Drive Me Nervous (Bruce/Cooper/Ezrin)
2. Yeah, Yeah, Yeah (Bruce /Cooper)
3. Dead Babies (Bruce/Buxton/Cooper/Dunaway/Smith)
4. Killer (Bruce/Dunaway)

Just as the cover of *Love It to Death* had successfully telegraphed the edgy, and at times dark and dangerous, content of the recording it housed, the carefully considered cover of *Killer* does so to even greater effect. Blood-red, the front cover features the head of a snake, its forked tongue extended and its cold, emotionless eye staring at the viewer. Above the snake is the band name written in black in a childlike scrawl using only lowercase lettering, while below is the album title, similarly scrawled and disturbing. Quite apart from the danger and repulsion widely associated with snakes, the presence of the reptile reinforces the band's notoriety for using a snake in their live shows, thereby linking their live and recorded work. Turning the cover over, the rear side displays a portrait of the band in Halloween green, backlit in blue, and with a snake dangling from the top of the frame. Alice is wearing his signature tarantula eye makeup and the total effect is, once again, dangerous and disturbing. It is when the gatefold cover is fully opened to reveal the photograph inside, however, that the album's true colors are revealed. In another telling linkage to the band's live show, the inside image is one of Alice alone, hanging lifeless with his neck in a noose and eyes closed as if in death. His jump suit is open to the waist, and a stab wound can be seen at his navel. Streaks of blood cross his stomach and chest. Beneath his picture is a 1972 calendar, the twelve months of the year printed orderly and neatly, in complete contrast to the violent chaos of the lead singer's demise above. In effect, Cooper is here shown as a gruesome Grand Guignol pinup.

The opening track and first single release from the album is the up-tempo, catchy "Under My Wheels." Failing to replicate the success of *Love It to Death's* "I'm Eighteen," reaching only a modest number fifty-nine on the Billboard chart, the lyrically minimalist song is hard to penetrate, but the notion of a hit-and-run automobile incident is a strong likelihood. The girl Alice is singing about certainly seems over-bearing and is justifiably put in her place: "'Cause when you call me on the telephone saying take me to the show. And then I say honey I just can't go—old lady's sick and I can't leave her home."

The Michael Bruce–penned "Be My Lover," the second single release from *Killer*, fared ten places better than the album's opening track, reaching number forty-nine in April 1972 and thus becoming the band's second top fifty single after "I'm Eighteen." Following a clear boy-meets-girl narrative structure, set in a musician/groupie context, Bruce's flair for lyric writing is evident, and contains a great example of wordplay in the line "But with a magnifying glance I just sort of look her over." In addition, the song is semi-autobiographical, notable for incorporating the band's name within the lyric: "She asked me why the singer's name was Alice." The incredulity and confusion the band—or at least the band's lead singer—must often have been met with is laid out in the next line: "I said listen, baby, you really wouldn't understand."

"Black Juju" and "Ballad of Dwight Fry" introduced a very dark, grotesque element to the Cooper band's recorded output, and in the third track of their fourth album they reinforce this with the tour de force that is the eight-minutes-plus "Halo of Flies." Not quite as invested in full-on horror, but every bit as theatrical as these earlier songs, a pattern is emerging of the band utilizing far longer songs in order to allow the space for narrative action to take place in such songs. While Ezrin's three-minute commercial formula is paying obvious dividends in streamlining the band's product and making Alice Cooper far easier to package for success, these longer Grand Guignol–type songs bring out the best in both the band and the producer, giving them the welcome scope to exhibit their collective love of, and talent for, theatricality. Here the theme is more James Bond–like subterfuge and spy references than grotesque imagery, and the song includes the highly memorable line, "I've got a watch that turns into a lifeboat."

"Desperado" closes out side one, and is an exploration of the outsider in society, a role that the Cooper band members were all too familiar with in real life as they became increasingly viewed as the freaks of rock 'n' roll. While couched in the fictitious scenario of a Western gunslinger, the lyrics contain the trademarks of the Cooper shtick with its references to the darker sides of humanity—the grotesque, the macabre, the dangerous: "I'm a picture of ugly stories. I'm a killer and I'm a clown." Just as the earlier "Be My Lover" name-dropped the band, by referring to himself as a killer here, "Desperado" similarly serves to name-drop the album, pre-empting the actual title track that later concludes the album.

Side two begins where side one ended with another critique of marginalization, but here the outlaw is situated within the more familiar territory of youth alienation. One of the most underrated tracks by the Alice Cooper band, the wittily titled "You Drive Me Nervous" is a fast-paced, hard-rocking triumph that comes and goes in a whirlwind, at less than two-and-a-half minutes long. The hapless youth begins the song being harassed by his parents who are waging the war of trying to control their independence-seeking offspring. "You run around with all that hair," they accuse, to which he responds by running away from home. However, penniless and stranded in another state, his parents are forced to come and bail him out of jail, asking the time-honored, generation-gap question, delivered here with a superb perfect rhyme: "Honey, where did we fail?" All that's left for the poor miscreant to do at this point is SCREAM! In terms of summing up universal youth angst, the band absolutely nail it in "You Drive Me Nervous."

In what might be seen as a parody of the Beatles and a fun-poke at the flower power generation, the next track, "Yeah, Yeah, Yeah," pivots around the Fab Four's famous harmonized antiphonal response to the title line in "She Loves You." But here when the phrase is sung, it is aggressive and ugly, not pretty and affirming. Cooper and Bruce's lyrics pit opposites against each other, running the full gamut of humankind's potential for good and evil: "You could be the devil, you could be the savior." With an endearing—and brave—lack of regard for songwriting convention, the succeeding line bends grammatical rules in the service of a fine rhyme: "Well I really can't tell by the way that your behavior."

One of the most notorious and controversial songs of the Alice Cooper band's career occupies the penultimate spot on *Killer*. The taboo-teasing "Dead Babies" drew many a frown and a muttered "tut-tut" from mainstream American mouths at the time of its release. Again reaching into the wellspring that produced Grand Guignol–styled, narrative-based tracks such as "Black Juju" and "Ballad of Dwight Fry," "Dead Babies" is not confined to a three-minute format but is instead given ample time to tell its story, and also gives Bob Ezrin free rein to bring his own theatrical arranging wizardry to bear. In their critique, *Rolling Stone* both admired and abhorred the track:

The key line is "Dead babies can take care of themselves"; I find this song a little repulsive myself, but then that's exactly the idea. Although if Alice Cooper thinks the idea of dead babies is somehow cute, then he's . . . he's . . . he's *succeeded*, I guess, although there are all kinds of motives and ways of offending people, some less justified than others. In any case, the songs arrangement is incredible, an almost cinematic sound.[6]

Ugly though the subject matter may be, "Dead Babies" has a strong moral basis, as two non-caring parents allow their baby daughter, Betty, to access and overdose on aspirin—the mainstay, every-home-has-them painkiller of middle America. With Ezrin's touch, we hear baby Betty cry, and it is a haunting moment. Such is their parental neglect, and most particularly their self-admission that they never really wanted her anyway, that the loathsome pair are brought before the court before the song's end: "Order in the court! Order in this court room!" shouts the judge as pandemonium breaks out in the public gallery. The song traverses the very same evil-deed-carried-out-and-justice-done scenario that Alice Cooper would typically endure in the band's live shows, at the conclusion of which he would typically be executed by the state. Many an image can be seen on the Internet of Alice Cooper stabbing or dismembering a doll during performances, and it is a sure bet that "Dead Babies" was in full force at the moment the shutter fell to capture these gruesome images.

The title track ends *Killer*, and it is another lengthy theatrical song ripe for narrative staging in the live shows. Here, Alice is found guilty of his crime(s) and the song addresses his final moments before execution. The songwriters, Bruce and Dunaway, had purposely set out to examine just such a scenario: "[We] tried to work ourselves into a really dark mood, we talked about when you know you are going to die—what is the scariest thing about that? What would the waiting be like?"[7] As he contemplates his imminent death, Alice reflects on his past: "I came into this life, looked all around. I saw just what I liked and took what I found."

Killer is the favorite album of many fans of the Alice Cooper group. Hard rocking, lyrically intense, and a fine mix of both the commercial and theatrical aspects of the band, its quality was reflected in both its success and critical acclaim. Alice himself believes *Killer* to be "our best album, according to a lot of critics, as far as pure rock 'n' roll goes. I agree with that."[8]

Certainly, on the back of *Love It to Death* and *Killer*, Alice Cooper was by now firmly established as a top American rock act, filling concert halls throughout the country, garnering much media attention and column space in the country's rock pages, as well as notoriety among the guardians of morality and good taste. Parents were worried. Alice himself reveled in the fact that they were adored by kids and hated by their parents. But, despite the band's popularity as a live act and the "I'm Eighteen" single achieving a meritorious number twenty-one spot on the Billboard chart, the band had not had a bona fide top ten, or even top twenty, hit single, and nor had their popularity at home transferred to the United Kingdom or Europe to anywhere near the same degree. *Killer* had reached only twenty-seven on the UK album charts, a mere one place higher than *Love It to Death* at twenty-eight. Certainly the band was known far beyond stateside, but was not yet in the top tier of acts. What Alice Cooper needed in order to keep progressing was a smash hit single that would take the world by storm, and an album that would ride on its coattails.

SCHOOL'S OUT, 1972 [US CHART #2 UK#4]

> Under the tutelage of Bob Ezrin, we now crafted better songs. Hit songs, the stuff that will put the icing on the cake.—Alice Cooper, *Alice Cooper: Golf Monster*, 2007

> I've been trying to figure this one out for months. As usual, it's got some of the rawest and cleverest hard rock ever recorded—the title hit is a masterpiece. It's also got a lot of soundtrack, and this part of it is lifted—with attribution, yet—from *West Side Story*. This bothered me until I admitted that as a middle-class adolescent I liked *West Side Story* quite a bit, and anyway, who better to steal a show tune than a showman like Alice? Still, even the best soundtrack—this is a lot more engaging than *A Clockwork Orange*—gets pretty boring fast. I wonder if an album of straight Cooper-rock would drive us out of our skulls. B+.—Anonymous, *Creem*, December 1972

Killer Alice they call him—and it's not surprising. Of all the American bands to have emerged in the past few years it's Alice Cooper that have captured the imagination of British audiences—pulling in sell out signs from every appearance, and featuring in both the singles and albums charts.—*Sounds*, December 1972

It was a good album, but not our best in my opinion. I think it was a bit overproduced with the horns and stuff. It was such a drastic leap from the hard edge of *Killer*, that I'm sure a lot of fans were turned off by it. It was a very Vaudeville kind of record.—Michael Bruce, *No More Mr Nice Guy*, 1996

Side One

1. School's Out (Bruce/Buxton/Cooper/Dunaway/Smith)
2. Luney Tune (Cooper/Dunaway)
3. Gutter Cat vs. the Jets (Bruce/Buxton/Bernstein/Sondheim)
4. Street Fight (Bruce/Buxton/Cooper/Dunaway/Smith)
5. Blue Turk (Bruce/Cooper)

Side Two

1. My Stars (Cooper/Ezrin)
2. Public Animal #9 (Bruce/Cooper)
3. Alma Mater (Smith)
4. Grande Finale (Bernstein/Bruce/Buxton/Cooper/David/Dun-away/Ezrin/Smith)

You wake up one morning during the summer of 1972. A summer that's hot, sticky, and full of discontentment. You're an early teen and you're bored, bored, bored; continually tossed around on the expectations and demands of adults, such as your parents, your paper-route boss, and your teachers. *Especially* your teachers—it is enough to make you scream. You roll over and turn on your transistor radio, fearing the usual MOR schlock that will make you feel even more disconnected from mainstream society's facade of "everything's all right." You have so little autonomy in your life, little power of any kind. Maybe dad will make you wash the car today, or mom might make you tidy your room (yawn); maybe you and your friends might kick a can around the park later. There's nothing to look forward to. But then . . . BANG! There it is. That riff! Like a saw cutting through steel, the guitar power of the opening of "School's Out" hits you like a blow to the chest. It's in-your-face and crude and aggressive, and when Alice Cooper begins to sing, he sums up your mood and your situation—and that of your friends—perfectly, straight away: "Well we got no choice." You sit up in bed, alert and with every sense aroused. Here it is—a musical talisman with which you can ward off the world. There are like-minded people out there. You are not alone after all. You have become a life-long Alice Cooper fan in the space of three glorious minutes.

The thrill of purchasing a copy of *School's Out* began long before getting the record home and putting needle to vinyl. The album cover was a masterpiece in its duplication of a school desk top complete with the names and initials of the AC band crudely carved into its surface along with the album title. It was an up-the-establishment pleasure to carry it out of the record store under your arm after forking over your hard-earned pocket money. It cannot be overemphasized—being an Alice Cooper fan was more than a music choice; it was a positioning statement. A badge. A touchstone for the alienated. More of a puzzle, however, to a twelve-year-old boy from the backwaters of Hamilton, New Zealand, was what do with the pair of white paper panties that came wrapped around the album. Much parental tut-tutting was heard. That was good, certainly. Viva the rock 'n' roll cornerstone of generational division. But again . . . what does a shy twelve-year-old boy who is still into gluing together model aircraft kits do with something as tantalizing, alluring, and downright puzzling as a pair of *gratis* paper knickers? Never mind. It's edjukational, right? Put them in your bottom drawer and earmark them for an exciting future time . . .

The opening, and title, track of *School's Out* is an enduring glam rock anthem that, in addition to being the smash hit of the summer of 1972 (number one in the United Kingdom and number seven in the United States), served to propel Alice Cooper to the top of the UK singles chart and beyond, placing him at the forefront of the burgeoning glam rock phenomenon alongside the likes of Marc Bolan and T Rex, and the UK king of theatrical art rock, David Bowie (then performing as Ziggy Stardust). Performing with similar success on the singles charts of numerous countries around the world, including my own native New Zealand, where it went top ten and immensely cheered up the midwinter schoolyards throughout the country, "School's Out" is the pièce de résistance of the Alice Cooper band, propelling the album that spawned it to number two stateside and number four on the UK chart, thus truly breaking the act into the top tier in that market. The most emphatic opening statement of any Cooper album, either group or solo, the masterpiece of rock infectiousness that is the title track is announced by one of the great guitar fanfare riffs of all time, one that sits easily alongside such great and instantly recognizable moments in rock history as the Rolling Stone's "Satisfaction" or Chuck Berry's "Johnny B Goode." It is the guitar equivalent of the teasing, sneering, schoolyard taunt "Nya nya nya nya nya": if ever an opening riff perfectly summed up the sentiment of the song that follows, then Glen Buxton's "School's Out" riff is it. Bristling with youth alienation and plainly irreverent disdain for their elders ("Well we can't salute ya—can't find a flag. If that don't suit ya, that's a drag"), the lyrics too are chanting and child-like, right down to the superb nursery-rhyme quality of the rhymes (choice/boys/noise/toys) and delivered to perfection by Alice in fine imitation of a naughty schoolboy heading gleefully for the school gates on the last day of term with the summer holidays stretching out before him. Perhaps the song's finest and most anarchic moment comes in verse two, when the abandonment of formal lyric structure effectively raises a middle finger to the efforts of teachers ("no more teacher's dirty looks") and authority figures everywhere with the words, "We can't even think of a word that rhymes." This is the 1972 precursor to the Sex Pistols' in-your-face punk taunt of 1977 when, in their signature single "Pretty Vacant," a sneering, obnoxious and defiant Jonny Rotten faced down the camera and growled, "And we don't caaaare!" "School's Out" is also extremely theatrical, bringing school-day imagery to the mind of the listener, even the cheesy blatancy of the school bell and children's screams of delight that herald the track's wind-down ending. The hand of Bob Ezrin is evident all over this theatricality. Hallmarks of the now established Alice Cooper shtick abound in "School's Out," a song that manages to be funny, sublimely catchy, edgy, and theatrical all at the same time, wrapped up in a made-for-the-charts, three-and-a-half min-ute, ride.

The unwelcome discipline and regimentation of school that gives this hit single title track its edgy impetuous is retained for the second song of the album, but here the location shifts to the far darker realm of a psychiatric ward in a youth detention center. In "Luney Tune" the joyful innocence of the opener dissipates all too quickly, despite the obvious, and positive, surface allusion to the Warner Brothers' Looney Tunes cartoons that were part and parcel of every American kid's youth experience of the era. "I slipped into my jeans, lookin' hard and feelin' mean," sings Alice with trademark snarl in the opening line, instantly evicting the likes of Tweety Bird, Bugs Bunny, and Daffy Duck from the song's proceedings. Alice is at his very darkest when he later sings, "I stole a razor from the commissary. I just couldn't take it no more." Although only the second track of the album, it has already been a long journey from the "No more pencils—no more books" of the preceding "School's Out." Innocence is lost.

Musical theater superstar writers Leonard Bernstein and Stephen Sondheim once again unexpectedly become Alice Cooper allies in the following track, "Gutter Cat vs. the Jets," with the verbatim borrowing of lyrics from *West Side Story*; the same lines were used in the *Easy Action* song "Still No Air," but here considerably extended. With turf-defending youth factions framed analogously as gangs of streetwise alley cats, the song serves as a setup for a highly effective segue into the instrumental track that follows, "Street Fight." "Some bad cats from fourth street come down to our alley," sneers Alice with menace. He then rallies his troops for the forthcoming fight with the *West Side Story* quote, fully acknowledged in the songwriting credits: "When you're a Jet you're a Jet all the way, from your first cigarette to your last dyin' day." Over an infectious repeating bass figure, the ensuing melee comes to life in "Street Fight," with the recorded sounds of violence prominently overlaying the music. With the screams and cries of the gang protagonists at the fore, alternately angry and pain-filled, bottles smash into pieces, thumps, crashes, and thuds are heard, and a police siren wails in the distance. An instrumental, at least in terms of having no distinct lyrics, the song is literally musical theater on vinyl, ending in the mournful repeated cries of a cat and thereby maintaining the "Gutter Cat" allusion.

The closing track of side one, "Blue Turk," surprisingly shifts the pace and feel of the album considerably for the listener. Sung in straight fashion by Alice, devoid of the sneering aggression of the earlier tracks, the brass-heavy arrangement features lengthy traded solos by sultry, sliding, suggestive saxophone and trombone that paint with good effect the heavily sexual lyrics of the song's opening verses: "I'm hurting, I'm wanting, I'm aching for another go. You're squirming wet, baby—nothin' bad comin' very slow."

After a deceptively tinkly and melodic piano introduction, side two of *School's Out* begins with the hard-hitting "My Stars," signaling a return to the sonic vibe and style of the opening tracks of the first side. Thematically difficult to pin down through any lyric analysis, one minute Cooper is playing the role of a lonely (false) prophet, "Living on my own," who promises much: "Come all ye faithful you know all you people should come to me. I'll make your arms work and I'll make your legs work, I'll make you see"; the next minute he has abandoned any such façade to reveal a much darker motivation: "All I need is a holocaust to make my day complete."

The second clear highlight of the album, behind the title track, follows. "Public Animal #9" gives the listener an insight into what the excited, delinquent, school leaver of the album's title track has become, and thereby begins to draw together the darker, kid-fallen-off-the-tracks threads of the previous songs. Full of reminiscences of school days, including cheating on a math test, carving dirty words into desks, and being led off to detention with "Mrs. Cranston," "Public Animal #9" contains one of the best raison d'être statements of Cooper's career in the line, "She wanted an Einstein but she got a Frankenstein." Better still, Cooper is unrepentant, proclaiming at the song's conclusion, "I'm proud to be Public Animal #9," throwing in animalistic growls for good measure to underscore his hard-earned status.

As suggested both by the title and its late placement on the album, "Alma Mater" finds Alice once and for all bidding goodbye to his high school, the final word on what has been the overriding theme of the album. The song acts as a complementary bookend to the album's opener, although the personal vignette of high school life that Cooper relates—the reference to putting a snake "down little Betsy's dress" much to Mrs. Axelrod's displeasure—was actually a true memory of Buxton's. The end of "Alma Mater" creates a wonderful moment of poignancy and humor, segueing into the final track, "Grande Finale," with Cooper appealing to his school buddies to keep in touch and not be strangers. Imploring them in unaffected, hesitant spoken rather than sung lines, the music changes completely at this point to a plodding, spaghetti Western feel, complete with clip-clopping horse hooves, howling dogs in the distance, and a mournful harmonica—a complete and utter musical depiction of loneliness and abandonment. The listener cannot help but insert cactuses into the visual picture that the soundscape creates, completing the Clint Eastwood scene. The we're-all-in-this-together shared, albeit forced, camaraderie of the high school experience is over for Alice, because "I finally grew up—they finally let me out of school." Alice is left alone to face the world, and it is a world as bleak as a desert, barren as far as the eye can see. It is an emotion-filled moment that has a wide universality for listeners, as we've all been there.

"Grande Finale"—the most portentously titled Cooper track since "Titanic Overture," the opening track of *Pretties for You*—closes the album once the horse hooves and harmonica of "Alma Mater" have faded away. It is a somewhat anticlimactic ending, an instrumental track with little obvious reason for being. Nevertheless, one cannot help but admire the arrangement skills of Bob Ezrin in the song's slowly climaxing, swirling brass and string sections, and the recapitulation of a theme heard back on side one in "Gutter Cat vs. the Jets," a linking device that provides the track with at least a semblance of justification.

All in all, *School's Out* is a highly effective concept album that tells its story of youth and innocence lost in a non-linear, convincing, and also ass-kicking way. Tapping effortlessly into the natural trepidation of soon-to-be school leavers the world over and, just as easily, the reminiscences of those who had already made that inevitable transition, the band's recognition in the recording studio of the fact that they had created a youth anthem was more than borne out. Cooper relates in his autobiography, *Alice Cooper: Golf Monster*, "As soon as we heard it, we looked at each other and gasped, 'This is gonna be a monster!'"[9]

Despite reaching number four on the UK album charts—a full seventeen places higher than its predecessor, *Killer*—*Schools Out* attracted criticism from some fans and critics for its obvious musical theater qualities and the clearly evident Ezrin fingerprints in the production. *Rolling Stone* suggested, "Not all of *School's Out* is . . . rock. A good half is Broadway or movie soundtrack music." The theatrical bent of the album was conscious and purposeful, as Michael Bruce confirms: "We were now really keen to display the showbiz side of the band."[10] Based on the success of the title track hit single, the album marked the entry point for many new fans into the world of Alice Cooper. In terms of successfully conveying the Cooper modus operandi to a new legion of fans, and selling by the truckload in the process, the album was a triumph. Disillusioned youth had a new champion, and as Alice himself confirms:

> *School's Out* was an artistic rock landslide success. We were bigger than ever. I strolled onstage wearing a top hat and cane, and kids started wearing top hats and makeup on the back streets of London. People actually wanted to look like Alice Cooper.[11]

BILLION DOLLAR BABIES, 1973 [US CHART #1, UK #1]

This is their most elaborate album project to date and is the basis of the stage show they are to take with them around America. In the past various artists working in rock have attempted to fuse the effects and devices of the theatre but to date none has succeeded in achieving the impressive shock tactics Cooper employs. Musically they are fairly limited and apart from brilliant orchestration jobs like "Elected" with added horns, the players are called upon to supply suitably creepy background to the "he's right behind you," "Oh no he isn't," pantomime of "Billion Dollar Babies," and "Unfinished Sweet." The guitars and drums do a competent enough job. The lyrics and Alice's voice are the main strength.—Anonymous, *New Musical Express*, March 1973

One of the best solid rock groups recording today have produced another set of unpretentious, straight rock. Cooper is a top vocalist and the band backs him ably, with this entire LP a bit tighter than previous efforts. Key to the group's success, besides top musical performances, seems to be the ability to draw the line between good fun and tastelessness, an ability they have mastered. Each member makes a contribution, be it in writing, singing or playing and this is another plus. Best cuts: "Hello Hooray" and "Elected" (both single hits), "No More Mr. Nice Guy" and "Generation Landslide."—Anonymous, *Billboard*, March 1973

Side One

1. Hello Hooray (Kempf)
2. Raped and Freezin' (Bruce/Cooper)
3. Elected (Bruce/Buxton/Cooper/Dunaway/Smith)

4. Billion Dollar Babies (Bruce/Cooper/Reggie)
5. Unfinished Sweet (Bruce/Cooper/Smith)

Side Two

1. No More Mr. Nice Guy (Bruce/Cooper)
2. Generation Landslide (Bruce/Buxton/Cooper/Dunaway/Smith)
3. Sick Things (Bruce/Cooper/Ezrin)
4. Mary Ann (Bruce/Cooper)
5. I Love the Dead (Cooper/Ezrin)

Topping the achievements of *School's Out* was an extremely tall order, and yet the Alice Cooper band and Bob Ezrin managed exactly that, producing an album that achieved the holy grail of number one on both the US and the UK charts. This was the absolute peak of success for either incarnation of Alice Cooper—both the band and the solo artist.

If the school desk of the *School's Out* album cover had been a masterpiece of marketing by virtue of being not only wonderfully representative of the album's contents, but also clever in its obvious association with the everyday reality of the band's school-age and recent school-leaver audience, then the well thought out cover of *Billion Dollar Babies* was similarly effective. Displaying a savvy recognition of the power of one of the most controversial and best-loved hallmarks of a Cooper live show—the obligatory live boa constrictor that Alice periodically wore around his neck—the cover was composed of a green snakeskin pattern fashioned to resemble a billfold. Within a circle of diamonds at center-right sat a gold crest or medallion featuring the band's name and the album title, with a picture of a baby sporting Alice's trademark black mascara'd eyes at its heart. The Cooper humor is writ large here, as the band of five newly wealthy outcasts of society fully recognized the irony in their newfound status. The tongue-in-cheek, wealth-centeredness of the cover seems all the more apt, in retrospect, given the fact that *Billion Dollar Babies* would mark the commercial peak of the band, never again surpassed in terms of sales by any other Cooper release even during Alice' solo career to follow.

One of the most elaborate album covers ever designed, extras included pop-out bubble-gum cards featuring photographs of the band members in both portrait form and live action, a money clip encrusted with a faux diamond–studded dollar sign, and an inner sleeve picturing the band dressed in white silk suits along with a crying baby and white rabbits standing behind piles of dollar bills and evoking memories of Scrooge McDuck playing in his money bin. And, to top it all off, a giant pull-out fake billion-dollar note picturing the band on the front. Flipping the bill over to the reverse side reveals a tellingly fun-poking image of an intercontinental missile being paraded through the streets of Washington before cheering, hat-waving crowds, beneath which was written the legend, "In God We Trust"—political hypocrisy writ large for all to see.

The alternately lauded and lamented theatricality of *School's Out* firmly remains the starting point for the album's successor, as *Billion Dollar Babies* kicks off with a cover version of Rolf Kempf's cabaret-styled "Hello Hooray." Previously covered by Judy Collins, the song was suggested by Bob Ezrin to the approval of the band who collectively gave it a significant reworking. As Alice puts it:

> We wanted our version to sound like Alice Cooper meets *Cabaret*, complete with that bawdy pre—World War II German burlesque sound from when Deutschland was oblivious and drinking, carousing and cross-dressing its way to decadent destruction. [12]

The ascending fanfare that greets the ear as the track begins is emphatic and declamatory; the guitar lines rising trumpet-like to usher in both the song and the album. "Hello, Hooray! Let the show begin," sings Alice, making it evident in the clearest possible terms that the band is about to put on a show in the very best top-hat-and-cane tradition of showbiz, confirming that theater is once more at the forefront of the band's work. In Cooper's hands the lyrics of the first verse are pure Grand Guignol in their sentiment: "Ready as this audience that's coming here to dream. Loving every second, every moment, every scream." As emphatic an opener as "School's Out" had been on the previous album, or "Under My Wheels" on *Killer*, it is a fine beginning as the band unequivocally make Kempf's song their own.

"Raped and Freezin'" kicks in sans introduction, with Alice's voice present from beat one as he relates his narrative of misfortune while hitchhiking in Mexico: "Finally got a ride, some old broad down from Santa Fe—she was a real go-getter." True to the song's provocative title, Alice is subsequently raped in the back seat, escapes through the back door and runs naked through the desert with the "broad" in hot pursuit, leaving him "Stranded in Chihuahua." From the Cooper stock-in-trade, up-tempo, full-on rock, the musical style shifts in the song's outro to a convincing, albeit humorous, Latin section that begins at the two-minute, forty-five-second mark, complete with drum section and maracas, reflecting the geographical location of the action.

The third song, and certainly one of the album's strongest tracks, follows. "Elected" is a complete reworking of the song "Reflected" from 1969's *Pretties for You*, resulting in a virtual tour de force. With prominent and busy snare drumming from Neal Smith employed throughout the verses, playing quaver beats eight to the bar and generously using military-styled rolls, the song has a political pomp to it. The Ezrin-arranged brass section remains to the fore and the listener can close his eyes and almost see images of a street procession unfolding with all the pizzazz, bunting, cheerleaders, placards and general razzmatazz of American political rallies and parades. If *School's Out* had given youth a new leader in Alice Cooper, here he relishes and flaunts his new status, raising his baton to declare: "Kids want a savior—don't need a fake. I wanna be elected!" Cooper's voice on the track is mixed well back, giving the impression that it is coming from afar and that the listener is situated well back from the singer's podium. With Cooper's voice at its growling, snarling best, at times he does not sing so much as the use the historic German vocal technique of *Sprechstimme* (sing-speech) or even, in the song's concluding moments, straight speech in lines such as "I promise the formation of a new party. A third party. The Wild Party!" Special effects are also to the fore in the song, with devices such as a mock radio broadcast to bringing the news of the candidate's landslide success to the populace, and "all ships at sea." All in all, "Elected" is the perfect marriage of the Cooper band's hard rock and songwriting prowess, and producer Ezrin's sublime arrangement prowess and theatrical bag of tricks.

The title track follows "Elected," and the subject matter here is typically twisted, in effect being a love ode to a blow-up doll: "Rubber little monster, baby, I adore you. Man or woman living couldn't love me like you, baby." Recorded in London, as was most of the album, Scottish folkie-turned-pop-singer Donovan was a celebrity guest in the studio and contributed falsetto backing vocals to "Billion Dollar Babies" while also taking turn-about with Alice on the spoken sections: "We go dancing nightly in the attic while the moon is rising in the sky." While a most unlikely pairing, the combination of Donovan and Cooper works well, with the former reputedly relishing the change of musical style.

One of Cooper's finest Grand Guignol moments closes the first side of the record. "Unfinished Sweet" is pure aural theater—"Candy everywhere, got chocolate in my hair, aching to get me. Sickly sweet suckers in the Halloween air." The story of Alice's dental health being ruined by an overly sweet tooth and his subsequent treatment at the hands of his dentist would become a firm audience favorite in the band's live shows, with Alice being chased around the stage by the demented, perverted, dentist wielding a giant, revolving drill. Tapping deeply into that universally held fear and in the best Halloween tradition of the Grand Guignol, perhaps the star turn of the song is not the band or the singer, but the all-too-realistic drilling sound that Ezrin lays over the track leading up to the tooth-pulling scene in the middle of the song. Not only is the shrill, terrifying sound of the dentist's drill to the fore in the mix, but one hears the dentist struggling to pull the tooth out with pliers. Back and forth he wobbles the tooth, straining to pull it from the patient's jaw, accompanied by the sickening sounds of creaking. When it finally gives way—within a musical gap cleared of other sounds/instruments and engineered to afford the moment its optimum impact—it is with a sickening, triumphant, wet sound: "PLOP!" The band re-enters the scene and the patient comes to, slowly and groggily, still struggling to discern real life from his drug-induced hallucinations: "I come off the gas but I'm still seeing spies, aching to get me." The song, and thus side one of *Billion Dollar Babies,* ends in groans of pain and utter misery.

The opening track of side two stands as an enduring testament to the songwriting combination of Michael Bruce and Alice Cooper. Full of the Alice Cooper band's hallmarks and their most successful US single, perhaps the most telling feature of "No More Mr. Nice Guy" is the parody-rich way in which the sentiment of the narrative-based lyric expresses with exactitude the very same distaste and suspicion with which mainstream, grown-up America regarded the Alice Cooper band. "He's sick! He's obscene!" are the accusations leveled during the song at the anti-hero, Alice, by society at large. The lyrics, mostly penned by Bruce, are oppositional and funny, comprising a playful continuation of the outcast theme of "Public Animal #9" from the *School's Out* album of the previous year. Here, Alice is presented as a hopeless outcast reviled by one and all, human and non-human: "My dog bit me on the leg today—my cat clawed my eyes."

"Generation Landslide" was the final song written for the album, after the band had left the United Kingdom and taken a brief hiatus to the Canary Islands with the specific aim of writing more material. As the title suggests, generational alienation is at the fore, and the children-versus-elders theme that was established so emphatically and with such success in both "I'm Eighteen" and "School's Out" predominates throughout. In "Generation Landslide," the battle lines are clearly drawn: "Militant mothers, hiding in the basement—using pots and pans as their shields and their helmets." The Cooper humor too is in evidence, with a reference to pop culture consumerism: "The Colgate invisible shield finally got 'em." Of additional note, the opportunity to name-drop themselves is taken in both hands, as Cooper sings, self-referentially, "And I laughed to myself at the men and the ladies who never conceived of us billion dollar babies," thereby keeping alive the album's (and cover's) central theme of society's outcasts being feted and fawned over by the moneyed/ruling classes.

Grand Guignol returns with gusto in the next track, "Sick Things," a funereally paced, minimalist reminder of the Alice Cooper band's avant-garde past. Here, Alice is an unnamed and unidentified yet deadly predator lurking within the dark shadows of the night: "You things are chilled with fright, for I am out tonight. You tell me where to bite, you whet my appetite." As atmospheric and darkly themed as "Black Juju" from *Love It to Death*, and as freaky as "10 Minutes before the Worm" from *Pretties for You*, "Sick Things" serves to remind the listener that one of the Cooper cornerstones is comic-book horror, lest anyone had forgotten in the slick production and ever-improving rock songwriting evident in *School's Out* and thus far on *Billion Dollar Babies*. Simply, it was still not safe to look under the bed . . .

The left-field weirdness continues with the next track, "Mary Ann," a short cabaret/parlor song with only five lines of lyrics accompanied only by piano, with Cooper's voice recorded close-up and earnest, suddenly devoid of pretension and role play. A world away from the rock gloss of side one, the song appears to be an unexpectedly predictable and square mainstream love song right up until the final lyric line when Alice croons, "I thought you were my man." It is a moment that bends gender as comprehensively as did David Bowie in the song "Lady Stardust" off his breakthrough 1972 album, *The Rise and Fall of Ziggy Stardust and the Spiders from Mars,* when he sang, "Lady Stardust sang his song of darkness and disgrace."

The final track of *Billion Dollar Babies* does not let up on side two's descent into Grand Guignol–styled macabre; rather, it takes it to the album's absolute peak. Indeed, not only is "I Love the Dead" the most Grand Guignol moment of the album, but it is also the band's career pièce de résistance in terms of merging music and horror. The song begins with a slow, exposed, atmospheric bass line that would be closely recapitulated on in the opening moments of Alice's 1975 solo debut album, *Welcome to My Nightmare.* In every way "I Love the Dead" is completely true to title, as Cooper croons lovingly, with reverence, and in his finest ghoul voice, "I love the dead before they're cold—their bluing flesh for me to hold." Any doubts that the song is referencing the extreme social taboo of necrophilia are quickly dispeled with the subsequent line, "While friends and lovers mourn your silly grave, I have other uses for you, Darling," the vocal inflection employed on "other uses" seductive and dripping with innuendo to the point where one can almost see Alice winking while speaking. As if in celebration of the band's status as rock's primary proponent of distastefulness, "I Love the Dead" ends in a triumphant, euphoric, repeated refrain of the chorus/title line.

In summation, *Billion Dollar Babies* built skillfully on the success of *School's Out* and gave the band its finest moment in terms of popularity and commercial success. The audience that had been drawn in, en masse, by the enormous success of the "School's Out" single and who bought the album that spawned it followed through by purchasing its successor, and were not disappointed. The band members too were ecstatic at their efforts, Michael Bruce recalling,

> I remember we were out on the road when the album finally came out in February 1973. I listened to it in my hotel room and just got this really big smile. I was thinking, "It's amazing, we're really pulling this off." The album was very, very unique and very, very different. I was really proud of the songs, especially "No More Mr. Nice Guy," "Billion Dollar Babies" and "Generation Landslide." I kind of had mixed feelings about "I Love the Dead"—it wasn't my personal taste—but I understood the importance of that macabre thing to the album.[13]

The album also marked the band's peak in terms of touring. As Bruce further recalls in his band memoir, "The *Billion Dollar Babies* tour was our biggest ever. We played seventy-plus cities in three months. With *Billion Dollar Babies* a number one album on both sides of the Atlantic, no expense was spared."[14]

MUSCLE OF LOVE, 1973 [US CHART #10, UK #34]

The Alice Cooper phenomenon, which began with the chart entry of "I'm Eighteen," rose to diabolical heights with *Killer* and *School's Out* and extravaganzaed in the show surrounding the *Billion Dollar Babies*, has now cooled itself down with *Muscle of Love*. While the album contains several highlights and wild-card experiments, its mood reveals that both the group and Alice are uncertain of what new directions they might turn to their own uses.—Lenny Kaye, *Rolling Stone*, January 1974

Muscle of Love is a magnificent effort from the only American act to be able to put theater back into rock and roll. It's always a good experience putting one of Alice Cooper's albums on.—Anonymous, *Creem*, March 1974

Side One

1. Big Apple Dreamin' (Hippo) (Bruce/Buxton/Cooper/Dunaway/Smith)
2. Never Been Sold Before (Bruce/Buxton/Cooper/Dunaway/Smith)
3. Hard Hearted Alice (Bruce/Cooper)
4. Crazy Little Child (Bruce/Cooper)

Side Two

1. Working Up a Sweat (Bruce/Cooper)
2. Muscle of Love (Bruce/Cooper)
3. The Man with the Golden Gun (Bruce/Buxton/Cooper/Dunaway/Smith)
4. Teenage Lament '74 (Cooper/Smith)
5. Woman Machine (Bruce/Buxton/Cooper/Dunaway/Smith)

With the unprecedented runaway success of first *School's Out* and then *Billion Dollar Babies*, the third album in the Alice-Cooper-band-as-superstars trilogy was always likely to be a difficult one, and so it was to prove. With the demands to maintain—and further build on—their enormous success, cracks began to appear within the group. As Alice recalls of this time when *Muscle of Love* was being written and recorded: "I could tell that the band was starting to fade. Either we needed to rest or we needed to take time off. . . . Unfortunately, we didn't. The price I would pay later would be practically immeasurable."[15]

Adding to the difficulty of maintaining such success was the fact that a rift had developed between Bob Ezrin and the band, the producer reportedly having reached an impasse with Michael Bruce, in particular, and the parties parting ways at the peak of their collaborative success as a result. While Jack Richardson subsequently assumed the producer's seat in the studio for the recording of the album, the explanation given at the time for the two parties going their separate ways was that Ezrin was exhausted from the recent recording of Lou Reed's *Berlin* album, a version of events that does seem to contain at least some elements of truth.

In terms of strictly commercial success, *Muscle of Love* still achieved sales that would have been considered credible under any circumstances other than falling under the shadow of the smash global hit that had been *Billion Dollar Babies*. The album reached number ten in the United States, but fared considerably less well in the United Kingdom, peaking at thirty-four.

The innovative approach to album cover design displayed on both *School's Out* and *Billion Dollar Babies* continued on *Muscle of Love*, with the outer sleeve designed to resemble a plain cardboard shipping package, made from corrugated cardboard, and stamped with the words, "ATTENTION: THIS CARTON CONTAINS ONE (1) ALICE COOPER MUSCLE OF LOVE." Across the bottom right hand corner appears the word "FRAGILE," On the rear side the ruse continues with the legend, "DO NOT BEND: AVOID EXCESSIVE HEAT," beneath which the track titles are listed as the package's "CONTENTS." The packaging—both revered and reviled in its reception—proved problematic in term of practicality, however, as it would not fit into standard record shop display racks. Bruce recounts:

> In fact the sleeve was one of the things that really killed the *Muscle of Love* album. That damn cardboard box for an album cover . . . the album wasn't well-received by the distributors because there were only twelve records to each box and it was difficult to fit into the album racks in the stores.[16]

While the album title has obvious sexual overtones, it is the inner sleeve that most potently conveys a carefully crafted message about the album and, with the front side showing a photograph of the band dressed as sailors and congregating outside a seedy strip establishment titled the "Institute of Nude Wrestling," it is a message of debauchery and excess. Advertising on the windows and door of the establishment promise entertainments within that are "XXX Rated" and for "Adults Only," and include the opportunity to "Wrestle a Nude Female." The band members look gleeful and excited and carry fistfuls of money, as if they have just been granted shore leave, received their pay, and are hell-bent on partying hard in the centuries-old tradition of such seafarers. At the door stands a bored and scantily clad prostitute nonchalantly chewing gum and blowing a bubble while holding what appears to be a wine glass. At her side is a dwarf, well dressed in hat, suit, and tie—the gatekeeper whose job it is to relieve the sailors of their money as they enter to partake in the carnal pleasures within. Turning the inner sleeve over, one sees an after-the-fact photograph confirming that the group have indeed fully indulged themselves in the establishment's pleasures, with the band members found here once again outside the strip joint, beaten up, disheveled, extremely drunk, and attracting the close attention of military police. The band's sailor uniforms are either bloodied and in shreds or else gone completely, with two members of the band clad in underpants only. Watching the mayhem at close quarters and standing just outside the door is a gorilla in a blond wig wearing bright red lipstick, possibly a bouncer who has thrown the band out of the club for, presumably, bad behavior.

The obvious sexual innuendo of the cover as a purposeful indication of the album's theme is confirmed in interviews Alice gave at the time. For instance, in the January 1974 issue of *Circus*, he explained, "As long as nobody gets pregnant or hurt . . . sex is healthy. *Muscle of Love* will tell millions of people all about it!" Assuring the reader that establishments just like the fictitious Institute of Nude Wrestling are commonplace, especially around Santa Monica Boulevard, he elaborates further on the album's theme: *"Muscle of Love* is interested in urban sex habits, but it doesn't particularly state that. It just points towards it, and it doesn't have one particular statement that says *this is what's happening.* It just says, isn't this funny and that this *is* happening."

Charged with opening the album, "Big Apple Dreamin' (Hippo)" is a more understated and groove-based opening track than had been the case on the previous three albums, where "Under My Wheels," "School's Out," and "Hello Hooray," respectively, made emphatic musical statements. As the title of this mid-paced opener suggests, the lyrics are about dreaming of New York, and the protagonists here are young, unworldly-wise men from Ohio: "We're so young and pretty, we're so young and clean. So many things that we have never seen." Tying in with the sailor imagery of the inner-sleeve photographs, they crave to experience the fleshpots of the big city, having "Heard about them massages, and all those dirty shows. I read somewhere some places never close." The song sets the thematic mood of the album, certainly, but it remains an unusual choice as an opener in that it is an obvious album cut rather than having the hook-laden, infectious, single potential of its predecessors, and with its extended outro and accompanying fade out it ends in a whisper rather than the fist-pumping scream that Cooper fans had become used to with each new album.

The second song of the album, "Never Been Sold Before," stays true to the sexually charged theme but turns the tables 180 degrees with a lyric sung from the perspective of a woman arguing with her man because he wants to pimp her: "I just can't believe that you're selling me, you never sold me before. I just can't become your lousy whore." The song is upbeat and direct, pulling no punches in its protestations: "I'm sick of streets, chicks and dicks, and I'm, I'm really sick of you." Overall, it is an empowering sentiment that is being expressed in the song, and with disdain the woman suggests that fifty dollars is not enough money to even buy her smile.

Displaying nothing of the underlying sexual theme of *Muscle of Love* that had been visited in the opening tracks, the next song, "Hard Hearted Alice," was written by Michael Bruce and Alice. Rather than being strictly autobiographical on the latter's part, in Bruce's recollection, "I think it was really about the band—I think my intuition was telling me that the band was breaking up."[17] Certainly, the song provides a less-than-cheerful account of the hard-touring musician's lifestyle in lines such as "Noise, seems logically right—ringing ears in the night, when you live in an airport," or the wistful, "Hard hearted Alice is what we want to be—hard hearted Alice is what you want to see."

If the album so far has seemed light on songs that could reasonably be considered single material—at least by the band's standards of the previous couple of years—the fourth and final song of side one does nothing to rectify the situation. The ploddingly paced "Crazy Little Child," performed in a New Orleans musical style and with appropriate instrumentation, is a narrative about a young boy, Jackson, growing up on the mean streets and turning to crime to escape his "bitch" mother and "rich" father: "He was a crazy little child—New Orleans alley playground. Grimy faced he watched the hookers cry." But his hired-gun lifestyle all went wrong during a botched safecracking job, and while his accomplices escaped and abandoned him to his fate, the teenager gets shot dead by police. It is an unremittingly bleak song, and stylistically an aberration for the Alice Cooper band. As Bruce puts it, "Let's face it this was a real step outside the normal Alice Cooper material."[18]

Side two starts off in a manner far more in keeping with what fans had come to expect from Alice Cooper, in the rocking, aggressive, catchy, and magnificent "Working Up a Sweat." In a return to the album's theme, the track is blatantly sexual from the very first line, "Aw, when you touch there, honey—makes my blood perspire," and it doesn't let up from there on. In the third verse the Cooper humor is very much at the fore as, when clearly talking in a thinly disguised manner about contracting a sexually transmitted disease, the final word of the description is comically delayed when Cooper exclaims, "The hardest part explaining all those blisters on my—nose!" The listener can almost see the singer's nod and accompanying wink as the line is delivered.

The title track sits as track two on the B side of the record and, as one might expect, is thematically entirely consistent with the album's central theme of exploring various sexual practices and mores—in this case, masturbation: "I read Dad's books like I did before—now things are crystal clear. Lock the door in the bathroom now—I just can't get caught in here." Confirming that the album title is indeed a euphemism for the penis, the Bruce and Cooper–penned song is a full-on rocker, a virtual paean to the practice of self-pleasuring—regarded as "a gift from above"—and one of the best tracks on the album.

As quickly as the return to the album's sexual theme had been re-established in the first two tracks of side two it was gone again, because next up, James Bond makes an unexpected appearance in the world of Alice Cooper in "[The] Man with the Golden Gun," an unsuccessful bid written with collaborative enthusiasm by the whole band to provide the theme song for the ninth Bond movie of the same name. As Bruce recalls:

> While in England we'd been approached by some people who asked us if we'd like a shot at writing the theme song. . . . The whole band were big James Bond fanatics and jumped at the chance to do it. With our love of soundtracks and showbiz, I guess we were looking forward to hearing our song playing over the distinctive opening credits. . . . Unfortunately it never made it into the film. They passed on our song and used Lulu's instead. I still think our song was fuck-ing great.[19]

A contrasting view is held by drummer Neal Smith, who considered the recording of the song to be substandard, describing it as "the one song, of all the albums we did, where I just wasn't happy with the basic track. It was supposed to be a contender for the Bond movie and all the parts were there, but it just wasn't as crisp as it should have been."[20] Meanwhile, Cooper biographer Dave Thompson is scathing in his appraisal, suggesting, "Perhaps no song better illustrates the depths to which the band's creativity had sunk than "The Man with the Golden Gun"."[21] Certainly the mid-tempo song lacks spark and is lyrically mini-malist, but perhaps its biggest flaw is that it appears to have no reason for being on the album, being essentially written for a different purpose but ultimately used as an album filler track.

The penultimate song on *Muscle of Love* is also the strongest song on the album, at least in terms of relevance to the youth culture of the day. "Teenage Lament '74," as other critics have also noted, can easily be read as a kind of ode to the passing of the heyday of glam/glitter rock. "What a drag it is—these gold lame jeans," sings Alice, later ex-plaining his feelings about the track to British rock weekly *New Musical Express* in February 2, 1974, article:

> My favourite track is "Teenage Lament '74" . . . It's about a kid growing up today who doesn't want red hair, or glitter on his face or,

flashy clothes, but he has to conform because it's a social thing. If I were a kid now, I'd rebel and go the other way. That's how the whole Alice thing started, only it became accepted. This poor kid is just stuck in the middle. He doesn't want to look like David Bowie or Alice. The song features the return of the individual . . . "Teenage Lament" stood out to me—it's reminiscent of "Eighteen."

Just as "I'm Eighteen" had humor embedded in the lyric (especially in the emphatic closing statement, "And I LIIIKE it!"), so too the central Cooper ingredient of humor adds spark to "Teenage Lament '74": "Well, I cut my hair weird—I read that it was in. I looked like a rooster that was drowned and raised again."

Also notable on the track is the superb quality of, and emphasis given to, the backing vocals, unsurprising when one notes the recruitment of Liza Minelli, the Pointer Sisters, Ronnie Spector, and Labelle to the task. As he opined to *New Musical Express* in the same article, "I wanted the best voices I could think of. Bette Midler was busy, but I got the Pointer Sisters to do scat vocals. Ronnie Spector did her 1960s voice. And we got Labelle and Liza."

In the United Kingdom, the epicenter of glam rock, the single release of "Teenage Lament '74" reached number twelve on the charts, taking its place alongside other late glam titles of a similar ilk, including "Teenage Rampage" by the Sweet, and most particularly, "Teenage Dream" by T Rex, which asked the question, "Whatever happened to the teenage dream?" and implying strongly that the golden years of glam were over. This good showing on the singles chart for "Teenage Lament '74" provided a measure of conciliatory success for the album. In addition to bidding farewell to glam rock, however, in hindsight the song also seems a fitting, albeit completely inadvertent, signing off from the Alice Cooper band, as it was the last success of the group's career. Tellingly, dissent was evident even between the songwriters, Cooper and Neal Smith, during the recording, especially with regard to its vibe: "It's too sweet . . . I wrote it and I don't like it," the latter recalled, adding, in regard to the celebrity singers who were invited to provide the backing vocals, "I am a purist and didn't like outsiders singing on our records."[22]

The final track of *Muscle of Love* and of the Alice Cooper band's fine career run of eight studio albums recorded over the course of five years fell to "Woman Machine," a song fittingly credited to the whole band

and, unlike the disconcerting diversions in evidence elsewhere on the album, fully consistent with the firmly established Cooper shtick in terms of its unabashed rock musical style and also thoroughly in keeping with the record's sexual theme, albeit unremittingly chauvinistic when viewed through post-2000 eyes. Almost certainly written with tongue placed firmly in cheek, the lyrics describe the delights of a robot woman who can work hard all day cleaning the house and still unreservedly take care of her man's sexual needs in the evening: "She goes to bed when her work is through—she'll do it all, just change the tubes." Tapping heavily into the timeworn sexist comedy concept of the nagging housewife, Cooper assures the listener, "She can't talk back with no playback, but she'll listen to all your woe."

There are moments of inspiration and Alice Cooper band brilliance on *Muscle of Love*, and for this critic these are most especially "Teenage Lament '74," "Working Up a Sweat," and the title track. However, in summation it was a disappointing way for the Alice Cooper band to end their reign. At times highly disjointed, there were big disparities within the sonic and thematic aspects of the work. Based on a very loose concept of exploring sexual practices that was present for only some of the time, and containing song choices that simply didn't fit—most especially "Crazy Little Child" and "The Man with the Golden Gun"—the consistency that had made *School's Out* and *Billion Dollar Babies* such fine albums was largely absent, and instead fans were faced with a virtual box of chocolates, as Forrest Gump might have described it. The absence of Bob Ezrin was a commonly visited point in reviews, and never more so than in producer/musician guru Kim Fowley's withering appraisal. Fowley also took the opportunity to acknowledge manager Shep Gordon's part in the whole Alice Cooper phenomenon:

> ALICE COOPER is an American International movie 10 years later set to music. But where is the director, Bob Ezrin? He directed such wow scenes as "I'm Eighteen," "School's Out" and "No More Mr. Nice Guy" and is nowhere to be found on this LP. When the Coasters lost Lieber and Stoller, they failed; when the Beatles lost Brian Epstein, they failed; and when the Rolling Stones lost Keith Richard (think about it) they failed! . . . Shep Gordon is a genius. Bob Ezrin is a genius. Alice Cooper is a genius. *Muscle of Love* isn't a genius piece of work. The LP by Queen on Elektra tries harder than *Muscle of Love*. Buy it instead.[23]

Much has been surmised, written, postulated on, and assumed about the end of the Alice Cooper band. While millions of fans worldwide continued to follow Alice (singular) through into his solo career and have stayed loyal supporters ever since, for many fans it is the clutch of early albums by the original band that are held closest to their collective hearts. There was certainly a magic in the combination of the five musicians, Cooper, Buxton, Dunaway, Bruce, and Smith, that resulted in a sublime—if all-too-truncated—body of work. Small wonder that they had such a unique and impossible to recreate chemistry, given their shared background from boys to men, and the rags-to-riches story of their elevation to one of rock music's top acts of the early 1970s. While this book does not attempt to retell the story—already recounted by Cooper, Bruce, and Dunaway in their autobiographies, albeit with unsurprising differences of opinion—it is clear that divisions had appeared, external problems compounding the rifts, and the experience of creating *Muscle of Love* had brought many factors to a head. Smith and Bruce wanted to do solo albums, Buxton was having all sorts of problems with addiction that were impacting significantly on the band, Alice wanted to go more theatrical—in close cahoots with Bob Ezrin—while the others wanted to move in the opposite direction . . . as Dave Thompson succinctly and summatively put it, "Disillusion kicked in."[24]

Michael Bruce recalls of this time:

> Alice Cooper, solo star, was really born around the time of *Muscle of Love*. Little by little he started spending less time with the band. . . . He was in a different league now. . . . There were times when the band would make an appearance and everyone would ignore us. They just wanted to take pictures and talk with Alice.[25]

The press began speculating; according to the August 1974 issue of *Melody Maker*, "Alice Cooper plus two members of his band—drummer Neal Smith and guitarist Michael Bruce—are planning separate solo albums. But reports of a split in the band are, according to a spokesman, 'hotly denied.'"

Perhaps the most telling portent of things to come during this period belongs to manager Shep Gordon, who warned Bruce and the other members of the band against embarking on solo ventures. Bruce recalls his warning: "I wouldn't advise you doing that Michael because once you open the door for Alice to do a solo thing he might not come back."[26]

3

ALICE DREAMS ALONE

Welcome to My Nightmare, 1975 [US #5, UK #19]

In my eyes the Alice Cooper band never broke up. There wasn't any yelling. Nobody accused anyone of anything or pointed any fingers. . . . None of the other band members wanted to take the ride with me as lead singer. After seven years of slaving, seven hard years on the road, they were tired. The last thing they wanted to hear was Alice and Shep were planning the production of all productions. . . . The rest of the band balked and backed out. Shep and I said, "Okay. We're pushing onward." *Welcome to My Nightmare* was our baby.—Alice Cooper, *Alice Cooper: Golf Monster,* 2008

Making his debut as a solo artist (without the rest of the group), the master of shockrock expands his musical direction toward more innovation and precision, blending fantasies and pathos with several thousand volts of electro-rock therapy. . . . Not many rock "idols" would voluntarily set themselves up for self-mockery. But Alice will. Alice will do anything. And he always has. So this time around, as Alice welcomes you to his nightmare, he's really welcoming you to another trek through a bizarrely all-American fun house of distorted mirrors and deliciously twisted thoughts. Dream on—and pleasant nightmares.—Meridee Merzer, *Penthouse,* September 1975

This poor kid wakes up and ugly demons are coming out of his toybox, a bevy of black widows are waiting to turn him into a succulent stew, and Cold Ethyl—a most seductive, but wholly stone cold stiff lady (necrophilia, anybody?)—languishes in the family fridge. Welcome to Alice Cooper's nightmare.—Lynn Van Matre, *Chicago Tribune*, April 2, 1975

Side One

1. Welcome to My Nightmare (Cooper/Wagner)
2. Devil's Food (Cooper/Ezrin/Jay)
3. The Black Widow (Cooper/Ezrin/Wagner)
4. Some Folks (Cooper/Ezrin/Gordon)
5. Only Women Bleed (Cooper/Wagner)

Side Two

1. Department of Youth (Cooper/Ezrin/Wagner)
2. Cold Ethyl (Cooper/Ezrin)
3. Years Ago (Cooper/Wagner)
4. Steven (Cooper/Ezrin)
5. The Awakening (Cooper/Ezrin/Wagner)
6. Escape (Anthony/Cooper/Fowley)

Welcome to My Nightmare is a watershed album for Alice Cooper; it was the moment when the band that bore the famous name became no more, despite there being no official breakup nor burial, leaving only the lead singer to carry on the name. Legions of fans were dismayed, while others were highly excited. The music press was intrigued and awaited the release with pens poised and eyebrows raised, while turbulence and rumors abounded. Alice wasted no time, however, and teamed up once again with producer Bob Ezrin, so conspicuously absent on *Muscle of Love*, in order to fully indulge the expansive theatrical creation that he sought to do with the full backing of manager Shep Gordon, but which had been the source of such division between himself and the original band members.

Like a spider creeping across the carpet into a darkened bedroom, the opening, and title, track, "Welcome to My Nightmare," does not announce its arrival with a crash, bang, wallop. Rather, it creeps into the listener's consciousness, beginning with a subtle downward glissando that leads into an acoustic guitar line fattened out with the addition of sparse root notes on the bass while off-beat cymbal taps keep time. The effect is immediately atmospheric and spooky, and when Alice's voice enters after four bars it is quiet and controlled, with none of the Alice Cooper signature rasp and edge evident. His opening words are the album's title, a literal welcome to his audience to share in the forthcoming "nocturnal vacation" experience, within which, he assures the listener, they will feel quite at home because "you belong," thereby immediately setting up an intimate rapport between himself and his audience. It is only when the album title is repeated at the end of the quietly understated, territory declaiming, first verse that the band enters in full and the timbre of Alice's voice takes on the familiar "Coop" quality of threat. Once the song is in full swing, the sound is a swirling, phasing, groove-driven dreamscape, the production crisp and clean, with the vocals to the forefront so that each word is clearly audible at the forefront of the mix. This is a soundtrack, a concept album in every sense of the word, and therefore the delivery of each word is critical. Expressing the hope that he hasn't already scared us, Alice lays out what awaits his audience within his nightmare, assuring us, "We sweat and laugh and scream here, 'cause life is just a dream here." As if not wishing to wake us up so early in the piece, the opening title song never becomes raucous or overbearing, instead remaining groove-based and controlled with no loud crescendos or shock moments apart from a single deep overdubbed explosion at the conclusion of the vocals. An extended outro with particularly striking horn parts—an Ezrin specialty—then completes the extraordinary scene-setting album opener, eventually fading out to silence; this is once again a carefully worked musical device, set to ensure the listener/dreamer does not get forced into wakefulness.

Now that the subject/victim is fully asleep, however, lulled by swirling, phasing guitars and banks of luscious consonant horns, he cannot wake up no matter how hard he tries, and so track two, "Devil's Food," begins with far more impact, the acoustic guitar intro of track one giving way to distorted rock guitar, menacing and angular. "Getting' ready for the lady!" bellows Alice in the song's opening line, before growling in his darkest Grand Guignol voice that fairly drips with venom, "She's gonna be a treat." Every line of lyrics in "Devil's Food" brings with it more threat and nightmarish imagery: "I knew your precious life and I know your death." Alice here is an actor as much as he is a singer, and while the entire song serves to set up what is to come— and it is abundantly clear that what follows cannot be good—the exact nature of the imminent threat is not made clear. At the two-minute mark Alice utters a loud, despairing scream that tapers off to reveal background noises of people chatting and plates clattering atop a restrained, walking-pace, military-style snare drum pattern. It is the beginning of the third track, "The Black Widow." Now, the threat is revealed. Suddenly a voice speaks over the soundtrack and it is instantly recognizable as that of famed horror-movie actor Vincent Price, veteran of numerous Hammer Horror films including *Theater of Blood, Dr. Phibes, The Comedy of Terrors, The Pit and the Pendulum, House of Wax*, and many others. Here, he quickly assumes the guise of a tour guide, moving his tour group along from lepidoptera to the arachnid display: "The spiders, our finest collection." Price describes a couple of lesser species with little enthusiasm before, with excitement starting to build in his voice, he turns to "my prize, the Black Widow. Isn't she lovely? And SO deadly!" With an increasingly manic edge to his voice, he goes on to triumphantly outline his horrific vision for a future in which Black Widow spiders will take over the world, because "man has ruled this world as a stumbling demented child-king long enough!" Immediately following Price's declamatory final word, there is a sudden pause before Alice affirms Price's statement and pledges his own allegiance to the Black Widow. The rest of the song is given over to nightmare images of the havoc that the giant spiders will wreak: "The horror that he'll bring, the horror of his sting," and at this point in the accompanying live show Alice would do battle with two huge spiders, their webs strung across the stage. Given most people's revulsion against spiders, "The Black Widow" brings to life a universally held fear on the rock stage for the first time ever.

In the following track, "Some Folks," Alice ponders the many different dark secrets that people may secretly relish, yet keep strictly to themselves. The musical underpinning is jaunty and benign, standing in purposeful contrast to the subject matter and providing clear testament to how such feelings, desires, and urges can be masked so effectively. Standing in lighter relief to the opening three tracks, in terms of musical style, the lyrics nevertheless still further the dark nuances of the story thus far: "Some folks love to feel pain . . . some folks die without a warning."

Completing side one of *Welcome to My Nightmare* is the seemingly somewhat incongruous but beautiful ballad, "Only Women Bleed."

Written by Cooper and Dick Wagner and recorded with the Toronto Symphony Orchestra with Ezrin at the baton, the song provided the surprise hit of the album, reaching number twelve on the US Billboard singles chart and soundly beating the performance of the title track, which reached a far more modest forty-fifth spot. While its place in the narrative of the album is tenuous at best, the sentiment is a telling one, with its message of abhorrence for domestic violence against women delivered in a frank and no-holds-barred manner as the male protagonist remains a monster no matter what his woman does to try to please him: "He lies right at you, you know you hate this game. He slaps you once in a while and you live and love in pain." And in the powerful bridge section, the visual imagery is equally strong: "Black eyes all of the time." Despite the song's lack of obvious context within the *Welcome to My Nightmare* narrative, its sheer power, vivid imagery, and sweeping range of dynamics made it a winner on the live stage, and the act of mock-beating a woman was the crime for which Alice would be executed in many an Alice Cooper show for years to come.

The opening track of side two, "Department of Youth," is for this reviewer one of the highlights of *Welcome to My Nightmare*. A youth anthem in the tradition of "I'm Eighteen" and "School's Out," this rallying cry with its powerful four-on-the-floor rhythm displays wonderfully Cooper's mastery of expressing in song form the feeling of difference and marginalization experienced by all youth. A generation-based call to arms, the rhymes form a key part of the songs catchy charm: "And we've never heard of Eisenhower, missile power, justice and truth. We're the Department of Youth." Impressive too is the obvious sense of humor that flows through the song, never better displayed than in the outro, which is set up as an antiphonal call and response between the leader (Alice) and his acolytes. When Alice asks who it was that had given the power to the kids, expecting them to answer emphatically that he had done so, he loudly exclaims with faux outrage, "What?" when they instead answer en masse, "Donny Osmond!"

"Cold Ethyl" is another out-and-out rocker, and is somewhat infamous for its none-too-subtle theme of necrophilia. Extremely fond of "making love by the refrigerator light" with her, it bothers Alice not one bit that "Ethyl's frigid as an Eskimo pie." Any doubt about Ethyl's state of being is completely removed in verse two: "She's cool in bed. Yeah she oughta be, 'cause Ethyl's dead." Again, humor is at the fore here, and given that his sexual partner is kept on ice until each time he needs her, the oft-used expression "I'm stuck on you" takes on a whole different meaning in Cooper's mischievous hands.

When "Years Ago" then begins, the pace dramatically changes from that of the duo of up-tempo rockers that had opened the flip side. In 3/4 time, and with a fairground organ predominating and ensuring an eerie sonic element, the scene is quickly and creepily set in an abandoned playground, the protagonist all alone and going up and down slowly on a swing while telling us from a first-person perspective how "all my friends went home years ago." One can only feel sympathy when he relates, "All my toys are broken, and so am I inside, mom." The horror factor steps up significantly in the song when, just after Alice has told us in his best little-boy voice that he is indeed a little boy, a big, booming, doom-laden, man's voice claims: "No, I'm a great big man!" Pleading to stay a little boy for longer, the song ends with the boy's mother calling him from afar in the distance, and we learn, at last, that his name is Steven.

"Years Ago" gently fades away until near silence before segueing smoothly into the victim's self-titled song, "Steven," where tinkling piano and plucked strings maintain the dreamlike mood. Alice continues to sing in the first person as Steven, his voice trembling and uncertain. As the song title suggests, at this point of the album the subject is caught in that disturbing middle ground between wakefulness and sleep: "I must be dreaming, please stop screaming!" The listener can feel the battle being waged as Steven tries desperately to wake up from his nightmare. "I think I hear a voice—it's outside the door!" Steven cries in anguish toward the end of the song. Given the critical point it serves within the narrative, "Steven" is afforded the longest track duration of the entire album.

From silence, abstract incidental noises and a looped piano fragment then usher in "The Awakening." Alice here abandons his adoption of a child's voice and, when his first vocal line is uttered, it is in his deep and menacing signature voice: "I wake up in the basement, I'm so hungry, I'm dry. I must be here sleepwalking, mustn't I?" But he is no longer asleep, and because of this fact the song takes the darkest twist of any on the album when he subsequently goes looking for his wife, sees through his "real eyes" a trail of blood spots on the floor, and realizes that blood is dripping from his hand. The intensity of the music builds through this procession through the house as he discovers what he has done in his sleep, but Cooper and Ezrin are not done with delivering frightening surprises to their audience yet. When he comes to the realization that it was him all along at the point where he spots his bloodied hand, instead of the music climaxing as it had been seemingly going to, it instead drops right away and Alice almost whispers the killer line, "And ooh it makes me feel like a man." Following this spine-chilling revelation, the track dissolves into sudden, sparse piano chords and loud, random, low drum beats. It is like the sound of an axe falling, and quietly in the mix we also hear small sounds like drops of liquid that come and go quickly. Suddenly, the track fades to nothing.

It is with quite some relief that the final song then kicks in, loud and celebratory, from the silence. A triumphant, strutting, and arrogant Rolling Stones–esque guitar riff that acts in the manner of a fanfare ushers in the sneering opening vocal lines of "Escape," the eleventh track of *Welcome to My Nightmare.* As if Alice is keen to put his hands up and exorcise the dark gravitas of what has gone before, the opening two lines give a clear insight into his role-playing performance methodology: "Paint on my cruel or happy face–hide me behind it. It takes me inside another place where no one can find it." As the song title suggests, it's all escapism. Just as he is markedly famous for in his live shows, where he always ends a performance with balloons, levity, and festiveness, here on his debut solo album he also leaves his audience on a high so that they go away uplifted and not downcast. In "Escape," simply, it is party time. In keeping with lightening the mood, humor is at the fore once again, and Alice tells of stealing his doctor's mascara and of ending his days black and blue (undoubtedly from being executed on stage every night). The nightmare ended emphatically with the previous song and now the real Alice is back in the room, having stepped out of the role, removed the fourth wall, and acknowledged the shared experience he has with the fans who come to see him and his job as an entertainer: "Just put on my makeup and get me to the show," he implores.

True to his stated goals, which had proven too much for the rest of the band to countenance, the Cooper and Ezrin–devised *Welcome to My Nightmare* had been the most theatrical album to bear the Alice Cooper name under any circumstances. And the stage show that it spawned would hugely raise the bar for all theatrical acts to follow.

Nevertheless, some critics, outraged by Cooper's in-your-face artifice and evident refusal to take rock music seriously, dismissed *Welcome to My Nightmare* as "mere" theater, derogatorily insisting that it broached some never-defined, once omnipresent, but now crumbling mythical edict of rock authenticity. Jaan Uhelszki, writing in the May 1975 issue of *Creem*, suggested, "*Nightmare* dangles between offensive pretensions and terminal cynicism; Alice is hung by his own rope." Meanwhile, Charles Shaar Murray, one of the most respected writers in the British music press, opined:

> The horrors that Cooper manufactures and then confronts on our behalf are all so obviously papier-mache that the liberating effect of the enactment of the confrontation is approximately zero, and it is the basic moral and social cowardice of Cooper's work that condemns him. [1]

Meanwhile, however, *Welcome to My Nightmare* sold by the truckload, reversing the backward sliding trend of the final Alice Cooper band album, *Muscle of Love*, and reached number five on the US Billboard charts. In the United Kingdom, the album scraped into the top twenty, achieving a number nineteen placing and again reversing the trend on that side of the Atlantic that had seen *Muscle of Love* reaching only number thirty-four. One might well imagine Alice chuckling into his Budweiser as he set out on his enormous global tour of the same name. While parents and rock purists linked arms to sputter and tut-tut, bigger-than-ever legions of "Coop" fans got on with the job of painting trademark black circles around their eyes and clutching precious concert tickets to their chests. For a brief time at least, such fans forgot the trials and tribulations of school, or dead-end jobs at fast-food counters, car washes, and grocery stores, and were indeed taken to "another place" by their scowling, cane-wielding anti-hero. Under the baleful glare of society's disapproval, Cooper and his fans united under the banner of their self-styled "Department of Youth." Rarely had teenagers and pre-teens been given such a cleverly concise and liberating rallying call. But this was no accident or fluke. The most potent previous example of such an anthem, "School's Out," from 1972, was also Cooper's. And preceding that, in 1970, his rallying cry had been "I'm Eighteen." Hats off to Alice Cooper, then—the indisputable champion of the disaffected and alienated, pied piper to the geeks, weirdos, losers, and the maladjusted. In short, all those caught in the twilight zone between childhood and adulthood. Disturbing for moms and dads, politicians and moral watchdogs, a new and very different role model to Elvis or the Beatles now held center stage. Cooper's message was simple: being on the outside was better than being one of the "in crowd." The worm had turned.

Visual analysis of the *Welcome to My Nightmare* album artwork, superbly created by Drew Struzan, provides iconography that acts as a crucial paratext in closely supporting the contents of the vinyl it housed. The top-hatted, tuxedo-wearing Cooper leans out of the front cover of the album in faux 3D, like a leering carnie trying to entice the unwitting to venture into the dangerous depths of the ominous inky-black triangle that surrounds him. Outside this, a plethora of bugs, spiders, flies, and other insects emphatically and creepily reinforces the nightmarish invitation. In short, the cover informs on the album's contents to an extent few other artists could match; in David Bowie terms, both sound and vision are in total synchronicity.

After watching Alice's *Welcome to My Nightmare* show in Detroit, the Alice Cooper group guitarist Michael Bruce, often-time songwriting collaborator with Alice, commented:

> I suppose it's just . . . Alice's trip, you know? I mean, when we first started out the reason we got into all the theatrics in the first place was because we couldn't play as well as other bands. I mean, that was around the time of the Doors and a whole lot of other bands that we knew we just couldn't compete with, and we figured that was the only way to get attention. And, while the rest of us have music to fall back on, Alice has to depend on the theatrical thing, so in a way he's kind of stuck with it. . . . No, I didn't resent any part of it. I like the guys in his band very much, they're incredible musicians. . . . But I do think there was something we had as a group after all those years together that can't exactly be duplicated overnight. You can do it differently, yes, but you can't really duplicate it. And when they did the songs that we had recorded together as a group, "I'm Eighteen" and the other ones, well, there I have to admit that was kind of a weird feeling. I mean, it was interesting to stand back objectively and hear somebody else doing your music, but I have to admit it did feel . . . strange.[2]

In Alice's eyes, *Welcome to My Nightmare* was an enormous breakthrough and, as he put it, the album and accompanying tour "remains one of the most iconic Alice Cooper moments in history."[3]

WELCOME TO MY NIGHTMARE CONCERT, WESTERN SPRINGS STADIUM, AUCKLAND

In 1977 Alice Cooper performed his *Welcome to My Nightmare* concert at Western Springs Stadium in Auckland, New Zealand, and I was there.

No, wait—that doesn't do it justice . . .

In 1977 Alice Cooper performed his *Welcome to My Nightmare* concert at Western Springs Stadium in Auckland, New Zealand, and I WAS THERE!

Auckland, and indeed, New Zealand, had never seen anything remotely like it. For many of his 20,000-strong audience on that balmy autumn night—including this writer, then aged seventeen—the bar was instantly, immeasurably, raised for every rock 'n' roll show that would ever come to visit our South Pacific shores forever after.

Close enough to the stage to dare to dream of catching a drop of Cooper sweat, a stray balloon, or—prince of hopes—part of a dismembered doll [swoon!], I watched the hour-and-a-quarter *Welcome to My Nightmare* concert unfold with an ever-increasing mix of awe and incredulity. With an intensity I had never previously experienced, and from the moment our favorite anti-hero entered the stage through a haze of red and green smoke, the concert brought to life in full visual and aural color the adventures of Steven—the boy who could not wake up from his nightmare, a story that I had heard told innumerable times through my headphones as I lay on my bed with my eyes closed, courtesy of my well-worn copy of the album of the same name. Short portions of the *Welcome to My Nightmare* concert were seen through the viewfinder of my Kodak Pocket Instamatic camera, accompanied by frequent silent curses at the necessity of having to juggle and insert, amid a heaving, jostling mob, a succession of fresh four-shot disposable flashcubes. Remaining ever mindful of the twenty-four-shot limit of my desperate endeavor to visually preserve this experience forever, I recognized only too well as the events of the evening unfolded that I was in the midst of a highly significant moment in my lifetime. A signpost. An epiphany. (For decades afterwards, I treasured the few grainy, blurry photos that actually turned out ok, only to eventually, tragically lose them somehow, somewhere.)

Neither I, nor my many thousands of fellow concertgoers, nor Auckland or indeed New Zealand at large, had ever seen such goings-on before. Giant spiders, a rampaging, lumbering Cyclops, choreographed domestic violence, a public execution . . . such things were far from de rigueur in our safe, distant land where Kiwis and sheep simply got on with their business without fuss, and shops remained closed by law all weekend, every weekend. Our touchstones or reference points for experiencing Alice Cooper's show in all its theatrical glory? There were none. The then-nascent, wacky, but endearing Split Enz perhaps? Er, no. While we remain exceptionally proud of our own mascara'd, groundbreaking clown troupe, Split Enz and Alice Cooper shared nothing bar the vague commonality of above-average theatrical investment.

"Welcome to my nightmare," Alice grotesquely and prophetically crooned at us as the show started, draping himself around the skull-imbued bedframe upon which Steven's nightmares took place. How powerful it was to hear those very same opening words in that very same voice with which he began the album that I had purchased so eagerly a year or so earlier and by then knew by heart, from first to last note. As a committed fan, this album was special—even more special than usual—because it was the Coop's debut solo effort and therefore far more of a *Welcome to HIS Nightmare* than the examples of winking debauchery, protest, and irreverence that the collectively named Alice Cooper band had produced in the past, sublime though they were. Just like David Bowie in Tin Machine many years later, this was an artist who could never really be just one of the boys. All things were not, in fact, always democratic and egalitarian in rock 'n' roll. And now, with the release of the *Welcome to My Nightmare* album and subsequent world tour, that uneasy situation had gone. Alice Cooper, solo artist with no peer, had finally arrived on the stage in all of his singular, disreputable, and controversial—but in so many ways magnificent and authenticity-shredding—glory. And he was doing it in my hometown at the bottom of the world. Unbelievable. A bootleg exists of that concert, preserving forever for those lucky enough to be able to find a copy, the evening that rock concerts in New Zealand became transformed into theater.

Set list for Alice Cooper's *Welcome to My Nightmare* Concert, April 4, 1977

Welcome to My Nightmare
Years Ago (excerpt)
No More Mr. Nice Guy
Years Ago (excerpt)
I Never Cry
Billion Dollar Babies
Years Ago (excerpt)
I'm Eighteen
Years Ago (excerpt)
Some Folks
Cold Ethyl
Only Women Bleed
Devil's Food
The Black Widow
Steven
Welcome to My Nightmare
Escape

Encore

School's Out
Department of Youth

4

CONFESSIONS FROM THE HEART OF THE MONSTER

Alice Cooper Goes to Hell, Lace and Whiskey, From the Inside, 1976–1978

ALICE COOPER GOES TO HELL, 1976
[US CHART #27, UK #23]

Very similar in overall concept to Alice's highly successful 1975 "Welcome to My Nightmare" LP, even down to the sequencing of hard rock and ballad cuts. "Hell" is at least the equal of its predecessor, with an even more ambitious storyline—Alice dreams he has gone down an endless black staircase to a disco hell because of his "criminal acts and violence on the stage." The crisply produced music he makes during his confinement in hades ranges from tearful balladry to humorous, semi-autobiographical heavy metal and include parodies of the disco sound and old vaudeville riffs. The promised winter stage-tour of this album should be something to look forward to. Meanwhile, Alice keeps moving toward becoming the James Joyce of commercial rock surrealism.—Anonymous, *Billboard*, July 1976

With a prologue on the inside of the sleeve addressed to Steven the central character from "Nightmare" this can loosely be described as a follow up. Basically it's all about Alice going (wouldja believe) to hell. "For criminal acts and violence on the stage"; as the opening line states. . . . The album then proceeds to take you through Alice's exploits down under. The whole thing is taken very tongue in cheek . . . it's still all strong stuff. No one does it like Alice.—Anonymous, *Sounds*, July 1976

Side One

1. Go to Hell (Cooper/Ezrin/Wagner)
2. You Gotta Dance (Cooper/Ezrin/Wagner)
3. I'm the Coolest (Cooper/Ezrin/Wagner)
4. Didn't We Meet? (Cooper/Ezrin/Wagner)
5. I Never Cry (Cooper/Wagner)

Side Two

1. Give the Kid a Break (Cooper/Ezrin/Wagner)
2. Guilty (Cooper/Ezrin/Wagner)
3. Wake Me Gently (Cooper/Ezrin/Wagner)
4. Wish You Were Here (Cooper/Ezrin/Wagner)
5. I'm Always Chasing Rainbows (Carroll/McCarthy)
6. Going Home (Cooper/Ezrin/Wagner)

It is always a difficult task in rock 'n' roll to follow up a highly successful album with another. The Alice Cooper band had learned that truism only too well when the loosely conceptualized *Muscle of Love* was charged with succeeding *Billion Dollar Babies*. For the newly solo Alice Cooper, the task was made even more difficult by virtue of the fact that the split with his much-revered band was still relatively fresh and, while *Welcome to My Nightmare* had silenced some critics, it had made others even more vocal as they lamented the loss of that original team chemistry and pondered the full and total embracing of theater. Alice's answer on *Alice Cooper Goes to Hell* was to further build on what he and Ezrin had begun with *Welcome to My Nightmare*, taking the concept still further and outlining with absolute clarity in the album's title the environs within which the next installment would take place: hell. Further, printed on the inner sleeve of the album is a letter titled "A Bedtime Story" and addressed to Steven, the boy who could not wake from his nightmare. Serving to bind the two albums tightly together, the letter informs the reader that what follows is a "very special story, that only special children will understand." Just as was the case on the preceding album, "It's a half-awake story," and Alice's letter assures us that "it will be better if you close your eyes." In summation, the letter invites Steven to join Alice as he descends the long staircase into the pit of hell. If Steven sings sweet songs to Alice, he is told, then he may end up freeing him. But if not, then Alice is destined to wander around aimlessly in hell searching for a non-existent exit and "forever chasing rainbows."

The album cover is in complete synergy with the work's title, despite its origins as a reworked photograph from the *Billion Dollar Babies* album cover shoot. Designed by Rod Dyer and Brian Hagiwara, Alice's front cover portrait screams HELL. His face is colored a Halloween green, his teeth and eyes an uber white, while his pupils are the jet black of his hair. His expression is more a leer than a smile, and he makes direct and unwavering eye contact with the viewer. The background to the left of the image is a fiery yellow and red, suggesting the fires of hell raging around him. The album title, *Alice Cooper Goes to Hell*, is written in gothic font at the top-left corner in split color—black where the background is yellow, and green where the background is black. Turing the cover over, on the rear the imagery contained in "A Bedtime Story" is graphically brought to life, as a black-clad Alice descends a long white stairway, the lower steps of which glow bright red as if he is close to reaching the bottom and hell's fires are close at hand.

Musically, the slow/mid-tempo opening track, "Go to Hell," doesn't have the immediate impact of the traditionally hard-hitting rock power of the Cooper band's first-up tracks, in keeping with the new complete and utter commitment to musical theatricality. The song acts in the same way that the opening title track of *Welcome to My Nightmare* did in presenting an almost filmic, atmospheric, scene setter on which the rest of the narrative is designed to sit. Full of dynamic and instrumentation shifts, the slick Ezrin production moves from an opening groove punctuated by the overdubbing of smashing bottles to successions of climactic chords that both punctuate and paint our hero's descent into the fiery inferno of hell. At times the track sounds like the listener is walking slowly, fearfully, through a jungle that is close, claustrophobically dense, humid, dangerous, and full of the sounds of insects. With the scene set, the opening vocal lines of "Go to Hell" inform us of just why Alice has been sentenced to hell: "For criminal acts and violence on the stage." Fair enough, too, as such charges were exactly what the Coop was both revered and reviled for. That it was time for some come-uppance seemed entirely just and, indeed, a juicy prospect to ponder. It is the next line, however, that allows us, the Cooper fans, to join him on that journey because, as teenagers, it is highly unlikely that any of us had avoided such allegations levelled against us by our elders/authority figures: "For being a brat, refusing to act your age." A subsequent line suggests it was Alice, too, who had caused us to doubt our parent's authority and, therefore, in the best traditions of "School's Out," "I'm Eighteen," "Department of Youth," and "Teenage Lament '74," the ever-fashionable topic of generational division sits firmly at the fore-front of an Alice Cooper album. In the third verse Alice takes on the roles—delivered in different voices—of his accusers, hurling further accusations at himself that include stealing the cane of a blind man and poisoning his dog, and sending a gift-wrapped leper to Aunt Jane. For all of this and more, Alice Cooper is sentenced to hell. The opening track has been a clear scene setter and served to most firmly—albeit done with humor—cast the singer once again in his familiar guise of "Public Animal #9."

In hell, as it transpires in the second song of the album, one must dance. "You Gotta Dance" conjures up childhood memories of "Ring around the rosy" and plants "dance of death" (danse macabre) imagery in the mind of the listener, as Alice is compelled to dance through some strange act of demonic possession. A theme he would return to in 1980 in the song "Dance Yourself to Death" from the *Flush the Fashion* album, here Alice and his hell-bound associates are "all slaves when we hear that sound." But "that sound" is the sound of slick funk/disco instead of rock; a comedic touch given that disco, for many a rock fan—and certainly for Alice Cooper—was indeed his/her idea of hell.

Song three of *Alice Cooper Goes to Hell* finds Alice assuming the role of the devil in "I'm the Coolest," singing in his lowest register, the microphone set close to his mouth in the studio for an uncharacteristi-cally intimate style of delivery. Purposefully hugely egocentric, the devil is cast in the lyrics as the coolest being in history: "You know that I'm the coolest that's ever come around. You'll notice things get hotter whenever I'm in town." Tongue pressed firmly into cheek throughout the song, there's a nod to world champion boxing icon Muhammad Ali, who was at the peak of his world-wide fame at the time, in the line, "I gotta be the greatest," which truncates by the song's end to become the exact statement frequently proffered by Ali—the emphatic "I AM the greatest." In addition, at the one-minute, forty-six second mark, when delivering the words "Yeah, baby," Alice's tone is pure Elvis Presley croon, thereby nodding in the direction of rock's greatest ever performer as well. Appropriately, for someone claiming to be "the coolest," the groove-based, cool-jazz, brushes-on-snare soft-shoe feel of the musical backing is suitably laid-back and smooth, bar the slightly more upbeat choruses. Reportedly, "I'm the Coolest" was originally intended as a duet with actor Henry Winkler, who was the epitome of cool in his role as the coolest dude in town, the Fonz, in the long-running television sitcom, *Happy Days*. However, Winkler ultimately withdrew from the contract due to concerns about being typecast in such roles.

In the following "Didn't We Meet?" Alice resumes being himself, his voice soft and dreamlike in the instrumentally sparse verses while assuming his signature Cooper rock edginess in the much heavier choruses. The narrative remains strongly linked to the preceding songs, as Alice now meets and holds a conversation with the devil himself, quizzically asking of the horned one, "Didn't we meet in the night in my sleep somewhere?" which is a clear reference to the recent dreamscape events of *Welcome to My Nightmare*. "To look at you, deja vu, chills me to the core," he sings, with trepidation building as his recollection grows. After a superb heavy rock interlude, Alice is left pondering his fate and wondering if his time in hell will end with him begging the devil to just let him die.

The trauma and angst of "Didn't We Meet?" is assuaged straight away with the fifth and final song of side one, the unexpectedly tender ballad "I Never Cry" which, in reaching number twelve on the Billboard singles chart, provided Alice with the surprise hit of the album and rekindled memories of the success of "Only Women Bleed" from *Welcome to My Nightmare*. Clearly, Cooper's songwriting talent, in collaboration with Dick Wagner, extended well beyond full-on rock. And yet, after four songs that sat easily and logically within the album's going-to-hell theme, it is undeniably hard to fit "I Never Cry" into the overall narrative, and the song sits almost as an intermission or, perhaps, a kind of musical sorbet before the record is turned over and the next course served up. While the song may be hard to fit into the album's concept, to Alice Cooper fans the autobiographical nature of the lyrics is both meaningful and poignant. "I Never Cry" is a soul-baring song; it is Alice admitting that he is experiencing a problem with alcohol addiction and is expressing his fears of the effect it may have on his relationship: "Sometimes I drink more than I need, until the TV's dead and gone."

In all, side one of *Alice Cooper Goes to Hell* has been the softest, the least consistently rock 'n' roll, of any side of an Alice Cooper al-bum—either band or solo—ever, with its forays into disco and jazz and the final tender confessional ballad. And yet the concept of the album has remained strong for the most part, and the trademark humor obvi-ous and endearing.

The opening of side two immediately returns the listener firmly to the album's storyline. In "Give the Kid a Break," a veritable musical theater piece in its call-and-response nature, Alice challenges why he has wound up in hell: "Must be something I said," and pleads for clem-ency from the devil himself: "Give me one good reason why I should!" Humor runs through the song, most especially when Alice says in exas-peration, "But for Heaven's sake!" to which the devil responds, "Watch your language, kid."

Unsuccessful and unpardoned, the next song emphatically states Alice's guilt, literally, in the most out-and-out, up-tempo, dirty rocker of the album, "Guilty." To fans of the original band, to hear the return of such powerful rock edginess was very welcome and the perfect vehicle for Alice to bare his soul and admit to the events that led him to hell: "I'm a dirt-talkin', beer-drinkin', woman-chasin' minister's son," he screams in almost celebratory fashion in his best signature snarl above the fast-and-fierce heavy rock backing. With references to his stage act and slapping on the makeup that transforms him into the on-stage Alice Cooper everyone knew and loved, his crime is described with typical wit and generational division: "Wake up the neighbors with a roar like a teenage heavy metal elephant gun."

As quickly as the rock tour de force of "Guilty" had resurrected the Alice of old, the moment is gone as balladry again takes center stage in the tranquil "Wake Me Gently." Beginning with a beautiful classical guitar introduction, it's all strings and understatement as Alice express-es his fears of being taken in the night: "No happy endings read—I think the hero's dead." The song explores the dream state of being not awake but not properly asleep, either, that had been prevalent on *Wel-come to My Nightmare* and remained a central theme of the current album: "And if I can't wake up will I be all alone?" For Steven/Alice, the nightmare continues . . .

And there is no letup when "Wish You Were Here," the fourth track on side two, begins and finds the incarcerated Alice once again at the mercy of hell's disco and funk rhythms. Sixteenth-note patterns on the hi-hat predominate in this humorous letter penned deep in the bowels of the earth and sent to his lover above, to whom he reports he's "having a hell of a time." The jokes come thick and fast as Alice relates the trials and tribulations of life in eternal damnation, where "It's pretty warm down here but it ain't sunny." A rock instrumental outro, complete with screaming guitar solo, that lasts for the final minute and a half of the track restores a degree of Cooper normality to proceedings and serves as a reminder—harkening back to the theme of "Guilty"—of what led to Alice's fall from grace in the first place; that is, his dirty rock 'n' roll past.

The album's only cover version, and seemingly a very odd choice, occupies the last but one position on *Alice Cooper Goes to Hell*. Back firmly into ballad territory, "I'm Always Chasing Rainbows," dating back to 1917 and credited to Harry Carroll and Joseph McCarthy but with its melody based on Chopin's *Fantasie Impromptu*, is a popular vaudeville standard and was featured in the 1918 Broadway musical, *Oh, Look!*

Covered by a great many artists, the most popular versions were by Charles W. Harrison in 1918 and Perry Como in 1946, though other well-known artists who covered the song include Tony Bennett, Harry James, Guy Lombardo, Petula Clark, Ray Conniff, Russ Conway, Bing Crosby, Sammy Davis Jr., Benny Goodman, Al Jolson, and Harry Nilsson. In addition, and perhaps more pertinently, Judy Garland sang the song in the 1941 movie *Ziegfeld Girl*. While seemingly incongruous on a rock album like *Alice Cooper Goes to Hell*—albeit a rock album that had already veered far from the norm—when one refers back to the carefully crafted liner notes, and in particular "A Bedtime Story," the letter written to Steven stating that Alice could only be freed if Steven sang sweet songs to secure his release, one can grasp the presence of "I'm Always Chasing Rainbows." Even so, as Dave Thompson points out, Alice "knew he was taking a chance—with his listeners' tolerance, if not the Prince of Darkness."[1] Alice plays the song straight down the middle, with no liberties taken to add nuances of humor or horror.

The aptly titled, happy ending–implying, "Going Home" closes out *Alice Cooper Goes to Hell*. Steven's magical, treacle-sweet rendition of "I'm Always Chasing Rainbows" clearly worked as "A Bedtime Story" foretold, and the devil released Alice Cooper from his dark, disco-riddled, realm. With its soaring choruses, dominance of piano, banks of lush strings, and finale vibe, the slow-moderate tempo "Going Home" is in the true tradition of a Broadway musical pre-curtain production number. Rock instrumentation is there throughout, to be sure, but it is a part of the mix only and does not drive the song à la traditional Alice Cooper. Perhaps some fans of the raw Cooper of old may have read rather more than the songwriters intended in the lines, "have I been gone so long they thought that I died?—How many said, I wonder what happened to Alice?" And yet, such pining for the rock edginess aside, given the remarkable musical and narrative journey of the album it can hardly be said—and it would be churlish to suggest such a thing—that such a grandiose, beautifully orchestrated ending is not entirely fitting.

Speaking as an avid Alice Cooper fan I can recall excitedly buying *Alice Cooper Goes to Hell*, taking it home under my arm, and spinning it on my bedroom turntable for the first time. "Guilty" aside, I didn't instantly love it, I confess. But it undeniably both opened my ears and impressed me at the same time. And I wondered what on earth Alice would do next.

LACE AND WHISKEY, 1977 [US CHART #42, UK #33]

Alice serves up a heaping plate of thumping, but well-thought-out rock here. In some ways the LP looks back to the days when Alice Cooper was a group, not a soloist. But today's Alice is a master of mixing smoothness with shock effects. And the current single, "You and Me," is another sensitive ballad that provides an effective contrast to the sleek heavy-metal sounds that otherwise dominate the LP. The jacket and sleeve graphics have Alice surrounded by the props of a Spillane-type detective-writer tough guy, but there is no conceptual storyline here, unlike the prior two "Nightmare" and "Hell" gold albums. Alice may rock with more sophistication now, but he hasn't lost any of his old demonic drive and inventiveness in his singing, writing and ease with killer rock rhythm sections.— Anonymous, *Billboard*, May 1977

Lace and Whiskey rings false, not only because its ideas probably originated from Alice's urinary tract (too much beer, I suppose), but because its conservatism is unfeeling. Honest, you might as well listen to the bubbly Abba or, for that matter, a blessed-out Wayne Newton. Even Alice's snarls on "Road Rats" are cautious and reserved—he sounds less cool than out of it. And his parody of a Hollywood starlet ("King of the Silver Screen") is oddly limp.—Anonymous, *Circus*, July 1977

Side One

1. It's Hot Tonight (Cooper/Ezrin/Wagner)
2. Lace and Whiskey (Cooper/Ezrin/Wagner)
3. Road Rats (Cooper/Ezrin/Wagner)
4. Damned If You Do (Cooper/Ezrin/Wagner)
5. You and Me (Cooper/Wagner)

Side Two

1. King of the Silver Screen (Cooper/Ezrin/Wagner)
2. Ubangi Stomp (Underwood)
3. (No More) Love at Your Convenience (Cooper/Ezrin/Wagner)
4. I Never Wrote Those Songs (Cooper/Ezrin/Wagner)
5. My God (Cooper/Ezrin/Wagner)

With *Lace and Whiskey* Alice Cooper tried something different. As Thompson puts it, "Working as usual with the Ezrin/Wagner/Hunter team, with Ezrin and Wagner his collaborators on every song, *Lace and Whiskey* seemed determined to eschew the formula laid down by its two predecessors."[2] While it was still conceptual, certainly, the album had no clear narrative like *Welcome to My Nightmare* and *Alice Cooper Goes to Hell* had done. The work was, this time, completely earthbound and totally devoid of malevolent things that went bump or boo in the dark of the night. Instead of exploring dichotomies such as awake/asleep, good/evil, fantasy/reality, the concept was to outline the life and times of a fictional 1940s/1950s hard-bitten, alcoholic private eye named Maurice Escargot. At least, such was the intention, as stated in interviews leading up to the album's release. However, and despite a strong beginning in the first couple of songs, in actuality the songs overall seemed to have very little direct relationship to such a theme, and certainly did not support the album's artwork in the synergetic way for which Alice Cooper albums had become renowned. This fact was picked up by commentators and critics: "Alice indicated that he was to portray a Forties detective, and, true, he does—in the album's packaging."[3] The black-and-white front cover certainly features appropriate iconography for the theme, including a revolver, scattered bullets, a whiskey bottle and glass, a cigarette and butts in an ashtray, plus an opened detective novel bearing the album's name, attributed to Alice Cooper as the writer, and described on the front cover as "The Outstanding Mystery Discovery of the Decade." On the rear, also in black and white, the fiction is maintained with three fake reviews of the novel, a posed photograph of Alice smoking a cigarette while sitting behind his typewriter, a half-full box of bullets, a crucifix, and the black lacy edge of an item of woman's underwear—perhaps panties or a bra—and thereby providing the lace of the album's title. The juxtaposition of the crucifix and the bullets begs comparison to the image on the billion-dollar note giveaway inside the *Billion Dollar Babies* album cover, where the legend "In God We Trust" was situated alongside the image of missile-laden trucks in a military parade.

The album begins with "It's Hot Tonight," a more up-tempo hard rock beginning than was the case on either of the first two solo albums. As a scene setter for a forties detective soundtrack, the song serves well with its imagery of a sweltering inner-city night where "Dogs are barkin', cats are screamin', streets are steaming." Lyrically minimal, the song paints a picture of the detective, Maurice Escargot, tossing and turning and unable to sleep, albeit without ever naming him.

The second song, and title track, is powerful hard rock made lush with the slick Ezrin hallmarks of banks of strings and soaring choral backing vocals, and serves to flesh out a fuller picture of the detective as a hard-drinking, tough womanizer who needs "a cure sometimes to knock out the pain, so I yell out for some kind of angel." However, he is self-aware enough to know that his lifestyle is one that will end in self-destruction: "I'll end up a broken old hobo with red and yellow eyes, swearing, and drunk and dyin'—no one's surprise."

At the moment the third song of the album begins, the just-established concept/story of Maurice Escargot is largely abandoned. While a great song in its own right, "Road Rats" is very clear in expressing its topic and it has nothing to do with being a private detective in a decades-past era, and everything to do with a group of rock 'n' roll band roadies plying their trade: "We move the drums and amps and junk. Road rats, we're a pack, and the road's our home." While this may be seen as a negative, "Road Rats" is high-energy heavy rock and is built around an infectious antiphonal (call-and-response) guitar hook of the kind that underpins the very best of rock 'n' roll. Already, at just three songs in, Alice Cooper fans have heard more signature Alice Cooper rock than on the entire *Alice Cooper Goes to Hell* album of just a year earlier.

The subsequent "Damned If You Do" can perhaps be seen as a kind of return to the album's original theme, with the womanizing Maurice Escargot caught in—or caught just after—the act, although the song is equally simply a fairly generic "loved-another-man's-woman" lament. "I'm gonna sign my name to a full confession—It seems the woman I loved last night belongs to another man," sings Alice over a fast, highly atypical retro honky-tonk, Jerry Lee Lewis–styled piano-driven backing.

In what has quickly become established as an Alice Cooper solo album pattern, another rock ballad occupies the now-strategic position of the final song on side one, and as had been the case with "Only Women Bleed" and "I Never Cry," its two similarly located predecessors, sure enough "You and Me" would become a major hit. A tender exposition of everyday life for salt-of-the-earth men and women everywhere, Alice celebrates his (pretend) lot with admirable universality: "You and me ain't no movie stars—what we are is what we are." So accurate and perceptive was the song in its depiction of everyday lovers' reality that it became a popular choice for a wedding song. Lines such as "We share a bed, lovin', and TV . . . and that's enough for a working man" struck at the hearts of many newly appreciative, nontraditional Cooper fans, and he still sounds genuinely bemused when recounting in *Alice Cooper: Golf Monster* that many people have told him over the years that "You and Me" was used for their wedding song. Nevertheless, despite the welcome chart success, in some ways the song's popularity was a double-edged sword; with three hit ballads in a row, his rock fans were now beginning to grumble.

Side two begins emphatically while once again completely eschewing any adherence to the album's tenuous Maurice Escargot concept. In the semi-autobiographical "King of the Silver Screen"—autobiographical because Cooper had long trumpeted his love for movies as one of his primary inspirations—the everyman empathy of "You and Me" is carried further, as here: "By day I'm a working man, laying bricks or laying pipe—I don't stand out in a crowd, just look like one of the guys." But the song carries more than what is immediately evident. More than being the dream of an everyday guy to miraculously become an Errol Flynn–type character, as the song goes on the protagonist reveals himself as a closet queen, desirous of becoming not King but "Queen of the silver screen . . . I'm going to Hollywood to be a starlet." Despite the obvious humor, which is gradually teased out in the manner of Monty Python's "Lumberjack Song" or Jim Stafford's "My Girl Bill," some all-too-real gender issues surface when Alice sings, "I don't care anymore. I'm tired of closets . . . just don't hit me again. All right guys?" As if to underscore the oppositional, confrontational aspects of the song, excerpts of a tune popular during the American Civil War, "John Brown's Body" (aka "The Battle Hymn of the Republic"), unexpectedly appear.

"King of the Silver Screen" gives way to "Ubangi Stomp," and just as *Alice Cooper Goes to Hell* had included one surprise cover version, "I'm Always Chasing Rainbows," the Charles Underwood–penned rockabilly staple "Ubangi Stomp" provides the cover version moment on *Lace and Whiskey*. Just as "Damned If You Do" had provided a highly atypical moment on side one of the album, "Ubangi Stomp" is similarly hard to square with Alice Cooper. Fun and frivolous, the song adds nothing at all to the concept of the album, and while Thompson may opine that the song, "allowed everybody to rock out with an absolute lack of self-consciousness,"[4] there would be few Cooper fans who would regard the song with anything less than a deserved incredulity.

If, as the saying goes, the wheels rather fell off *Lace and Whiskey* with "Ubangi Stomp," then the following "(No More) Love at Your Convenience" does nothing to get the show back on the road. "We wrote it as a satire. Unfortunately, we weren't clever enough to let the audience know it was a satire,"[5] claimed Alice. A return to the disco vibe of *Alice Cooper Goes to Hell*, on *Lace and Whiskey* the song appeared without the humorous justification that the style had enjoyed on the preceding album. The irony of the track is that it is a fine disco song in its own right, but it is so out of context on *Lace and Whiskey* that it—perhaps undeservedly—remains a Cooper curiosity more than anything.

And as if Alice knew it all along, the following song is the very aptly titled, "I Never Wrote Those Songs." A schmaltzy Broadway ballad with all of the grandiose attendant instrumentation is the musical framework for lyrics that equate to a denial of previous penmanship but without identifying any specific song or songs: "And oh, that music, I hate those lyrics . . . the melody, it goes nowhere pointlessly . . . and I swear to you I never wrote that song."

Finally, with Maurice Escargot having been long forgotten in the scheme of things, in the final song there is still time for one more surprise on an album full of surprises. In "My God," ushered in with a full church organ introduction with pipes blazing in all their hymnal glory, Alice lays bare his personal faith in an unmistakeable, highly reverent, manner. "When sheep like me, have drifted lost—all frightened children who are tempest tossed—down flies his wrath like an albatross, my God!" While rock instrumentation provides cut and thrust to the track, it is the organ that carries the song, while a many-voiced, angelic-sounding church choir joins Alice in exaltation, resulting in an evangelical tour de force. Alice, famously (for a rock villain) the son of a minister, had certainly given indications in the past that Christian faith was a part of his creative makeup and that critiquing the topic provided him with rich songwriting subject matter. Both *Welcome to My Nightmare* and, even more so, *Alice Cooper Goes to Hell*, explore and problematize Christian theology. But it is not until the final track of *Lace and Whisky* that an out-and-out song of praise is put before fans. It is a masterpiece of a song, and a hallmark in Christian heavy rock.

Lace and Whiskey, then, was a surprise package in many ways. Achieving nowhere near the critical success of *Welcome to My Nightmare*, and in sales terms failing to address the slide down the charts experienced by *Alice Cooper Goes to Hell*—indeed faring significantly worse than that second solo album—it must have set commercial alarm bells ringing. Yet, the one thing that this inconsistently focused work does show is an artist prepared to think outside the box and experiment. Some hallmarks of established Alice Cooper remain present, such as the intrinsic humor, while other are absent—most especially the macabre/horror touches. But in terms of being prepared to fearlessly try out new musical styles, and demonstrating the considerable courage required to present to his audience an overt, glory-to-God song of praise, one cannot help but admire *Lace and Whiskey*.

FROM THE INSIDE, 1978 [US CHART #60, UK #68]

This concept album that chronicles Cooper's self-imposed stay in a rehabilitation center to cure his alcohol addiction, is without a doubt his most ambitious statement to date. The subject is not an easy thing to publicize, yet Cooper, with the writing assistance of Bernie Taupin, has come up with a moving, often emotional autobiographical rock record with more lyrical sting than anything he's ever done.— Anonymous, *Billboard*, December 1978

Alice has always had a way of treating something that scared his psyche: he put it in a song to exorcise it. So it's not surprising that this album is full of murder, mayhem, madness and memories. And, typically, he even manages to make fun of his own experiences: blowing them up to life-size near surreal portraits in technicolour and cinemascope. . . So here we are, smack in the middle of Alice's nightmare, for real. Some of it is rubbish. . . . But some is brilliant.— Penny Valentine, *Melody Maker*, December 1978

Side One

1. From the Inside (Cooper/Foster/Taupin/Wagner)
2. Wish I Were Born in Beverly Hills (Cooper/Taupin/Wagner)
3. The Quiet Room (Cooper/Taupin/Wagner)
4. Nurse Rozetta (Cooper/Foster/Lukather/Taupin)
5. Millie and Billie (Cooper/Roberts/Taupin)

Side Two

1. Serious (Cooper/Foster/Lukather/Taupin)
2. How You Gonna See Me Now? (Cooper/Taupin/Wagner)
3. For Veronica's Sake (Cooper/Taupin/Wagner)
4. Jackknife Johnny (Cooper/Taupin/Wagner)
5. Inmates (We're All Crazy) (Cooper/Taupin/Wagner)

The first thing that strikes the purchaser of *From the Inside* is the highly elaborate album cover. Harking back to the wonderful gimmickry of *School's Out* and *Billion Dollar Babies* with, respectively, their panties and billion-dollar note, and to a lesser extent *Muscle of Love* with its faux outer packaging that didn't quite work in a practical sense despite looking great, the cover of *From the Inside* raises the bar even higher. A gatefold cover, it has surprises galore that take it well beyond the standard gatefold design. The front has a split down the middle that bisects into exact halves the extreme closeup of Alice's heavily made-up face. Faintly visible squares around each of his eyes suggest separation and incarceration. In addition to the obvious function of providing an opening door to what lay inside, the division down the middle also carries with it the inference of a split personality in much the same way that David Bowie's *Aladdin Sane* cover achieved, with the now iconic red lightening flash bisecting Bowie's face. Inside Cooper's gatefold cover is a scene that might well be a still frame from the movie *One Flew Over the Cuckoo's Nest*, as sixteen inmates and staff of an asylum are pictured in various states of bizarre activity amid the stark, polished white and light-blue walls and linoleum of a common room. At the rear is visible a door bearing the legend, "Quiet Room." This door too opens, and inside we see a half-naked Alice sitting against a stark-white wall in solitary confinement. Turning the cover over, the rear features a set of exit doors which, when opened, show Alice and a bunch of other inmates rushing out wearing broad smiles and clutching official-looking documents that proclaim, "Released."

Once again, a carefully designed and elaborate Alice Cooper album cover functions not only to protect the vinyl recording it houses within, but also acts as a highly communicative paratext that is designed to not only shed light on but to advance the storyline contained in the music. Despite that storyline or concept being a very strong one, the producer who excelled in such territory, long-time collaborator Bob Ezrin, was not at the recording desk for *From the Inside*, his role filled instead by David Foster.

Song one is the title track and, fittingly, "From the Inside" lays out much of the territory just as the opening scene of a movie would do. Instantly autobiographical, it is very clear that Alice is singing about himself: "I'm stuck here on the inside looking out. I'm just another case—where's my makeup, where's my face? On the inside." In addition to singing in first-person perspective about himself, he also includes his audience in the events that led him to this dark place, recalling that whenever onstage, "You were screaming for the villain up there."

With the scene now set by the album's mid-tempo opener, "Wish I Were Born in Beverly Hills" goes on to up the ante with a fast, high-energy performance complete with hallmark sneer and the edginess of old. Here, Alice turns the spotlight not on himself but on a fellow inmate, a certifiable teenaged delinquent who "says that she's an actress, just never got a part. Well now she's a teenage mess with a burned-out Gucci heart." The lyrics are strong, clever, and image-laden throughout, and carry with ease the message that being born into privilege is no deterrent to mental instability. "Wish I Were Born in Beverly Hills" is classic Alice Cooper at his best.

The third song of the album, "The Quiet Room," a visual feature of the inside sleeve with its opening door that reveals an alienated, isolated Alice within, is highly confessional and contains some of the darkest imagery the artist ever put to music: "I have confessed my life. The Quiet Room knows more about me than my wife," sings Alice in this heartfelt song that veers between piano or piano/synthesizer ballad verses and full-on rock choruses. Further, "I can't get my wrists to bleed. Just don't know why suicide appeals to me." A stark, beautiful song that also features on backing vocals the treacle-smooth voice of Earth, Wind & Fire's Maurice White, nevertheless it is almost hard to listen to, such is its brutal honesty, telling Alice Cooper fans more than they ever expected to hear from their hero.

Track four, "Nurse Rozetta," is a song full of sexual frustration and suppression, with much suggestive lyricism as Cooper the recovering alcoholic inmate lusts uncontrollably after one of his caregivers: "Nurse Rozetta, I won't let her catch me peering down her sweater, fantasizing silk suspenders on her thighs." The song is notable for presenting the most sexually graphic of any Cooper song as he proclaims, "I'm suddenly twice my size—My pants are all wet inside." Full of signature Cooper snarl, the contrasting bridge passage in Alice's unforced, natural voice stands out like a beacon, injecting the song with a disturbing honesty that makes it clear he really is baring his soul.

"Millie and Billie" concludes side one of *From the Inside*, and it is a very curious closer. A bitterly twisted yet initially disguised love duet with Marcy Levy (aka Marcella Detroit), the song is dark in the extreme, leaving its gory clincher until the final verse, at which point we find out the two are killers who colluded in murdering Millie's children and also her husband: "I liked your late husband Donald, but such torture his memory brings. All sliced up and sealed tight in baggies—guess love makes you do funny things." Despite the fact that the name Alice Cooper had by this time become synonymous with Grand Guignol–style horror, in its MOR blandness—devoid of all the qualities of inherent weirdness that were a prerequisite feature of all previous Cooper visitations to the dark side, and made it somehow okay—"Millie and Billie" comes across as genuinely disturbing.

"Serious" is side two's opening track, and while the subject matter remains true to the song's title, the vibe signals a welcome return to what Alice Cooper does best—rocking hard and fast. With a fine guitar riff reminiscent of the cornerstone of "Life's Been Good" by Joe Walsh, but sped up by two-thirds, and Alice at his finest snarling best, it is this reviewer's favorite song on the album. While in its own way as confessional as "The Quiet Room" had been earlier on the album, the Cooper-of-old musical nuances make it a much easier listen despite Alice's candidness in relating: "All of my life was a laugh and a joke and a drink and a smoke, and then I passed out on the floor again and again and again and again and again." In terms of the album's narrative flow, perhaps "Serious" would have been better placed early on side one, given that it fills in the gaps regarding what had led to Alice's incarceration. Nevertheless, its placement completely reinvigorates *From the Inside*.

Sitting in complete contrast to the rock power of "Serious," and breaking with the recently established and highly successful tradition of placing the album's primary ballad and single release as the last track on side one, as had been the case on the first three solo albums, "How You Gonna See Me Now?" occupies the second position on the flip side. Reaching number twelve on the Billboard singles chart and thereby extending even further his seemingly unlikely string of ballad successes, the song is an achingly tender and beautifully constructed admission of the singer's trepidation regarding how his wife Sheryl would regard him in his newly cleaned up, sober, post-rehab state.

It's hard to imagine that any other premier-league rock star would compare his or her lot to that of a mentally unstable, but much-loved pet dog languishing locked up in a city pound, and yet that's exactly what Alice Cooper does in the magnificent "For Veronica's Sake." While in many ways a by-the-numbers rocker in terms of songwriting framework and instrumentation, the Cooper humor is the driving force that carries this track: "We've both been put in cages—we got our shots and tags. I got my sweating fist to shake—she's got her tail to wag." After the overt seriousness of the album to this point, "For Veronica's Sake" comes as welcome light relief without sacrificing the integrity of the album as a whole.

The ninth, and second-to-last track on *From the Inside*, "Jackknife Johnny" came about as the result of an idea of Bernie Taupin that was based on the real-life experience of a shell-shocked Vietnam War veteran and asylum inmate who had brought a Vietnamese woman back to the United States as his wife, and had been maligned for it. Brought to fruition as a song by the full creative team of Cooper/Taupin/Wagner, here Alice steps back from autobiography and considers the lot of someone else experiencing life on the inside for different reasons to his own: "Jackknife Johnny, welcome to our world."

The album's finale, "Inmates (We're All Crazy)," effectively sums up the album's message. In modern society, who is really crazy and, beyond that, who has the sanction and authority to determine such a diagnosis in others? The childlike chant of "We're all crazy"—taking the world of the (adult) lunatic asylum back to the ream of the schoolyard— is extraordinarily effective in the questions it raises, but doesn't profess to provide any solution(s). Perhaps the most effective and telling couplet in the entire song is "We just talk to our shrinks—Huh! They talk to their shrinks." Universality is writ large in "Inmates (We're All Crazy)," and while the song itself may not be much beyond workmanlike, just what it poses is powerful in the extreme. Included as a free giveaway with the album was a signed certificate from Alice Cooper, pictured on the document as a doctor, on which the recipient could write his or her name and become officially, certifiably, insane, as endorsed by the "Alice Cooper School for the Hopelessly Insane, Founded 1978."

From the Inside might have been an essential catharsis for Alice Cooper, but it was not a commercial triumph, seeing Cooper's fortunes slide even further from the heady days of the Alice Cooper band and the highly promising success of his first solo album, *Welcome to My Nightmare*. But *From the Inside* was a very strong album, and both a risky and highly important work in the artist's career. Perhaps fans were not prepared for such soul-searching and earnest honesty from rock's premier ghoul? Others have suggested that the Taupin collaboration introduced an Elton John MOR element that did not sit well with the

Cooper style of old. Regardless, *From the Inside* contains many fine moments and is worthy of positive reappraisal.

5

THE DEMISE OF ALICE COOPER

*Flush the Fashion, Special Forces, Zipper Catches Skin,
DaDa, 1980–1983*

FLUSH THE FASHION, 1980 [US CHART #44, UK #96]

Cooper is out to prove he was shocking parents long before any of
the punk/new wave bands even thought of going into music. No
ballads are present this time as all songs are up-tempo rockers with
typical new wave lyrics about world problems and desolation. . . . For
the most part though, the material is tame and won't shock anybody
who has been listening to any new music over the past two years.—
Anonymous, *Billboard,* May 1980

Raise that curtain, hello hurray, old snake eyes is back with a two-
sided disc-dose that's more fun than freebasing with a polyester shirt
on. After years of scamming us with a tightrope walk between rock
'n' roll and bleeding-women bull, Alice has finally dug down, come
up, and put his money where his meat is.—Jeffrey Morgan, *Creem,*
September 1980

Side One

1. Talk Talk (Bonniwell)
2. Clones (We're All) (Carron)
3. Pain (Cooper/Johnstone/Mandel)
4. Leather Boots (Wester)

5. Aspirin Damage (Cooper/Johnstone/Mandel)

Side Two

1. Nuclear Infected (Cooper/Johnstone/Mandel)
2. Grim Facts (Cooper/Johnstone/Mandel)
3. Model Citizen (Cooper/Johnstone/Mandel)
4. Dance Yourself to Death (Cooper/Crandall)
5. Headlines (Cooper/Johnstone/Mandel)

The band called Alice Cooper had formed, experimented, and percolated during the mid- to late 1960s, becoming well aware of the important differences that stood them apart from their peers and developing the confidence to further mine these differences. Finding enormous success in the early 1970s, particularly in their partnership with Bob Ezrin, by the middle of the decade Alice Cooper had shrunk to a solo act. While his debut, *Welcome to My Nightmare*, had achieved considerable initial solo success, each of the three subsequent solo albums during the latter years of the decade had struggled to maintain that level of success despite a run of highly successful rock-ballad singles. Because of all this, 1980, then, took on some significance as Cooper looked to reverse his slide and begin the new decade in style. So important was this, in fact, that the cover art for his first effort of the decade, *Flush the Fashion*, highly unusual but proudly carried the date alongside his name at the top of the front cover: ALICE COOPER '80. With an album cover infinitely less elaborate than had been the case with its predecessor, the 1978 alcoholic-confessional *From the Inside*—aside from his name and the year, the cover of *Flush the Fashion* carried only the graffiti-styled handwritten album title—it appeared the artist was intent on embracing the new decade as a new beginning and, accordingly, taking a new approach. If a dark cloud was visible anywhere, it was well behind the scenes, with Cooper having relapsed in his fight with alcohol. Nevertheless, Cooper's desire for a new lease on his musical life is borne out further when one considers that the album is free of any linking concept—concept albums being an established Alice Cooper hallmark—and includes three songs in which Alice played no compositional hand at all.

According to Dale Sherman, change for Cooper was absolutely necessary at this time due to the altered nature of the popular music marketplace, which meant that certain styles were in, others were out, and niche marketing was the key to success:

> By the beginning of 1980, there were only three ways to go: Disco, punk/new wave or pop. Alice fell into the center of things. He was too heavy for pop fans to want him, and too commercial for the punkers to identify with him. . . . Instead of scrounging to find a niche, Alice instead embraced the new decade with a passion. He'd been wanting to advance his "Alice" character past the well known "killer" mode, and 1978's *From the Inside* album helped him to develop another side to the character and show more of its inner workings. The punk and new wave movements helped propel the character into a new area, into an area that dealt more with psychological ideas and nightmares, with world problems and personal struggles. The world saw a post-nuclear Alice—an "Apocalypse Alice."[1]

Change is evident from the moment the needle hits the vinyl on side one of *Flush the Fashion*. The opening track of any album is critical as a scene setter and style indicator, and here, remarkably, Cooper gives the opening statement of his first album of the 1980s over to a cover version. "Talk Talk" was a 1966 hit for garage band the Music Machine, and written by their lead vocalist, Sean Bonniwell. Long before the Alice Cooper band recorded their first album, "Talk Talk" had been one of the cover songs in their repertoire. As bassist Dennis Dunaway would go on to ruefully remark in his 2015 autobiography, "Years later, Vince would finally record 'Talk Talk,' but it was with a new band, the one that replaced us."[2]

Cars producer Roy Thomas Baker took on the producer's role for *Flush the Fashion*, and as soon as "Talk Talk" begins one hears the stripped-back, new wave edge in the production. The short album opener conveys much in its shade-over-two-minutes duration. The synth line is pure Cars, while the lyrics—despite not being written by Alice—seem to clearly admit to his quest of re-establishing himself in a changed musical landscape: "Now here's my situation. And how it really stands. I'm out of circulation . . . I guess I'm down to size."

Song two, "Clones (We're All)," while not a cover version, is also not written by Alice, creating the remarkable situation of the singer's compositional voice remaining unheard in the opening tracks of *Flush the Fashion*. Nevertheless, it is a fine song that, although Gary Numan–ish in musical style and sonics is nevertheless highly in keeping with the Cooper thematic ethos in its referencing of classic science-fiction television, most particularly the BBC series *Doctor Who*. "Clones (We're All)" would prove to be the album's only single success, albeit a minor one with its number forty placing on the US Billboard singles chart. It is hard to not read a biographical nuance into the lyrics regarding Cooper's displacement from the current rock elite: "Six is having problems adjusting to his clone status. Have to put him on a shelf (please don't put me on the shelf)."

"Pain" is song three and is notable for being the first song of the album to feature the artist as a cowriter. Notwithstanding the easy surface alliance to the Grand Guignol–esque subject matter of the Cooper of old, here the topic is every kind of pain imaginable as a tidal wave of physical, emotional, and mental pain sweeps over the listener: "I'm the salt in the sweat on the cuts of the slaves. I was the wound in the side while Jesus prayed. I was the filthiest word at the vandalized grave." In the manner of a religious savior, Alice proclaims: "I'm your pain!" although it is never clear if he is on the side of heaven or hell, such is the relish with which he seems to be taking on the massed pain of others in this mid-tempo and, frankly, workman-like rocker.

The following track, "Leather Boots," is a frenetic new wave stab lasting just one minute, thirty-eight seconds that views life from the perspective of a scared young cop drawing strength from his leather boots and his comrades in arms. A rail against fascism, factionism, and military-style justice from those whose uniforms empower them to commit excess in the name of maintaining order, the song takes the view that such protagonists are "frightened by the real world," and only by enforcing such order can they feel at ease. With the lyrics delivered at such a fast pace, there is no space for the signature Alice Cooper snarl or edge, and if one heard the song in isolation you would be hard pressed to recognize the singer, such is the deviation from the norm in both style and delivery. Simply, "Leather Boots" could have been performed by anyone. And once again, as it was for the opening two songs of the album, the singer had no part in the writing of the song.

The dangers of overdoing it when self-medicating provides the subject matter for the concluding song of side one, "Aspirin Damage." When Cooper sings "I balance my Excedrin and Anacins in stacks. I'm a pain reliever junkie—I got a Bayer on my back," he is commenting on the medicated, life-denying, habit of modern-day Americans to bliss themselves into a better place by masking pain. Perhaps, too, his own recent—and, indeed, current, problems with alcohol informed this song to a large extent. But, while the lyrics may offer a valuable critique of a damaging social problem, the musical underpinning is bland and strictly by the numbers, while the songwriting lacks any of the Cooper spark of old. "Aspirin Damage" provides a weak ending to the first half of *Flush the Fashion*.

The promisingly titled "Nuclear Infected" begins side two. Another very short song at two minutes and fifteen seconds, it provides a punchy, infectious, and welcome return to one of the Cooper corner-stones—humor. Every verse is funny, as the nuclear infected protagonist describes his life as a glowing man clearing out ball games, going out on a date in a lead suit, choosing a radioactive salad, and choosing an appropriate place to live: "I want to live on Three Mile Island where things are clean and neat. 'Cause we don't have no health freaks cluttering up our streets." The musical style is less new wave and more bona fide Cooper rock than has been heard on the album to this point, and with the stripped-back production values, the return of the signature growl and an inherent rawness to the sound, there are similarities to be discerned between "Nuclear Infected" and Alice's *Love It to Death*–era work when the band was just starting to find its feet. Simply, "Nuclear Infected" is a terrific start to side two of *Flush the Fashion*.

"Grim Facts" is, as the title suggests, an unrelenting presentation of dark subject matter; specifically, a succession of youth problems presented as facts that, as Alice opines, "every parent better know." Ranging from a schoolboy with a gun in his desk and a pregnant girlfriend, to a young girl groupie looking to live out a thousand fantasies with musicians, to a teenage prostituting herself in order to support a drug habit, the last verse finds the singer angry, afflicted by a sexually transmitted disease, and stalking the streets about to crash and burn: "And I'm feeling itchy—got a fire down below. I'm a walking loaded time bomb just about to blow." Another highly credible slice of rock, the song is built around a clichéd but highly effective guitar riff, and continues the stronger showing of the second side of the album.

In a song that revisits the kind of public face/private face conundrums that provided the subject matter of earlier gems such as "Public Animal #9" and "No More Mr. Nice Guy," the midpoint on side two is occupied by "Model Citizen." Jumping between first-person and third-person perspective throughout—the latter sung as a gang vocal by the backing musicians—Alice outlines the importance of keeping up pretenses in modern American society: "I won't let down my disguise." (Group: "He's a model citizen.") "Just keep believing that my friends. I'm a model citizen." But the song also has some touches of Cooper humor that add much to the track: "They'd like to kill me slow and bury me." (Group: "Deep in the heart of Texas").

"Dance Yourself to Death" follows, and for Cooper fans the immediate thematic referent is "You Gotta Dance" from *Alice Cooper Goes to Hell*. But while the former track was couched in disco-from-hell, here the sound is one of pure Rolling Stones raunch, and it works well. Given that the subject matter is the behavior of the young protagonist's embarrassing hippy parents, the musical homage to those icons of the counterculture is both highly appropriate and funny. Alice struts his way through the song with Mick Jagger nuance and inflection as he hopes his pot-smoking parents will have coronaries on the dance floor and fulfill the command of the song's title: "Come on mama, come on daddy. Come on skinny, come on fatty. Shake it Martha, shake it Larry. Shake it Mr. Coronary."

Finally, the last track on *Flush the Fashion* is "Headlines," and it's a straightforward rocker run through in equal measure with humor and cynicism. Critiquing the duality and hypocrisy of modern American life has always been fertile ground for Alice Cooper, and "Headlines" is the best installment since "Elected," with its cutting quality evident right from the opening lines: "Do a show, save a child—raise a million bucks that'll last a while. Fight at parties, buy a horse—lose a couple, win that big divorce." Through the presentation of a range of scenarios both believable and bizarre, Alice purports to do anything at all to stay in the headlines. A cynic might say that in reinventing his musical product to embrace the 1980s and new wave, Cooper was perhaps practicing exactly what he was preaching in "Headlines." Cooper biographer Dave Thompson suggests: "*Flush the Fashion* emerged as a desperate album . . . Alice Cooper was a lot of things, but he was not the new Gary Numan."[3] This is perhaps somewhat harsh as, while some of the new wave–flavored tracks on side one made little impact, the evidence elsewhere, particularly on side two, did not suggest desperation, with a succession of strong songs and some fine lyric writing. Perhaps the biggest hurdle for critics and fans alike was the lack of a concept for the album. After all, concept albums were the Cooper stock in trade, and fans had come to expect exactly that, so to have disparate songs simply lumped together in the manner of myriad other artists meant one of the Coop's strongest points of difference was absent.

SPECIAL FORCES, 1981 [US CHART #125, UK #96]

"Special Forces" is an appropriate follow up to "Flush the Fashion" in that Cooper continues his exploration of sparser sounding audio techniques. His vocal delivery is cool and distant while the instrumentation is minimal.—Anonymous, *Billboard*, September 1981

An underground LA vibe percolated to the surface as Alice dug back into the closet and unearthed his old Love and Doors albums. For a time, a new concept presented itself, a virtual history of Los Angeles rock, from the garage blast of the mid-sixties, full-circle to the punk noise of the eighties.—Dave Thompson, *Alice Cooper: Welcome to My Nightmare*, 2012

Side One

1. Who Do You Think We Are (Cooper/Hitchings)
2. Seven and Seven Is (Lee)
3. Skeletons in the Closet (Cooper/Hitchings)
4. You're a Movie (Cooper/Hitchings)
5. You Want It, You Got It (Cooper/Kaz/Krampf/Scott/Steele)

Side Two

1. Vicious Rumours (Cooper/Hitchings/Pinera/Scott)
2. Prettiest Cop on the Block (Cooper/Johnstone/Mandel)
3. Generation Landslide '81 (live) (Bruce/Buxton/Cooper/Dunaway/Smith)
4. You Look Good in Rags (Cooper/Hitchings)
5. Don't Talk Old to Me (Cooper/Johnstone/Mandel)

The cover of *Special Forces* is striking, and a welcome development from the new wave blandness of *Flush the Fashion* with its graffiti-rendered album title standing alone. Here, a portrait of a serious Alice, shot by Jonathan Exley, sits in a gilded frame atop a red surface and against a blue wall with his head held high. Decorated with military medals and wearing a studded collar, he appears in the same iconographical style in which military heroes the world over have been preserved in picture, staring straight ahead, his lips pursed in a depiction of strength and defiance. In such portraits, war heroes often carry in one hand their weapon of choice. Here, however, weapons appear outside the frame as two swords are crossed above Alice's portrait. Crossed swords have been commonly used in military applications, with the symbol often appearing on the gravestones of fallen soldiers, and also appearing on unit insignias the world over. In the United States, cavalry units would often feature this symbol. Historically, crossed swords pictured with their points upwards symbolize a readiness and willingness to go into battle, whereas swords pictured with their points down indicate a state of, or desire for, peace. So in the case of *Special Forces*, the implication of the cover is certainly one of imminent conflict, with military general Alice Cooper at the fore.

"Who Do You Think We Are" begins the album with a dark and brooding synth line turning into the sound of helicopter blades, and once the band kicks in and the track proper begins the military nuances of the cover are immediately strongly also present in the lyrics. "I'm machinery with a semi-automatic heart," sings Alice, before threateningly confirming his active service status at the end of verse one with, "My finger squeezes off the final shot—say goodbye." Verse two depicts him further as a blood-crazed killer, recounting how he has murdered and terrorized without remorse or conscience, doing things too horrific to relate and then concluding the verse with the chilling information that he is sanctioned to act in this way by his government: "I am licensed, trained and bona fide." The question in the song's title is asked repeatedly throughout the song, while the chorus makes it clear that Cooper and his comrades in arms don't give a damn anyway. Alice sings in his most threatening voice to deliver sonically the full extent of the threat present throughout every aspect of the song. "Who Do You Think We Are" is a strong beginning.

Track two of *Special Forces* is the album's only cover version, but in this context it appears well selected and fits with ease the military concept jointly set up by the artwork and opening song. "Seven and Seven

Is" was written by Arthur Lee in 1966 and performed and recorded by his band Love who, along with the Doors, were an iconic part of the counterculture's Los Angeles heyday. However, in Cooper's hands there remains very little evidence of flowers in anyone's hair. Driven by the fast rolls of a military-sounding snare, the track fairly races along: "When I was a boy I thought that someday I would be a man," sings Alice, conjuring up imagery of a boy standing on the sidewalk watching a military parade going by and idolizing the uniformed soldiers marching past in unison. And now that he is indeed a soldier who has seen and done too much, it is an easy task to apply Lee's lyrics to his situation: "My heart lies in the fireplace . . . and I'm trapped inside a night."

"Skeletons in the Closet" is up third, and for Alice Cooper fans there is an instant moment of recognition and nostalgia in the tinkly harpsichord introduction that conjures up Steven's can't-wake-up traumas from *Welcome to My Nightmare*, six years earlier. Whatever war crimes Cooper and his accomplices have committed, in "Skeletons in the Closet" the ghosts of those they have wronged come back to visit. Alice's voice here is unforced and held back, reminiscent of the half speak/half whisper that he had employed on similarly atmospheric tracks in the past. "Ooh, I see bones, icy bones. Say boys, don't you see them bones?" At the end of the song, Alice appears to wake up, the music stops abruptly, and one can imagine him sitting up in bed and bathed in a cold sweat as he yells in fear, "What? Whaddya want?"

"You're a Movie" occupies the fourth spot on the album and is, again, strongly conceptual. The lack of a concept on *Flush the Fashion* has been well and truly rectified thus far on *Special Forces*. "You're a Movie" offers insight into the mind of a soldier, or in this case clearly a general or some kind of leader—presumably the decorated Alice we see on the album's cover—and suggests that, as a coping mechanism for the horrors of battle, one might imagine it is all simply a movie and not real life. The lyrics are full of immortality references: "The bullets repel off my medals and my men are in awe when I speak." With such a distancing mechanism in place, even killing can become the equivalent of just another day at the office: "Another day, another victory, another gold stripe, another star." At three minutes, as Alice self-importantly commends himself on being the best in the business, the music stops and the sound of soldiers' boots marching in formation takes over for a time until the music resumes and the backing vocals repeat "movie movie movie," over and over, to reinforce the concept.

Side one's final song is the lyrically minimalist and musically light-weight "You Want It, You Got It." Highly synth-driven, and thereby harking back to new wave—but here far more pop than the rock of *Flush the Fashion*—the lyrics imply that Alice can get you anything you desire, from money to sex to a Ferrari, to "Chateau Breyon for breakfast every day." Whether from the ill-gotten stolen gains of military triumph or from black-market racketeering is unclear, but Alice is the wheeler and dealer.

Side two of *Special Forces* begins with the powerful "Vicious Rumours," and it is here that the personal toll of being an ordinary man turned soldier-killer is assessed, as everyday normality is turned on its head and chaos, death, and destruction take their toll: "All of this is getting normal now—You'll never go back to your farming plough." Typical dark Cooper is in clear evidence in lines such as "Sometimes you duck when you see your pet canary turn into a Sabre jet." Three minutes into the track the music stops, and there is a recapitulation of the helicopter sounds from "Who Do You Think We Are," leading into a brief return of the title line from that earlier song and ending on the all-important denial "we don't care," implying that the simplest response to dealing with the psychological damage is to simply proclaim indifference.

Instead of military, in "Prettiest Cop on the Block" Alice dons a policeman's uniform. Many an ex-soldier found gainful post-hostilities employment in the police force, and this appears to be the undercurrent of the song as the bullying and cruelty dished out on the battlefield is here transferred to an inner-city, urban setting. There is gender confusion in the song's title and this is furthered in lines such as "I'm a queen on the street and a king at the station," while sexual violence is implied by "I've handcuffed your desire—I got a stiff reputation with a stick like a rock." With police sirens in the mix, the song carries the same qualities of theatricality and visuality that had been the hallmark of Bob Ezrin's production efforts. While *Special Forces* was produced by Richard Podolor and retained the stripped-back urgency of new wave, the presence of scene-setting special effects such as the sirens and the helicopter blades ensured that theatricality remained a key component of the album.

Although the following track, "Generation Landslide '81," is listed in the album credits as a live recording, Sherman notes that "it was actual-ly re-recorded in the studio during the making of *Special Forces* and not in front of an audience."[4] A seemingly unusual inclusion, the *Billion Dollar Babies* track withstands the updated treatment extremely well, and its message is certainly not out of keeping with the violence, con-flict, and division that fuel the rest of the album.

Just two tracks remain on *Special Forces*, and the first of these, "You Look Good in Rags," is the first song on the album to have no obvious link to the central concept. Bearing an uncanny chordal resemblance to Blondie's "Atomic," ostensibly the song is a critique of the behavior and dress habits of rich women versus that of the poor central subject and singer's love interest—from the stage Alice has seen "the women up front, way down below." But regardless of how the classy women look and behave, in Alice's eyes, "Ah, you look good in anything—mmm, I don't care." At the two-minute, nineteen-second mark an unexpected and unusual section begins that continues for over a minute, during which the word "rags" is performed over and over in comedic fashion, first as an a capella call-and-response and then, once the musical back-ing returns, simply as an extended outro. In terms of keeping faith with the themes visited through the course of listening to *Special Forces*, "You Look Good in Rags" is hard to reconcile, despite being catchy enough in its own right.

Completing the album is "Don't Talk Old to Me," and while its relationship to the *Special Forces* storyline is not overt in the way that the songs on the first three-quarters of the album had been, the song still fits and, in many ways, provides a fitting conclusion. Sung from the perspective of a military veteran, the prickly, feisty subject is having trouble leaving the past behind and getting on with the mundaneness of his post-military, retired life: "Don't shake that finger in my face no more, 'cause I might bite it off and spit it on the floor." It is with some resignation that he concedes, "Better sell my bike, my leather coats, those city auto parts and all my guns." The aggression of the musical underpinning leaves no doubt that the retiree is certainly not going to settle for a life of fluffy slippers and hot milk drinks in front of the television, most especially when he growls late in the track, "That's the last time I'm gonna say please."

Special Forces performed poorly on the charts and, in addition to the lack of an accompanying hit single to put a spotlight on the larger work, this may be partly explained by a reported rift at the time between Cooper and his record company. Regardless, any fan who did not get themselves a copy might well rue that fact because it is a hidden gem in the Cooper catalog and should not be overlooked purely on the basis of its commercial performance. Strong in terms of its songwriting, concept, and overriding cohesiveness, and with the newly stripped-back directness in terms of production and instrumentation at the core of its sound, the album deserved better.

ZIPPER CATCHES SKIN, 1982 [US CHART —, UK —]

"Ouch," Alice seems to whimper from the back cover; "ouch," thought I listening to this. Alice is not a healthy man as the last couple of albums have shown and this doesn't do much to convince me he's getting any better. . . . I suspect Vincent Furnier has lost all control over the monster that is Alice, and, unleashed, the creature appears to be floundering aimlessly without much idea how to use his freedom. A return to "The Inside," Vincent, would probably do you and Alice the world of good.—Dave Dickson, *Kerrang!*, November 1982

At the age of 34, Alice Cooper is moving faster than ever, and his latest album, *Zipper Catches Skin*, bears the defiant trademark of a guy who'd choose to burn out before he'd ever rust.—Toby Goldstein, *Hit Parader*, March 1983

Side One

1. Zorro's Ascent (Cooper/Nitzinger/Scott/Steele)
2. Make That Money (Scrooge's Song) (Cooper/Wagner)
3. I Am the Future (Osborne/Schifrin)
4. No Baloney Homosapiens (Cooper/Wagner)

Side Two

1. Adaptable (Anything for You) (Cooper/Scott/Steele)
2. I Like Girls (Cooper/Nitzinger/Scott)

3. Remarkably Insincere (Cooper/Nitzinger/Scott)
4. Tag, You're It (Cooper/Nitzinger/Scott)
5. I Better Be Good (Cooper/Scott/Wagner)
6. I'm Alive (That Was the Day My Dead Pet Returned to Save My Life) (Cooper/Scott/Wagner)

The cover of *Zipper Catches Skin* is both innovative and divisive, with many Cooper fans disliking it. Consisting of a page of unrelenting lines of the album's song lyrics written in a small font, the album's title appears toward the top right and stands out only by virtue of appearing in red while all other text surrounding it is black. Underneath is what appears to be a smear of blood acting like a crude underlining. At the top of the cover, a red background beneath the lines of text subtly spells out "Alice Cooper." On the rear cover is a photograph of an extraordinarily clean-cut Alice, sans makeup, against a blood-red background wearing a business shirt and tie, staring straight ahead and directly at the viewer while bearing a pained expression, his arm and hand directed toward his groin where, presumably (although out of shot), he has caught himself while in the act of zipping up the fly of his trousers, thus acting out the album's title.

The producer's chair for *Zipper Catches Skin*, the first Alice Cooper album since 1970's *Easy Action* to not chart in either the United States or the United Kingdom, was shared by Erik Scott and Alice himself after plans to use Richard Podolor once again fell through. Another of the group of four albums that Cooper barely remembers recording, Dick Wagner recalled on the 2014 documentary *Super Duper Alice Cooper* that the recording sessions for the album were heavily drug affected, with Cooper and other band members smoking crack cocaine between takes behind a curtain set up in the studio for the purpose.

"Zorro's Ascent" begins *Zipper Catches Skin*, and is a very visual account of the famous fictional outlaw's demise as he lays dying on the ground, complete with the sound of castanets, swishing swords, and guns being cocked: "Now there's only minutes left for the cunning El Zorro. Go fetch my sword . . . my horse, I'll ride out death, Diablo." Also featuring vocalist Patty Donahue (credited on the album sleeve with "Vocal and Sarcasm"), Cooper fully role plays his part by adopting a Hollywood-styled Spanish accent. With a loping, busy snare pattern that resembles the sound of horse's hooves, the virtuosic guitar solo too

carries Spanish inflections. "Zorro's Ascent" is an unusual beginning to
the album and, given that Alice Cooper albums so often begin with a
scene setter that outlines the wider concept of the work, the listener is
left wondering at the track's end just what concept is being mined on
Zipper Catches Skin.

The following track, "Make That Money (Scrooge's Song)," cowritten with longtime songwriting collaborator, Dick Wagner, immediately
sounds remarkably like "The Black Widow" from *Welcome to My
Nightmare*, a song that the pair had written with Bob Ezrin. But any
similarity begins and ends there as, thematically, "Make That Money
(Scrooge's Song)" is an ode to hard-nosed, money-making businessmen.
The lyrics are consistently witty: "But when it's time for me to croak,
bury me with all my dough. And where there should've been an oak, my
private money tree will grow." A solid enough song in its own right, it
bears little or no obvious synergy with the opening track.

The proclamation-titled "I Am the Future" is the third track and the
only song on *Zipper Catches Skin* in which the singer had no compositional hand. Veering between positive, encouraging messages such as
"And you got to learn just how to survive—you've got to learn how to
keep your dream alive," to ominous threats: "Take a look at my face—I
belong to the future, and you belong to me," the song is nevertheless
something of a mystery and leaves more questions unanswered than
answered. Just who is the tyrannical despot that is speaking? What is
the dream in question, and how is it under threat? The slow, almost
ballad-tempo musical accompaniment is bland and uninspired, and the
track comes across as a filler. Nevertheless, while the album was to lack
a hit single once again, this song was used in a movie, *Class of 1984*. Its
appearance in the movie was not well received, and the review in *Kerrang!* noted that "I Am the Future" was a "limp soundtrack from the
one time master of menace—re-mixed especially for the occasion. As
much as I would really like to like this (being a total fan of the man) it's
nothing more than a cliched cop out, aiming for the charts and MOR
fans. This was not made for Alice Cooper fans."[5]

With three songs down and no evident cohesive direction making
itself evident on the album, it is becoming clear that *Zipper Catches
Skin* may well be following in the tracks of *Flush the Fashion* in having
no overriding concept, unlike the immediately preceding *Special Forces*

with its strong military centrality. Perhaps track four will provide something?

"No Baloney Homosapiens" ends the rather short side one, and once again the lyrics are witty in this open address to aliens in outer space: "Oh, we're fun and games, just guys and just dames. But don't call us names and most of all, please don't eat us." Alice is at his snarly unmistakable best in terms of his vocal delivery, and the song is strongly written. Reminiscent in style of "Sweet Transvestite" from *The Rocky Horror Show*, its anthemic touches allow Alice a full range of dynamics to show off the many sides to his vocal prowess. The best song of the album so far, Alice's childhood love affair with trashy science fiction runs free: "My blood's thick red—you bleed black glue. So, let's not bleed at all, is that all right with you?" However, with its out-of-the-blue thematic content, the track confirms that *Zipper Catches Skin* is indeed another album without focus—without a central concept.

Side two is kicked off by "Adaptable (Anything for You)," and it's a love song with a difference—a song that it's hard to imagine anyone other than Alice Cooper coming up with. While straightforward in terms of its mid-tempo rock instrumentation and feel, the point of difference lies in the lyrics, in which Alice lists the many Cooper-flavored ways in which he is prepared to demonstrate his love and commitment: "Say you're Vampira and needed plasma, and I was dying from chronic asthma. I'd leave my death bed to draw some blood for you."

The subsequent "I Like Girls" is self-explanatory, a duet with Patty Donahue that lives up to the shallowness of its title but doing no more than that. In a frankly embarrassing lyric ("Does she have a nice pair?") that describes how the self-styled Valentino dumps Sheila, Melissa, Donna, Shauna, Amanda, Sandra, Kay, Patty, Katy, and Carrie, the sole highlight is perhaps the oblique nod to earlier, more successful, days with the Alice Cooper group when Alice professes "I like girls—I love 'em to death."

The third song on side two is "Remarkably Insincere," and on an album that lacks any sort of cohesive concept at least it might be said that this song links closely to the preceding "I Like Girls." The details of his charlatanism are laid bare in the lyrics, but for all that, "Remarkably Insincere" is no less embarrassing than its predecessor: "My dearest darling. You know that luggage? It belonged to the blond with the really nice pair." Fast paced but completely unmemorable when compared to the quality of work the artist is known for, the song does not improve as it goes on: "If I would rate you—not that I hate you. But you would end up eighth, maybe ninth in your class."

Track four on side two is "Tag, You're It," and by this point side two of *Zipper Catches Skin* is in dire need of a lift. Thankfully, "Tag, You're It" provides exactly that. A Grand Guignol–themed horror romp in terms of accessing the Alice Cooper vault of career-defining thematic material, this track—a pastiche of every cheap slasher horror film ever made—stands head and shoulders above anything else on the album. When a young, beautiful bride named Debbie realizes on the night of her wedding that the man she has married is a crazed killer, she does anything she can to stay alive: "He shifts his glance, you see your chance, you grab the needle and you plunge it in his ear." But in the manner of so many B-grade horror movies—the lyrics even name-drop *Halloween*—it is never really over until it's over, and in the final verse he reappears from nowhere, and the last sentence Debbie ever hears is the chilling "Tag, you're it, Sweetie." Extremely filmic and theatrical, special effects enhance the mood of the track, including ominous foot-steps and the sound of scissors. By quite some distance "Tag, You're It" is the best track of *Zipper Catches Skin* up to this point.

The last song but one is "I Better Be Good," and the new standard set by "Tag, You're It" is in no danger of being surpassed by the penulti-mate track. A broad lesson in what to expect if one does not behave oneself, the track is the closest the album has to a title track when Alice sings the line: "If zipper grabs skin I'll know I had it out when I should've kept it in. Ow." Elsewhere, he weighs up the consequences of annoying or offending his father, his doctor, his teacher, his girl-friend . . . the list goes on. The fast, stop/start track quickly dates, and the blistering guitar solo toward the end does little to maintain or ex-tend listener interest.

By far the most interesting song title on the album—and perhaps even in the history of popular music, grand claim though that is—is saved for the final word on *Zipper Catches Skin*. "I'm Alive (That Was the Day My Dead Pet Returned to Save My Life)" closes the work and, as its title suggests, its Stephen King *Pet Sematary*–sensibility is one that sits easily with Alice Cooper. During the song Alice is saved in the midst of a succession of life-threatening scenarios by a) his deceased dog, "good ol' Blue"; b) his deceased horse; and c) his deceased rat. Lightweight, the song is nevertheless enormously endearing in its audacity and its total investment in macabre humor. As had been the case earlier on the album with "Adaptable (Anything for You)," one would be extremely hard pressed to think of another major rock artist who would have tackled—let alone pulled off—such a song. While not enough to redeem the entire album, "I'm Alive (That Was the Day My Dead Pet Returned to Save My Life)" is a wonderful closer.

Zipper Catches Skin is not a strong Alice Cooper album despite its highlights, which are, most notably, the final track and "Tag, You're It." Tellingly, these two songs are the ones that tap most heavily into the old, established, Cooper trait of Grand Guignol–style macabre. At other moments on the album, songs that are uncharacteristically cringeworthy—especially "I Like Girls" and "Remarkably Insincere"—unprecedentedly made the cut for the final track listing. The album's lack of any central theme removes an established cornerstone, here even more damagingly than had been the case on *Flush the Fashion*. Unfortunately, *Zipper Catches Skin* is a low point in the discography of Alice Cooper.

DADA, 1983 [US CHART —, UK #93]

This record, his umpteenth at last count, has Alice continuing through his third vinyl decade as gracefully, yet tastelessly, as his terminally twisted mind will allow. . . . His tongue-in-cheek sick sense of humour is brilliantly to the fore in the lyrics. . . . With further spinning, this could well become a latter day A.C. classic because *DaDa* already sounds better than anything he's done in yonks. Thank goodness for Alice!!!—Neil Jeffries, *Kerrang!*, December 1983.

DaDa stands at a stylistic crossroads that Alice had not visited in a decade; since that moment when the band stood poised between *Easy Action* and *Love It to Death*, or maybe *Killer* and *School's Out*. "I Love America" even sounds like a *Billion Dollar Babies* outtake.—Dave Thompson, *Alice Cooper: Welcome to My Nightmare*, 2012

Side One

1. DaDa (Ezrin)
2. Enough's Enough (Cooper/Ezrin/Shaw/Wagner)
3. Former Lee Warmer (Cooper/Ezrin/Wagner)
4. No Man's Land (Cooper/Ezrin/Wagner)
5. Dyslexia (Cooper/Ezrin/Shaw/Wagner)

Side Two

1. Scarlet and Sheba (Cooper/Ezrin/Wagner)
2. I Love America (Cooper/Shaw)
3. Fresh Blood (Cooper/Ezrin/Wagner)
4. Pass the Gun Around (Cooper/Wagner)

That Alice Cooper should be a fan of Dada, the European avant-garde art movement of the early twentieth century, comes as no surprise. David Bowie, the British artist to whom he was so often, at times tiresomely, compared, was also a fan, and both imbued their work with the artistic freedom, humor, and absurdity that the movement espoused. While Bowie might never have gone so far as to name an album *DaDa*, its influence was clear in critical aspects of his work, most evidently in costuming and the freedom with which he at times approached his lyric writing. That sanction to put together disparate entities and influences drawn from many contrasting sources was a Dada cornerstone, and both Bowie and Cooper saw it as a bona fide way to expand their creative palette.

The album art pays immediate tribute to one of Dada's greatest latter-day enthusiasts and a personal friend of Cooper, surrealist artist Salvador Dali, with the image by Glen McKenzie featured on the front cover a reworked portion of a Dali painting titled "Slave Market with the Disappearing Bust of Voltaire." As in the Dali original, the image presents the viewer with an optical illusion; depending on how it is viewed, the picture can either be of two seated figures or the bust of an old man.

On the rear side of the cover the song titles are listed down the left-hand side, while to the right sits an open locket featuring two photographs; on the left a picture of a young, adolescent Alice smiling broadly and holding a puppy, and on the right, a smiling old man wearing glasses.

For *DaDa*, longtime Cooper collaborator Bob Ezrin was brought back into the fold to produce the album, the first time this had happened since 1977's *Lace and Whiskey*. In addition, Cooper and Ezrin had a new ally that they would use extensively on the album, a CMJ Fairlight computer which was used primarily for programming drum tracks.

Ezrin's return immediately flavors the album, as it is his solo-composed title track that opens the album. "DaDa" is a hypnotic, dreamy, and lengthy opener, lasting four minutes and forty-six seconds. Introduced by a childlike baby-doll voice uttering the album title, "DaDa" (which introduces the inherent duality of the word—despite the album cover, maybe in this song DaDa means daddy?), from there on the CMJ Fairlight computer provides the base on which a wonderful display develops of Ezrin's talent for building a theatrical soundscape. Over this, but always in the background rather than the foreground and thereby maintaining the dreamlike atmosphere, Alice is heard being questioned by a doctor or psychiatrist. Alice wants to talk about his son who, he says, looks after him. But then he recalls that he has a daughter too, to which the counselor responds, "You don't have a daughter." But Alice insists he does: "I have a son and a daughter." Is this Vince Furnier on the couch, trying to make sense of his world-famous performance persona, the boy named Alice Cooper? The lyrics confirm nothing, and the therapy session is abandoned when the subject professes tiredness, but the song ends with the question, "Who's my boy?" "DaDa" has been a highly successful opening track, the most eerie and atmospheric track since the *Welcome to My Nightmare* days, and a welcome return for fans of the unique quality that Bob Ezrin brings to Cooper's work.

The scene setter over, side one of *DaDa* continues with "Enough's Enough," and it's a creepy song. The musical backing is clean and unthreatening throughout the carefully crafted, slow-tempo track, and Alice's vocal delivery is likewise. Cleverly, the disturbing lyrics sit in complete opposition to the musical mise-en-scène, making for an unsettling listening experience as the story is told of a boy losing his mother to an unnamed cause—an event that makes his father smile ("a smile he tried to hide"), and after which he threateningly declares, "Son, I've really got you now, boy." The song takes on a further dark nuance of sexual exploitation and child abuse when the father goes on to say: "Go buck and buck and make a buck—Come and show me how, boy." An additional disturbing element exists when the boy asks his father why he hid his brother away.

"Former Lee Warmer" continues and builds further on the theme of extreme dysfunctionality, and the unanswered question from the preceding track is immediately answered when we learn: "In an upstairs room, under lock and key—It's my brother, Former Lee." Beneath the humor of the word play (Former Lee/formerly) sits a story of pure Grand Guignol–styled horror as the prisoner exists in his father-imposed solitude, his only amusement an old piano: "Former Lee Warmer peeks out the window when he feels really brave—Former Lee Warmer waves at his father out in the family grave." Over a beautiful, lush, evocative, and ever-evolving musical arrangement complete with orchestral gravitas, small production touches such as the solitude of a lonely whistled figure late in the piece combine to create a filmic, image-laden masterpiece of loneliness.

The fourth track on what is already an impressive piece of work is "No Man's Land," and here it is Alice's twisted sense of humor that permeates the track. Singing in the guise of a reluctant shopping mall Santa, who got the job only because the suit would fit no one else, the daily torture of enduring lines of little kids with sticky fingers pulling at his beard is unexpectedly alleviated when a sexually frustrated twenty-three-year-old woman sits on his lap and delivers to him her far more adult-themed Xmas wish, to which he readily accedes—leaving fifty kids crying in line along with their outraged mothers. For the majority of the song—a cheery tambourine adding a festive flavor throughout—the inference is laid that the song title refers to the fact that the young woman has no man in her life: "She said 'I'm in no man's land.'" But the song has a twist in its tail in the final verse when the woman takes him home, and it is revealed to both her and the listener that the reluctant Santa is not the man he seems: "She didn't notice I was thin with a delicate chin, nor the softness of my skin, nor the scent of my other personalities." Further revealing that he has no less than four personalities within him, it now becomes clear that he, and not she, that is the subject of the song's title, because he doesn't know which of the personalities is "the real me." Therefore, *he* is the one in "No Man's Land."

"Dyslexia" concludes side one of *DaDa*, and the investment in humor is immediately evident once more. "Is dis love or is dyslexia?" inquires Alice in the chorus of the computer-founded song. Atop the uncharacteristically metronomic electronic backing, Alice ponders the topsy-turvy world he inhabits before revealing that the cause of his discombobulation is simply good, old-fashioned, love: "But since I bumped into you, I bump into walls. And no one knows what's wrong with me."

Side one of *DaDa* has been a highly enjoyable experience. While no constant character has been present, the overarching theme of psychological unsettlement has maintained a conceptual thread that sits in welcome contrast to the album's predecessor, *Zipper Catches Skin*, and it is with relish that the listener contemplates the rest of the album still to come.

Side two begins with "Scarlet and Sheba," an erotic tribute to the bondage and discipline talents of the two women named in the title, who were rumored to be real women previously encountered by the artist: "I'm crossed with longitude and latitude upon my back with a crack!" But the one-minute, eleven-second introduction before Alice's vocal appears is a masterpiece in its own right. As powerful a piece of music as the beginning of any rock opera, containing every Ezrin theatrical rock trick in the book and a master class in the art of dynamic manipulation, Thompson gets it right when he gushes that the "BDSM-battered 'Scarlet and Sheba' is sheer grandiosity, so cinematic in its soundscapes that when Alice's vocal finally kicks in, everything has to rise up a few notches simply to make it count."[6] But remarkably, despite the power of the introduction, Ezrin leaves enough in reserve to ensure that Alice is not overshadowed, and "Scarlet And Sheba" maintains its beautifully harnessed release of energy right until the end.

Charged with the unenviable task of following side two's astounding opener is "I Love America," and thankfully, in its own quite different way, it is as strong as the first track. Emphatically in the tongue-firmly-in-cheek tradition of "Elected"—indeed, the two songs would have made a terrific couplet if "I Love America" had appeared ten years earlier alongside "Elected" on *Billion Dollar Babies*—Alice manages to both celebrate and laugh at aspects and features of American society that help define it in the eyes of the rest of the world. Anthemic in the repeated hand-on-heart group singing of the title slogan, Alice adopts an exaggerated American accent to make his point, while the main guitar hook that introduces the song and returns again later is in the style of Jimi Hendrix's iconic rendition of the "Star Spangled Banner." All of the old prejudices and attitudes are given an airing: "I love a commie if he's good and dead, yup . . . I think them Ruskies should be sterilized," as Alice lays out his version of blue-collar American values and likes: "I love the bomb, hot dogs and mustard . . . I love my bar and I love my truck." In all, "I Love America" hits the mark on every count.

If Alice's irreverent ode to the great US of A tapped into his past, then the horror-themed title of the second-to-last track on *DaDa* does likewise. "Fresh Blood" could not be more aligned to what made him famous in the 1970s, and sure enough, just as many of the horror-themed songs of the Alice Cooper group were allowed to unfold courtesy of extended durations, such is the case here too as "Fresh Blood" is given almost six minutes to carry its tale. The central protagonist is the Renfield-like assistant to a serial killer, who may or may not be a vampire but nevertheless drinks the blood of his victims: "He gets hungry, I go hunting in the moonlit streets for somebody that's right." Not particularly selective in their choice of victims, the psychopathic duo prey on "Showgirls, businessmen in suits . . . bad girls, cops on the beat," and basically anyone caught out alone late at night.

The last track on *DaDa* is the similarly ominously titled, "Pass the Gun Around." A portrait of a loser named Sonny, given the struggles Cooper was having at the time with alcohol addiction, the big impact that was having on his marriage and personal life, and his seemingly endless downward slide in the music industry, it is hard to not read an element of desperate autobiography into the work. The song begins without music as the cold hard sound of a gun being loaded is heard. The trigger is pulled and a click is heard as, presumably, Russian roulette is being played. Alice begins, "Sonny wakes up in the morning feeling kinda sick. Needs a little Stoli vodka, needs it really quick. Sees a little blood run from his eyes—feels a little hotel paralyzed." Should he be the one to pull the trigger on the full chamber, Alice implores his unnamed colleagues to dump his body in the local river. Throughout the lengthy song—another one clocking in at almost six minutes—the downward chord progression of the verses maintains a gloomy inevitability, given considerable additional pathos by the virtuosic and extremely lengthy guitar solo that cries anguish and despair. The conclusion of the song comes suddenly and unexpectedly with the sound of a gunshot. Silence ensues for a few seconds, and then the album ends as it began, with the childlike baby-doll voice uttering its creepy two syllables . . . "DaDa."

DaDa was Alice's final album for Warner Brothers, a parting of ways brought about by his commercial fortunes continuing to fall. *DaDa* did not alleviate that situation despite bringing Alice a reappearance on the UK album charts with its number ninety-three placing. Nevertheless, it is a fine album that is unrelenting in its depiction of the multiple dysfunctionalities displayed by a diverse cast of characters.

6

THE WORM THAT TURNED

Constrictor, Raise Your Fist and Yell, Trash, 1986–1989

Having hit rock bottom and severed ties with his record company, Warner Brothers, after a twenty-five-year association that had seen both phenomenal success and abject failure, Alice Cooper took a much-needed break to sort himself out. Alcohol had once again become a huge problem for him, his health was poor, and he was having difficulties in his marriage to Sheryl because of his addiction. Simply, it was time to take stock on multiple fronts. Entering Camelback Treatment Hospital for a month at the beginning of September 1983, he would emerge clean; completely cured, and with a new healthy addiction in golf.

A new record deal with MCA provided the opportunity for Alice Cooper to revive his fortunes, and he was ready for the challenge, being sober, reinvigorated, and with a clean slate. Teaming up with Ratt producer Beau Hill, the result was *Constrictor*.

CONSTRICTOR, 1986 [US CHART #59, UK #41]

Master of rock horror returns with highly refreshing debut MCA set. With Beau (Ratt) Hill producing, Cooper has gone for harder edge and delivered rock solid package that should hold strong appeal to fans from the *Billion Dollar Babies/School's Out* days, as well as younger metal ears.—Anonymous, *Billboard*, October 1986

The teeny-idol, creative genius and master of the eccentric who has kept so quiet for ten years has turned up sounding rockier than ever before and has managed to put behind him the weak albums that were his efforts of the late seventies and early eighties. . . . Basically this is an album that the old master sorely needed. Hopefully this will bring him back the success that he missed and, without doubt, deserves. Cooper goes to the front of the class and gets a 7.—Oliver Klemm, *Metal Hammer*, November 1986

Side One

1. Teenage Frankenstein (Cooper/Roberts)
2. Give It Up (Cooper/Roberts)
3. Thrill My Gorilla (Cooper/Roberts)
4. Life and Death of the Party (Cooper/Roberts)
5. Simple Disobedience (Cooper/Roberts)

Side Two

1. The World Needs Guts (Cooper/Roberts)
2. Trick Bag (Cooper/Roberts/Wagener)
3. Crawlin' (Cooper/Roberts)
4. The Great American Success Story (Cooper/Hill/Roberts)
5. He's Back (The Man behind the Mask) (Cooper/Kelly/Roberts)

The front cover of *Constrictor* immediately conveys a return or reconnection with the past, as a snake is pictured wrapped around the neck and face of the singer, completely covering his mouth, while his widened eyes feature the classic Alice Cooper barbs at the top and bottom of the wide black mascara circles. This is a revisitation of the *Killer*, *School's Out*–era Alice; a welcome return to his most iconic of images, underlined by the presence of a snake which had in itself become iconic in Cooper iconography due to the *Killer* album cover and innumerable live concert appearances.

On track one of *Constrictor*, "Teenage Frankenstein," the first of seven written by the new songwriting duo of Alice and Kane Roberts, three cornerstones of Cooper's success are expertly drawn together into a powerhouse beginning to the album. Youth estrangement, horror, and mental fragility/instability intertwine: "I'm a teenage Frankenstein—the local freak with the twisted mind." The musical underpinning is pure 1980s glam metal, à la Mötley Crüe, Twisted Sister, KISS, and, indeed, Ratt. It is the snarling, confident, Alice of old atop a metal platform that sparkles with power and energy. ROCK in capital letters (Alice himself referred to it as "monster rock 'n' roll"),[1] but still showing the trademark humor in lines such as "I'm the state of the art—got a brain à la carte," while elsewhere in the song he makes women faint and babies cry.

The second track, "Give It Up," maintains the pace and metal onslaught of the album's opener, while taking potshots at the American/ Western way of life: "Just when you got it made and all your bills are paid you stumble and fall into your grave. Ah, too bad." Delivered in a call-and-response manner, Alice's urgings are each time answered by a wall of gang vocals commanding the listener to "Give it up."

"Thrill My Gorilla" occupies the third place on the album and, while it is harder to initially pin down the thematic direction of this track than was the case for its two predecessors, in its urgings to return to primitive times and values a link can be drawn to the eschewing of modern life as espoused in "Give It Up." "Sukie honey, we're gonna turn back the clock to a time when we danced to volcanic rock," Alice sings in the opening lines, going right back to the time "when monkey turned to man." Again there is no letup in the pace or ferocious onslaught of the spikey metal backing—as primitive and tribal as rock could be, and thereby musically painting the lyrics with great effect.

"Life and Death of the Party" occupies the penultimate placing on side one, providing another fine Cooper-esque title. "You got my heart right by the throat," sings Alice in a line that links back to the album cover image of the singer with the snake around his neck. But the subject here is an unnamed and unattainable object of Alice's desire: "You take a walk right across my soul—you're in control and everybody down here knows." Once again maintaining the fierce pace and aggression set up during the course of the first three tracks, *Constrictor*, while thus far certainly light on dynamic or stylistic changes, is consistently rocking with a raw, bloody-steak quality that Alice Cooper had not shown for years.

"Simple Disobedience" completes side one, and here the destruction of the system identified and encouraged in "Give It Up" is fully realized. A crazy, anarchic, free-for-all metal assault serves as the introduction to the song, upping the ante of the album's aural assault on the listener to a degree that one would not have thought possible after the energy of the previous four tracks, and consigning to history the one-time Alice Cooper pattern of reserving such spots on his albums for ballads. Following this hammer blow, Alice opens with a sneering taunt: "Looks like all your laws are broken, all your lines are down. And all your officers are shook-up babbling little clowns." Alice aligns himself with the revolutionaries throughout, as "all the hungry outlaws have taken up a stance," and behind him throughout the song the outlaws are heard chanting the song's title in the background, spitting the syllables of the words out with boot-camp marching precision. With screaming guitar solos, drums bigger than a Kenworth truck . . . side one of *Constrictor* has introduced a new Alice Cooper to the world, and here he is now a heavy-metal killer.

Side two is led off by "The World Needs Guts," an unspecific, highly aggressive call to arms to anyone who has ever been wronged and failed to fight back: "Hey you! You gonna let some scumbag stab you in the back? Hey you! Turn around kicking and rearrange your sack." A song that would have sat well extremely on the *Special Forces* album, Alice aligns himself to an unnamed band of brothers and declares: "The world needs guts—the world needs us!" Another track of unrelenting hard rock using the same technique of call and response between Alice and his gang vocal comrades, "The World Needs Guts" takes no prisoners and ensures that side two of *Constrictor* begins exactly where side one left off.

On any other Alice Cooper album the mid-tempo "Trick Bag" would not be described as relaxing the intensity, but it does exactly that on *Constrictor* due to everything that has preceded it. A sexual innuendo–heavy ode to a Hollywood groupie, "Little Miss Hollywood," borne atop a fairly by-the-numbers heavy rock song form, Alice peppers the track with iconography drawn from the strongest of his images: "I'm in the mood for my leather boots with the leopard spots . . . pet you nice with my velvet glove."

"Crawlin'," the third track on side two, is a clear follow-on from "Trick Bag," beginning with the after-the-fact lines, "Your dress is hangin' on a hook on the door—my jeans are lying in a pile on the floor." A further lyrical link is made to the album cover when Alice sings: "You come crawling to me like a snake in a tree," but once again the track fails to quite match the power of the tracks on side one, or the opener of side two.

Given the Cooper fondness for identifying, pointing the finger, and laughing uproariously at the more absurd and ridiculous sides of American society, the promisingly titled fourth track, "The Great American Success Story"—although the title is never uttered in the song itself—is, on the surface, a tantalizing prospect for the long-time Alice Cooper listener. But the humor that had made irreverent gems like "Elected" and "I Love America" is absent here. The opening lines lay out the territory: "He was born in a depressed nation. Started tough and worked his way right off the street," and rather than the Cooper tongue being anywhere near his cheek during the song, as it was in those aforementioned songs from earlier in his career, the story continues on to paint a picture of a man going back to school in adulthood to gain the education he missed the first time around. A pale antithesis of "School's Out," without the catchiness or humor, it is hard for the listener to take much from the track beyond perhaps the hook of the repeated chorus line, "Back to school," which would have made a far more sensible song title given its prominent placing and the frequency of its repetition.

Much then relies on the final track, "He's Back (The Man behind the Mask)," to resurrect the fortunes of *Constrictor*, which had impressed and promised so much initially on side one but then rather waned in intensity and focus over the course of the last few tracks. And the final track does indeed deliver, although in an unexpected way. Alice had been asked to contribute tracks to the soundtrack of the latest *Friday the 13th* movie, *Part IV: Jason Lives*. "Teenage Frankenstein" was duly selected, as was a song recorded at this time but did not make the final track listing for *Constrictor*, "Hard Rock Summer" (which was included as an extra/bonus track on CD versions of the album). But it was "He's Back (The Man behind the Mask)" that garnered the most attention, appearing in full in the movie and becoming the much-publicized theme song. However, in order to cater to the requirements of the film's producers, who felt the initial recording of the track was too heavy for their purposes, "He's Back" had to be re-recorded with Michael Wagener in the producer's chair. The result was a more keyboard and synth–flavored track that, while perfect for the purposes of *Jason Lives*, meant *Constrictor* ended with an atypical track compared to the rest of the heavy metal songs that played before it. Still, full of look-out-behind-you moments, the track works and, despite its odd-one-out status, nevertheless provides a strong ending to *Constrictor*: "He's back! He's the man behind the mask and he's out of control."

Achieving exactly what he so earnestly set out to do, the uber-heavy *Constrictor* revived the fortunes of Alice Cooper, reaching number fifty-nine in the United States and forty-one in the United Kingdom. Despite its occasional patchiness and lack of a strong central concept—so damaging on previous occasions—the album was carried by sheer musical power and newly invigorated songwriting, and it soon attracted well-deserved critical acclaim on release. Much of this was couched in a very fond "Welcome back!" manner, epitomized by Dave Dickson in *Kerrang!*: "Yes, my beauties, he's back: Uncle Alice, and he's brought with him some of your worst nightmares, the kind that made you wake up sweating in the middle of the night screaming for your mummy! Yes, he's back . . . and the fun has only just begun!"[2]

Indeed, the Coop was back. And there was a lot more to come . . .

RAISE YOUR FIST AND YELL, 1987 [US CHART #73, UK #48]

The nightmare returns! Alice Cooper is back and, boy, is he mad. . . . The pretenders had better beware. Alice is in top form here, and second best just ain't gonna do.—David Ling, *Metal Hammer*, October 1987

Heavy metal pioneer returns—bedecked in horror-show imagery—to prove once again that he can be just as snotty as the young 'uns. Such raw-knuckled rockers as "Step on You" and "Prince of Darkness" and solid heavy metal pop tunes like "Not That Kind of Love" and "Freedom" say it all.—Anonymous, *Billboard*, November 1987

Sound-wise, it's the logical step on from *Constrictor*. *Constrictor* was a good first album—and I looked on it as a first album after those three or four years off after the *DaDa* LP. *DaDa* was like the end of an era, the end of the old Alice. *Constrictor* was the beginning of the new Alice.—Alice Cooper, interviewed by Dave Dickson, *Kerrang!*, October 1987

Side One

1. Freedom (Cooper/Roberts)
2. Lock Me Up (Cooper/Roberts)
3. Give the Radio Back (Cooper/Roberts)
4. Step on You (Cooper/Roberts)
5. Not That Kind of Love (Cooper/Roberts)

Side Two

1. Prince of Darkness (Cooper/Roberts)
2. Time to Kill (Cooper/Roberts)
3. Chop, Chop, Chop (Cooper/Roberts)
4. Gail (Cooper/Roberts/Winger)
5. Roses on White Lace (Cooper/Roberts)

Healthy, drug- and alcohol-free, and newly confident after the improved commercial fortunes and critical acclaim for *Constrictor* and the accompanying "The Nightmare Returns" tour, Alice Cooper had a new lease on life and enthusiastically tackled a second album, collaborating with guitarist/songwriter Kane Roberts. At the time, heavy metal in particular had come under a very public challenge from a highly organized and politically well-connected lobbying group named the Parent's Music Resource Center, which advocated censorship and paraded Alice Cooper as one of the worst purveyors of sex and violence in music. Alice retaliated:

> This group [the PMRC] mustn't be taken too seriously. Really, they are just four old ladies in Washington who try and get as much publicity as possible for their husbands, who are all influential politicians. Since the main man behind the PMRC, Albert Gore, has admitted himself that he used to smoke pot and listen to loud rock music when he was a kid (something which was discovered while he was working on the President's election campaign) the movement won't last long anyway.[3]

Alice's ire is highly visible on the striking album cover, both loved and reviled by Cooper fans in equal measure, which consists of a picture created by Jim Warren of a closed fist featuring Alice' face on the palm, eyes wide and mouth open as if captured in the act of yelling, and the artist's name written in dripping blood-red above.

Like the Alice of old, *Raise Your Fist and Yell* has a very strong central theme or concept, with its doomsday plot of a horror-movie fan living out his fantasies while remaining unaware of the dividing lines between reality and fiction. However, this concept does not feature throughout the entire album. Instead, it is the PMRC who are the targets of the opening salvos of *Raise Your Fist and Yell*, led off by the aptly titled, "Freedom." According to Cooper,

> "Freedom" is a song against all organized power, although I wrote it mainly as a protest about the PMRC. Alice was right at the top of their hit list. Alice is supposed to print all his lyrics on his sleeve and have them approved. Not that I mind printing my lyrics on the sleeve, but I don't think I should have to. I wrote the song "Freedom" instead of a letter of complaint to let the PMRC and everyone they stand for know what I think about them.[4]

And the rightful ire of Alice Cooper rings clear, loud, and long in this emphatic, declamatory opening track of *Raise Your Fist and Yell*, as he even manages to drag no less than George Orwell into the fracas: "You change the lyrics and become Big Brother—this ain't Russia, you ain't my dad or mother." Speaking on behalf of himself, his fellow musicians, and most importantly, the legions of metal fans, Cooper thunders in outrage: "We're a makeup metal generation—we're not as stupid as you want to make us!" And true to the "metal generation" description, "Freedom" takes up where *Constrictor* left off, kicking off the album with an unrelenting aural assault on top of which Alice' vocals are as powerful and sneering and acerbic as they had ever been. With the chrome-clean production ensuring that every word uttered is crystal clear, the message is delivered and sustained right up until the end of the track where the repeated call-to-arms urging to "Make a fist!" dominates the fade-out. As reviewer David Ling said in the quote that begins this section, Alice Cooper is back and, boy, is he mad!

Following "Freedom" is the thematically related "Lock Me Up," and here the rock star's outrage at the puritanical meddling of the Parent's Music Resource Center doesn't pale or waver for an instant. Opening with a mock judge accusing the singer in court of committing "mass mental cruelty" and asking how he pleads to the charge, Alice answers with spitting defiance, "Guilty," before going on to rail at the unfortunate authority figure: "I'm back with a rage—I want them to write in the paper each night how I bloodied the stage. Oh, if you don't like it you can lock me up!" Describing in highly emotive and descriptive terms the experience of an Alice Cooper concert, he is gloriously unrepentant, and the track stands as a solar plexus–thumping celebration of the live metal concert experience, Alice Cooper style.

Just as *Constrictor* had been consistently unrelenting with track after track going for the jugular from the outset, so too on *Raise Your Fist and Yell* the third track keeps up the pace with aplomb. Titled "Give the Radio Back," authority figures—in this case, teachers—are once again given a firmly extended middle finger: "You think I'm wasting all my precious time? You say my music oughta be a crime."

Fourth song in, and the sights move away from the PMRC and authority figures to hone in on substance abusers and drug addicts. Over a chugging four-strums-per-bar power base punctuated by gang vocals chanting "Step," Alice attacks his targets: "The snow in your nose and the crack in your brain—it used to be cool, now it's just insane." While certainly delivering a powerful anti-drug message, at least a small hint of irony exists given the artist's own struggles of years past.

"Not That Kind of Love" ends side one, and the song begins with pure Cooper lyricism in the spoken, self-knowing, and self-deprecating introduction: "Hello, my little pretty. My, don't we look YUCK!" However, once up and running, "Not That Kind of Love" emerges as the weakest of a strong opening clutch of songs, despite its fast pace and metal edge. The topic is cheap, shallow, and nasty sex, and the lyric evinces that shallowness while acknowledging that another, presumably deeper, kind of love does exist. However, it's not for Alice in this current guise as a snarling metal god: "Don't cry your heart out, don't tell your preacher, don't get ideas, this won't last forever."

If side one ended a little disappointingly given what had gone before, the beginning of side two rectifies the situation with a weighty visitation of Alice's career-long fascination with Christian/biblical depictions of good and evil. In "Prince of Darkness," the devil "spits on God," and the final lines summarize the overall content of the track: "He smells the breath of sweet human sin and deeply breathes it in, Prince of Darkness." At this point one feels the album changing shape. The howls against authority that kicked things off have come and gone, as has the filler of "Not That Kind of Love," and now Alice is accessing significantly deeper and darker territory. It is a powerful opening to the second side completely in keeping with its subject matter, and if ever a guitar solo successfully accessed the foul and fiery crevice of Satan's bottom, then it is the solo on this track that does it.

With the concept of evil now firmly introduced to the album, it's just a small step to the succeeding track, the riff-heavy "Time to Kill." If the "Prince of Darkness," better known as the devil, is evil writ large, then on this track we meet the earthly human personification of him in the guise of a disaffected, estranged, disturbed, psychotic character whose name we do not learn, but whose intention could not be more plainly spelled out: "I had enough of long goodbyes, I only got time to kill—I feel the fire in my eyes, I only got time to kill." In the now well-established technique employed extensively on *Constrictor* and again on the current album, vocals swap between Alice and the gang, the latter reinforcing the mood throughout with group utterings of the song's title. Just who his target might be remains unclear by the song's end, but the seeds have been well and truly sown for dark deeds to transpire in the tracks to come.

And here it is—extreme violence enters the fray at the mid-point of side two of *Raise Your Fist and Yell* in the graphically titled "Chop, Chop, Chop." Describing himself as a "homicidal genius" in verse one, Alice all too chillingly adopts the role of a serial killer, describing the city's other residents as "game" and comparing himself to Jack the Ripper, the notorious serial killer of prostitutes in the Whitechapel area of London in the 1880s. Acknowledging that much of his inspiration comes from the movie screen, sure enough, prostitutes are Alice's target too in "Chop, Chop, Chop"; when "Women on the streets want money when we meet—I take them for a little ride." A twist lies at the end of the highly disturbing song when the killer discovers an ankle bracelet on his victim identifying her as Mary (two of Jack the Ripper's victims were named Mary), but this only incites Alice to mysteriously cry "Gail" over and over again in anguish as the track ends, implying that he is actually looking for someone called Gail. Throughout "Chop, Chop, Chop" the backing music remains firmly a support for the story-telling, and even the obligatory glam metal guitar solo is absent. When a half-minute break in the vocals occurs between one minute, thirty-three seconds and two minutes, seven seconds, only riffing ensues, heightening the tension for the rest of the story to be told.

The reason for the despairing, repeated utterances of "Gail" on "Chop, Chop, Chop" becomes clear on the next track, "Gail," and in Alice's explanation of the song during a subsequent interview he makes it clear that, despite killing a woman called Mary, in the killer's twisted, dysfunctional mind she was somebody else called Gail:

> He just keeps killing them, and he can't discern between actors in the videos and real victims! And at the end, when he's killed this girl in the song "Gail," and he's thinking about her bones in the ground and about how the bugs are inside her ribcage, and the dog is digging up the bones—he wonders how the dog remembers Gail.[5]

Alice sings reflectively, "A tree has grown on the spot where her body did rest—blood seeped in the soil from the knife in her chest," while throughout the atmospheric track—glam metal temporarily shelved—we hear the hallmarks of an established modus operandi that Cooper has employed at such moments, with tinkling harpsichord and austere church organ adding a touch of religiosity and aural gravitas to proceedings. In this moment, for Alice Cooper fans, this could be 1975 and *Welcome to My Nightmare* all over again: "A dog dug up a bone and wagged his tail—I wonder how the dog remembers Gail?"

Raise Your Fist and Yell ends with "Roses on White Lace"; Alice explains:

> And he sees this wedding dress and it's got blood-stains on it every-where—but he doesn't see the blood-stains, he sees roses! This guy's a romantic y'know? He's so crazy, he looks at this blood and all he sees are roses. "Roses on White Lace" is this whole thing about him not knowing that it's really blood. For him, he's painted these lovely roses on this white dress. So he's really a psycho.[6]

"Roses on White Lace" is not the reflective, reverent track one might expect given such subject matter. Instead, the album ends where it began with a full-on metal assault that ticks all the genre boxes, including a guitar solo blistering enough to melt paint (or flesh). When Alice sings "Blood drops look like roses on white lace, they won't wash away—in my mind they're roses on white lace straight from the heart," it is in his full-blooded growl with nothing held back. The track ends via an extended fade-out, and once again the listener hears an Alice versus gang vocal trade-off, a notable feature of the new, glam metal version of the artist.

Picking up on, and developing further, the confidence and newly updated stylistic allegiance established through *Constrictor*, the *Raise Your Fist and Yell* album solidified Alice Cooper's re-emergence into the upper echelons of modern rock. While on paper his commercial fortunes slipped back in both the major US and UK markets, critical acclaim remained high, and the artist was footing it relatively easily with the acts in the upper echelons of glam metal.

TRASH, 1989 [US CHARTS #20, UK #2]

When Alice Cooper (real name: Vincent Furnier) first turned up in record racks back in 1969, the public wasn't quite prepared for his painted face, his uncompromising music, and his outrageous stage shows. Now, the King of Shock Rock has a new release, *Trash*, selling by the crateload. Boasting a guest list that includes members of Aerosmith, Bon Jovi and Winger, is it any wonder that his new platter has already moved a million units?—Anonymous, *Circus*, 1989

Alice Cooper is not a woman's name any longer. The meaning, as with the threat, is long gone. With *Trash* the prime mover behind those still challenging pop landmarks, "School's Out" and "Elected," has seen the light and switched it on. Old hits and past glories don't necessarily add up to a great pension—*Trash* does. . . . *Trash* is so safe—Tina Turner could comfortably cover every track. And yes, now Alice could play Woodstock. Danger, excitement—Alice doesn't live there any more.—Andy Ross, *Sounds*, August 1989

Side One

1. Poison (Child/Cooper/McCurry)
2. Spark in the Dark (Child/Cooper)
3. House of Fire (Child/Cooper/Jett)
4. Why Trust You (Child/Cooper)
5. Only My Heart Talkin' (Cooper/Goldmark/Roberts)

Side Two

1. Bed of Nails (Child/Cooper/Warren)
2. This Maniac's in Love with You (Child/Cooper/Held/Teeley)
3. Trash (Child/Cooper/Frazier/Sever)
4. Hell Is Living without You (Child/Cooper/Bon Jovi/Sambora)
5. I'm Your Gun (Child/Cooper/McCurry)

Following the *Raise Your Fist and Yell* tour while vacationing in Hawaii with his wife Sheryl, Alice received an unexpected and generous offer from Epic Records to record an album with them. Given a deal that offered almost no financial restraints and complete artistic freedom on the condition that Alice delivered a hit album, he immediately began collaborating with renown hit-writer Desmond Child, whose work he had long admired and who had delivered hits for KISS (cowriting "I Was Made for Loving You"), Aerosmith (cowriting "Dude Looks Like a Lady") and other luminaries including Jon Bon Jovi and Joan Jett, while an amicable severance with MCA was brokered by manager Shep Gordon. The end result was *Trash*. Alice Cooper's resurrection album, produced by Child, restored his fortunes in both commercial and critical senses to a level akin to the dizzy heights of the Alice Cooper band in their prime and the performance of his solo debut, *Welcome to My Nightmare*. Borne on the wings of a smash hit single, "Poison," *Trash* achieved top twenty status in both the US and UK markets—reaching number two in the latter—and fared extremely well in numerous other countries around the world. While *Trash* remained in a glam metal stylistic vein similar to its two predecessors, its architects, Cooper and Child, looked to an earlier reference point in the Alice Cooper catalog for their inspiration: *Love It to Death*.

The album cover is one of Alice's simplest, most uncluttered, and best. Standing with his hands in his pockets and looking down reflectively in a pose of studied nonchalance against a mottled grey background, the image conveys much to the viewer, but without seemingly trying hard; with controlled subtlety. The white T-shirt he is wearing bears his own oversized image in a caricature sourced from the innersleeve artwork of *Raise Your Fist and Yell*. His face, displaying the full grotesque signature black makeup, is half flesh and half gleaming white skull, thereby conveying the horror for which he is renowned, while his black leather jacket with its chainmail, zip, and studs, along with his black bondage leggings with brown belt buckle, locate him effortlessly once again within the glam metal realm established by the *Constrictor* and *Raise Your Fist and Yell* albums. With his own face mostly hidden by his head-down pose, it is the face on his T-shirt that stands in for the real thing, creating a wonderful amalgamation of the real Alice and the fantasy Alice in the viewer's gaze, blurring fact and fiction. His name appears at the top right of the cover in cream-colored white letters over which is superimposed the album title in slasher-style blood-red lettering, creating another highly effective juxtaposition.

"Poison" is the first track and was the album's most successful single, equaling the number seven placing of "School's Out" on the US singles chart while rising all the way to number two on the UK chart. The hand of Desmond Child is clearly evident on "Poison." Child had cowritten the 1986 smash-hit "Livin' on a Prayer" with Jon Bon Jovi and Richie Sambora and, as shown in that signature song, he was a master of incorporating infectious key changes into his work. And indeed, much of the magic of "Poison" lies in the unsettling string of three changes of key that occur in the first half of each chorus, with each modulation using the same I / VI / iii / VII chord sequence. The first vocal line occurs over a I (Gm) / VI (E-flat) / iii (B-flat) / VII (F) pattern; the second modulates up to a I (Cm) / VI (A-flat) / iii (E-flat) / VII (B-flat) pattern; the third vocal line modulates again down to a I (Am) / VI (F) / iii (C) / VII (G); and the fourth vocal line modulates up to the home key of Dm, using a I (Dm) / VI (B-flat) / iii (F) / VII (C), where it finally stays for the remainder. Each key change comes as a surprise to the listener, with no subtle Bach-like preparation in the harmony to disguise and ease the shift, a dynamic technique that drives forward momentum. While a cleverly prepared key change can at times be barely discernible to the listener, here the effect is brutal and obvious, much like changing gear at high revs in an automobile. Lyrically, the song features ingenious syllable pairings in lines such as: "Your cruel, device. Your blood, like ice. One look, could kill. My pain, your thrill." A very basic but highly effective technique, the pairings mirror the utterances in the choruses of the two-syllable song title, "Poi-son," which is itself masterfully positioned to fall at the moment where the three key changes identified above have finally coalesced on the home chord of

Dm. The subject matter of the song is in total keeping with Cooper's career-long investment in Grand Guignol–styled horror themes, and he uses his Ezrin-assisted signature voice. On all counts, his first block-buster hit since 1972 masterfully draws together the Alice Cooper hall-marks on which his success was founded.

Tasked with the unenviable job of following the smash hit single is the second track, "Spark in the Dark," and were it not for the singer's instantly recognizable sneering vocal style, frankly this by-the-book song could have been performed by any one of the many other glam metal exponents of the era. The tone is set in the opening lines, and the message of lust and sexual liaison is as deep as the track ever gets: "Oh, welcome to the party. It's only me and you. Tell the world to go away babe, and I'll tell you what to do." A hint of underage sex adds a token element of danger: "'Cause if your mom and dad find out they'll skin me to the bone." But "Spark in the Dark" pales in comparison to its lofty predecessor, and even another Desmond Child key change only elevates the pitch rather than lifting the song to any greater heights. While "Poison" possessed brilliance enough to elevate it beyond MOR, "Spark in the Dark" cannot escape that fate.

The third track, "House of Fire," remains in a similar vein, albeit veering more toward love than sex: "Building a house of fire, baby, building it with our love. We are building a house of fire every time we touch." Released as a single, it performed moderately well, peaking at number sixty-five in the United Kingdom and fifty-six in the United States on their respective singles charts. Again, however, trademark Cooper touches such as horror and/or the all-important element of tongue-in-cheek humor are totally absent, resulting in a track that is generic glam metal rather than bona fide Alice Cooper material.

"Why Trust You" is the fourth song on *Trash*, and it has small touches of vintage Cooper here and there within the lyrics. Religiosity surfaces briefly in the line "You'd try to sell the Bible to the devil himself," while a dash of very welcome humor (and, indeed, a nice, nostalgic, gallows moment) appears in "The noose is getting tighter, your face is turning whiter—You can stuff it up your muffin and go stick it in the fire." While the song content goes no deeper than a critique of untrustworthiness, these flashes, and others, lift the song above its two predecessors.

Last on side one comes "Only My Heart Talkin'," and it sees a return to the end-side-one-with-a-ballad rule of earlier days. "I never said the words out loud," sings Alice, "I guess I couldn't get 'em straight. Baby, give me one more chance before you walk away." Sure enough, a key change occurs late in the piece to maintain/enhance listener interest, but while all of the elements of a rock ballad are present and the production is spot-on perfect, the uniqueness of Alice's ballad hits of yesteryear is absent, replaced by an MOR sameness. Whereas in "Only Women Bleed," "You and Me," and "I Never Cry," the listener felt like Alice was singing his heart out and expressing truths he held close to his soul, here it seems like Alice is just, well, singing a song. Despite the evidence of the song's title, "Only My Heart Talkin'," it appears to fans that Alice's heart did a lot more talking on those far less formulaic and heartfelt songs from back in the 1970s.

Side two starts with a hiss and a roar and a dose of pure rock 'n' roll raunch. While plying basically the same subject matter as the earlier "Spark in the Dark," "Bed of Nails," like "Poison," is a textbook example of how to write a glam metal hit and it is no surprise that the song was selected as another single from the album. Surprisingly, given that it reached a respectable number thirty-eight in the United Kingdom and moved as high as number thirteen in Australia, making it the second most successful single after "Poison," "Bed of Nails" was not released as a single in the United States. Multilayered gang vocals soar in the choruses, dynamic shifts occur throughout, the whole glam metal box of tricks is employed by Child, and Alice sound just plain nasty, dirty, and dangerous on lines such as "Love hurts good on a bed of nails. I'll lay you down and when all else fails, I'll drive you like a hammer on a bed of nails."

In the following track, "This Maniac's in Love with You," threads of Alice's experiences during his therapy for addiction filter through despite the song being about, once again, primarily love but with a side order of sex: "My heart has been strapped in a straitjacket love. The therapy boys say it fits like a glove." At the same time, the sadomasochistic nuances of "Bed of Nails" are also present: "I'm crossing the line in my brain, the line between pleasure and pain." The extensive use of echoed vocal lines and, once again, gang vocals that respond to Alice's words in a call-and-response manner, fail to ignite this medium-paced track, and the listener is hard pressed to not begin singing in one's head the J. Geils Band's "Centerfold," or perhaps Huey Lewis's 1983 "I Want a New Drug," such is the similarity in pace and vibe with these other MOR classics.

The title track is third up on side two, and "Trash" is Alice's most overtly sexual song ever: "C'mon momma, help me climb aboard. . . . If my love was like a lollipop would you lick it until you get to the chewy center?" The rest of the lyrics echo this sentiment in various guises and scenarios, with the summative line being "When you hit the sheets you just turn to trash." There are at least two songs that the mature Alice Cooper refuses to perform any longer: "I can no longer go onstage and represent something I don't believe in. There are a few songs, like 'Trash' and 'Spark in the Dark' that I won't do any more."[7] It's completely accurate that, as Alice claims in his autobiography, his Christian faith has seldom been at odds with his product. But "Trash" is clearly on, or over, the line. And, once again, "Trash" could just as easily have been a Mötley Crüe song, sitting easily alongside their stock-in-trade songs about sex such as "Piece of Your Action," "Girls, Girls, Girls," or "Slice of Your Pie."

The penultimate song on *Trash* is "Hell Is Living without You." Just why the object of his affection is absent, Alice doesn't say. All we know is that she's "gone without a trace in a sea of faceless imitators." Without any reference points or a glimpse into the missing woman's motives, it is hard to empathize with the theme of this ballad and easier to accept it as a universal "missing you" kind of tale with no specificity.

Last up on *Trash* is "I'm Your Gun," and it's another track that Alice might well have on his list of songs he no longer wishes to perform. In the long-established innuendo tradition of the Beatles' "Happiness Is a Warm Gun," but with the sleaze factor increased at least tenfold from that much more innocent time, Alice encourages his "scared little girl in this big, bad town," to "be the target on the bed," where he'll "be shooting hot lead." More precisely, "Pull my trigger, I get bigger, then I'm lots of fun—I'm your gun." A furiously fast-paced track with an obligatory screaming guitar solo that orgasmically crescendos at its end, "I'm Your Gun" is a fittingly glam-metal-by-the-book end to Alice's knowingly titled album. *Trash* has delivered stylistic perfection, but it is not to everyone's approval.

In many ways, if searching for an adequate comparison, *Trash* is to Alice Cooper what *Let's Dance* (1983) was to David Bowie. *Let's Dance* was an album that took Bowie back to the top of the pop charts after a long absence with songs such as the title track as well as "Modern Love" and "China Girl." Both albums restored their respective artists to top-of-the-charts relevancy and its associated commercial success, but in the process, they were accused by hard-core fans and critics who had followed the artists over the years through thick and thin of selling out to the mainstream in order to achieve that success. Hit songwriter/producer Desmond Child was perhaps to Alice Cooper what Nile Rodgers had been to David Bowie. Typical of the tone of the many detractors was the following review:

> Alice Cooper's comeback seemed to be on solid artistic ground with '87's *Raise Your Fist and Yell*, a passionate aural horror story that bristled with intricate musicianship and wonderfully sick gothic lyrics. But . . . Cooper changed labels and collaborated with Bon Jovi/Aerosmith/Joan Jett hit doctor Desmond Child. The result is a confusing and listless group of catchy tunes calculated for airplay, kinda like Bon Jovi death metal. (Jon, don't try this at home.) And Alice's heart's not in it. Spend that cash for his early works on CD instead.[8]

In his book *The Complete David Bowie* (to continue the comparison just a little further), Nicholas Pegg describes *Let's Dance* thus: "*Let's Dance* is an album on which anything remotely resembling a rough edge had been sanded down and polished up until the glare is dazzling . . . he plays it safe in every department."[9]

For two artists whose reputations were built upon anything but "playing it safe," such criticism may be justified to an extent. But this is perhaps also largely unfair as—for any other artist—success on such a level would have surely been shouted from the rooftops and celebrated. The fact is, *Trash* and *Let's Dance* are both wonderful examples of pop/rock perfection, and should surely be admired in that light. Certainly, their respective successes brought both artists a host of new fans, even if providing an uncomfortable moment—and an ongoing talking point—for existing ones. Perhaps the bottom line with *Trash* is that Cooper had a plan, and executed it magnificently: "It was an extremely commercial album, geared toward the legion of fans flocking to see Mötley Crüe and Guns N' Roses on stage and *Friday the 13th* and *The Evil Dead* on movie screens." Undeniably, whatever one's views, in the wake of *Trash* there was no longer any doubt about the fact that Alice Cooper was back and as popular as ever.

7

TAKING STOCK AGAIN IN THE 1990s

Hey Stoopid, The Last Temptation, 1991–1994

HEY STOOPID, 1991 [US CHART #47, UK #4]

Hey Stoopid isn't the greatest, but it's great enough. That ol' black humour is greyin' but, thankfully, Alice is growing old disgracefully.—Ray Zell, *Kerrang!*, June 1991

I feel there's a lot of fun on this album. It sounds like a good, fun summer album to me—I'm in a good mood at this point. Even the nasty songs have got a nice sense of black humour to them.—Alice Cooper, interviewed by Drew Masters, *Meat*, July 1991

Side One

1. Hey Stoopid (Cooper/Pepe/Pfeifer/Ponti)
2. Love's a Loaded Gun (Cooper/Pepe/Ponti)
3. Snakebite (Bulen/Cooper/Kelling/Pepe/Pfeifer/Ponti)
4. Burning Our Bed (Cooper/Patrelli/Pfeifer/West)
5. Dangerous Tonight (Child/Cooper)
6. Might as Well Be on Mars (Child/Cooper/Wagner)

Side Two

1. Feed My Frankenstein (Coler/Cooper/Mindwarp/Richardson)
2. Hurricane Years (Cooper/Pepe/Pfeifer/Ponti)

3. Little by Little (Cooper/Pepe/Pfeifer/Ponti)
4. Die for You (Cooper/Mars/Sixx/Vallance)
5. Dirty Dreams (Cooper/Pfeifer/Vallance)
6. Wind-Up Toy (Cooper/Pepe/Pfeifer/Ponti)

Justifiably, Alice Cooper and Epic Records felt on a roll after the success of *Trash* and moved confidently on following it up with Cooper's first album of the new decade. Produced by Peter Collins and featuring a who's who of top guest artists, a notable near-total absence on *Hey Stoopid* was Desmond Child, cowriter of nine of the ten songs on *Trash* as well as producer. On *Hey Stoopid*, Child is present on only two tracks as a cowriter.

The lurid album cover created by Mike McNeilly (his work is described as "lethal art" in the credits) immediately grabs the attention. At the center lays a grinning white skull with a shock of black hair bearing Alice's trademark makeup around the eyes and mouth, while a pair of green bulging eyes make full contact with the viewer. Two metallic mannequin arms cross beneath this, bearing in their hands a wad of cash and a bunch of diamonds and precious stones. A snake is wound around the black lace-adorned arm on the left, while a chain encircles the arm on the right. Smaller items lie scattered around the image, including spiders, spiderwebs, hearts, more precious stones, badges, and baubles of various kinds and colors. Two makeup brushes lay at front right, while nails fringe the image. The logo appearing at the top right of the cover is done in exactly in the same style as the logo on *Trash*. Once again attributed to David Coleman, the only difference here is the pink block lettering of the artist's name while the album title is in bright yellow. Simply, the cover of *Hey Stoopid* is a veritable grab-bag of Alice Cooper iconography, and a marketing masterpiece.

As soon as it begins, *Hey Stoopid* tackles heavier ground than the sex- and love-themed *Trash*, with the title track's clear anti-suicide message placed right at the beginning of the album and delivered with absolute clarity of meaning: "Now I know you've been seeing red—don't put a pistol to your head. Sometimes your answer's heaven sent—your way is so damn permanent." With the first verse addressing a male, "Hey bro," and the second a female, "C'mon girl," Alice ensure he leaves no one out of his heartfelt message, and the notion that salvation lies above is a clear portent of a growing preparedness to incorporate his Christian beliefs into his music. Every bit as catchy as "Poison" and very close to the preceding hit in terms of vibe, instrumentation, and attitude, and featuring guest stars Slash, Ozzy Osbourne, and Joe Satriani, it is something of a surprise that it didn't fare better as a single, achieving a respectable number twenty-one on the UK chart but only a lowly seventy-eight in the United States.

The second track, "Love's a Loaded Gun," was also released as a single and fared moderately in the United Kingdom, reaching number thirty-eight on the chart. Acting somewhat against the obvious positivity of the title track, the theme is that of a man driven to violence by the ongoing sexual betrayal being perpetrated by his girlfriend: "I tried to look the other way and fake it—you know, you push me right to the limit, I can't take it." Adhering once again to the standard glam metal formula of teasing out the action in the lyrics for the first half of the song, erupting into a ten-fingers-and-forelock guitar solo, and rounding it off with a beefed-up chorus, there is little to tease out of "Love's a Loaded Gun."

"Snakebite" follows, introduced by several seconds of shaking maracas designed to sound like a rattlesnake, thus simultaneously referencing the album cover, the song title, and Alice's reputation as rock's premier snake enthusiast. The song title turns out to be the name of the song's protagonist who is, seemingly, a biker: "My face is tattooed on your shoulder, an' your name is scratched into my bike, yeah." Snakebite has a bad reputation and is in a bad mood as he contemplates the prospect of anyone else taking his woman, who seems to be of a mind to leave him: "I'll break 'em like a matchstick 'cause baby that's the kind of mood I'm in." Another straight-down-the-middle, glam metal track, it's hard to judge if "Snakebite" is supposed to build upon the narrative from "Love's a Loaded Gun" or not.

A beautiful, sparse, and intimate acoustic guitar introduction announces "Burning Our Bed," track number four and a ballad, which finds an unnamed (perhaps it's Snakebite, but the characterization seems quite different) jilted lover trying to erase the memory of his ex-partner by carrying out the action mooted in the title. The full band kicks in from the end of the first verse, and the song is given the full rock ballad treatment. There are a couple of self-referential moments in the lyrics, the first occurring when Alice name-drops the title of the previous album: "You talked a lot of trash and ya lied to me." The second, more oblique but funnier for Cooper fans who are well aware that their hero has been guillotined more times than anyone else on the planet, is in the clearly intentional line: "Maybe I might lose my head— aw, wouldn't be the first time." Now THAT is the Alice Cooper humor we all love, and the element most missed when it is absent.

One of the two Cooper/Child collaborations, "Dangerous Tonight," occupies the fifth spot on *Hey Stoopid*, and the track sees a return to the edgy sex/love theme of *Trash*: "If you let me I'll untie your sensuality—I'll open up your heart and satisfy my greed." Painting the ugly picture of a self-centered sexual predator, Cooper growls out the nature of his character: "I'm a flesh fanatic psychopath."

Ending side one is the other Cooper/Child collaboration—here joined by longtime collaborator Dick Wagner—"Might as Well Be on Mars," and it is a much better song. A tale of urban alienation and emotional estrangement, the track is noir-like in its images of city streets "wet with rain" and a woman—the object of the protagonist's desire—unattainable behind the glass window of a "favorite corner bar" because "to reach is just too far, and I might as well be on Mars." Swirling synthesizer, strings, and fragile piano set up an appropriately distant and lonesome introduction, and when the track proper begins, the mood is maintained despite the wall of instrumentation. Alice sounds convincingly alienated throughout; when he sings of being on the roof and staring down at the cars, the listener can feel the desperation in the situation with an almost filmic clarity. Indeed, "Might as Well Be on Mars" sounds like a film score and is highly effective in all regards.

A number twenty-seven hit on the UK chart, "Feed My Frankenstein" begins side two and is in many ways a classic Alice Cooper song. Included on the soundtrack of the movie *Wayne's World*, with Scooby Doo–like cartoon-horror at its core, the track begins with the sound of a growling monster and exhibits inherent humor throughout. Cooper fans could delight in lines that contained the traditional Cooper wink, such as: "Well, I ain't no veggie, like my flesh on the bone/Alive and lickin' on your ice cream cone." As sexual in content as the *Trash* material, as well as "Dangerous Tonight" just two tracks earlier, the lyrics of "Feed My Frankenstein" are far more clever, interesting, funny, and endearing, as Alice pleads of his love conquest to "let me drink the wine from your fur tea cup." The line has historical significance in its reference to an actual fur-covered tea cup made in 1936 by Swiss Dada/surrealist artist Meret Oppenheim, an object that has, both at the time and throughout art history, continually drawn sexual connotations in its interpretation. With a straightforward but highly effective chorus that repeats the song title again and again, the mid-paced rocker featuring guest stars Steve Vai, Joe Satriani, and Nikki Sixx is one of the most simplistic songs of Cooper's glam metal years, but is also one of his best with its four-on-the-floor infectiousness. In addition, the brief appearance on vocals of US pop culture icon Elvira, Mistress of the Dark, aka actress and musician Cassandra Peterson, is a clear nod to the influence of, and Alice's love for, trash TV/movie horror.

Alice's growing confidence in expressing his Christian faith through his music shows itself once again in the second track of side two, "Hurricane Years": "Turn my eyes to heaven, watching all the clouds roll by—I see the blood moon rising; I know I'm way too young to die." With underlying religiosity and the desire for salvation the most notable feature of the track, the protagonist is a lost cause with no investment or regard for past or future but aware that, unless he changes his ways, the impending doom he sees approaching will swallow him up. "I need a preacher," he cries, wishing to be relieved of his sins.

Given the many explorations of notions and scenarios of love and sex, especially on *Trash* but prevalent elsewhere on Alice Cooper albums, on the following "Little by Little," the vast difference between the two states is here spelled out with absolute clarity: "Push and shove, sex is sex, but honey love is love." Having started out as seemingly yet another portrayal of dangerous sexual behavior—"You're bad, you're so hardcore. Pull me down here on the killing floor"—when this soul-searching line is delivered, it takes the song to a new level by introducing the age-old dichotomous moral dilemma. Musically, the glam-sleaze instrumentation of sinuous distorted guitar over reverb-heavy snare on the two and four of the bar serves the slow/mid-tempo song extremely well, leaving much space for Alice to imbue his vocals with equally sleazy nuances. However, when he delivers his "love is love" line, it is without any such undercurrent; his voice here low in his register, and serious.

"Die for You" follows and is another song notable for the quality of its guest artists, with Nikki Sixx and Mick Mars of Mötley Crüe cowriting and the latter performing on the track along with Bon Jovi's sometime bassist Hugh McDonald. A piano introduces the standard rock-formula ballad with its message of lament for a love that might have been: "A million memories flood my brain—Drown my sorrow, kill my pain."

Second to last on *Hey Stoopid* is the self-evidently titled "Dirty Dreams" which, following a powerhouse instrumental opening reminiscent of the Sex Pistol's "God Save the Queen," returns the album to the theme of dangerous, edgy sex. "Dirty dreams—how you wanna do me?" growls Alice in a lyric that at one point amusingly and subtly harks back to the necrophilia days of "Cold Ethyl" from the *Welcome to My Nightmare* album sixteen years earlier in the line: "You can turn yourself blue and I don't care." The call-and-response technique of gang vocals singing the album title in the chorus, to which Alice responds, is used to excellent effect. "You oughta be ashamed of yourself," admonishes Alice in the closing line, after which the song is left hanging on a fade-out power chord.

Hey Stoopid ends very strongly with "Wind Up Toy," visiting the familiar Cooper thematic territory of horror and alienation, the latter both generational and psychological/mental. More remarkably, however, it also reintroduces a character from the past—the young boy Steven from *Welcome to My Nightmare*. Beginning with the sound of a wind-up music box, which quickly gives way to ominous synthesizer swirls, the song successfully merges the glam metal sound of Cooper's present and recent past while allowing elements of the more distant past to permeate. "I'm lost in a nightmare," Alice cries, cementing the recapitulation of the setting of his 1975 solo debut. The final section of the song here is in spoken word form featuring two voices, a man's and a child's, overlaid on one another, the same technique used to such eerie effect on that earlier album: "You know they come here every night—I see them, don't you see them?" Seconds after the final line informs us that the protagonist is tired and that it is bedtime, the ensuing silence is broken when a woman's voice from far-off calls out a spine tingling . . . "Steven!" Also revisiting the past, more specifically the *From the Inside* album of 1978, are the images of institutional forced incarceration in lines such as: "Solitary confinement—chained in a cell," and these also conjure up in the listener's mind even earlier Alice Cooper band tracks such as "Ballad of Dwight Fry" with its overtones of madness. In all,

"Wind Up Toy," along with the album's title track and "Feed My Frankenstein," shows Alice at his strongest both musically and thematically.

While it may not have fared quite as well as its critically divisive but commercially restorative predecessor, there is more quintessential Alice Cooper on *Hey Stoopid* and, as a result, the album is deservedly regarded by many fans to be among his best solo albums. Dave Thompson suggests: "*Hey Stoopid* stands now as the last gasp of the good ship glam metal,"[1] and this is certainly true, in Cooper's case, as he was about to embark on a significant change of direction that would forge new ground while simultaneously recapitulating the past.

THE LAST TEMPTATION, 1994 [US CHART #68, UK #6]

Screw the concept, the really important message this album has to convey is that Alice Cooper is back with his strongest collection of gen-u-wine, wrap-around-your-brain-more-than-once songs since his *Billion Dollar Babies* mid 70s heyday. I realise, of course, that a statement like that will mean doodly-squat to most of you twenty-somethings-and-unders reading this, having come in, as you probably did, with Alice's 1989 "Poison" hit single, or even his all-too-worthy appearance in the first Wayne's World movie. But as someone who was just out of short trousers the first time I saw Alice miming "School's Out" on *Top of the Pops*—my soon-to-be-felt-penned eyes nearly popping out of my teen skull as my mum tutted along (always a good sign)—you'll just have to take my word for it.—Mick Wall, *Raw*, May 1994

This is the strongest collection of tunes by the worthy snake-charmer in quite a year, bringing to mind comparisons of his early '70s heyday. . . . Whether or not you get the album's decay-of-society moral concept (or even care) is beside the point, because the better tracks stand up on their own.—Anonymous, *Toronto Star*, June 1994

Track Listing

1. Sideshow (Brooks/Cooper/Norwood/Saylor/Smith/Wexler)
2. Nothing's Free (Cooper/Saylor/Wexler)
3. Lost in America (Cooper/Saylor/Wexler)
4. Bad Place Alone (Cooper/Saylor/Wexler)

5. You're My Temptation (Blades/Cooper/Shaw)
6. Stolen Prayer (Cooper/Cornell)
7. Unholy War (Cornell)
8. Lullaby (Cooper/Vallance)
9. It's Me (Blades/Cooper/Shaw)
10. Cleansed by Fire (Cooper/Dudas/Hudson/Saylor)

The unexpected but very welcome return of Steven in the the final track of *Hey Stoopid* set the scene for *The Last Temptation* magnificently. But, unlike the earlier *Welcome to My Nightmare* concept, here the young victim is not caught in a dream from which he cannot awaken but is instead caught in the traveling Grand Guignol theater of a mysterious and dangerous showman who is based on the villainous yet curiously endearing Alice Cooper character of old. Set during Halloween week, Steven is subjected to an array of the evil Showman's temptations. In addition to resurrecting Steven, one of his most powerful characters, *The Last Temptation* also draws together and makes plain two more intrinsic threads of influence, Grand Guignol–style horror and comic books, making the album a highly important landmark in the history of Alice Cooper.

Crucially, Alice collaborated with author Neil Gaiman in order to bring to full fruition his strongest concept album in twenty years. Gaiman was a very well-known figure, a multiple-award-winning writer renowned for bringing to life Alice Cooper–esque horror on the pages of numerous best-selling short works of fiction, comic books, graphic novels, and other forms of popular media, including film. Fans of each other's work for many years, the collaboration went beyond the album itself, resulting in a spin-off, three-part comic book series illustrated by Mike Zulli and published by comic giant Marvel, the first issue of which was made available as a limited edition bonus with the initial pressing of *The Last Temptation.*

The evocative front cover of the album, created by Dave McKean, appropriately sets the scene with its montage of images drawn from multiple performance media around the world: religious iconography, masking, death symbolism and, at the center, a photograph of Alice in his signature black makeup making full eye contact with viewers, his hand outstretched beneath his face as if reaching out to pull them into the image. At the center bottom of the picture a fiery cauldron burns fiercely, a clear symbol of the hell that awaits anyone unfortunate enough to venture inside the Showman's theater.

From the moment the album begins with the lengthy opening track, "Sideshow," the concept is laid out for the listener with absolute clarity as Steven, bored and clearly a prime candidate for the Showman's attentions, bemoans his lot and is found scouting around looking for adventure: "I need a sideshow . . . some kinda creepshow, oh yeah . . . I want a scary ride, oh yeah—see Jekyll turn to Hyde." The song is peppered with Cooper humor, including some obvious references to US pop culture such as Kentucky Fried Chicken ("Some finger lickin' chicken-eating geek") and television ("Not a 90210"). Immediately noticeable to the listener is the changed sound of the music, with the reverb-heavy, flawless chrome production of his recent glam metal albums replaced by a much more raw-sounding rock quality somewhat reminiscent of the days of the Alice Cooper band. Having outlined his disillusionment with his everyday life through the course of six-and-a-half-plus minutes, as the tracks fades out a carnival organ takes over and Steven receives a spoken invitation from the Showman to enter his realm.

"Nothing's Free" then takes up the story, told by a sneering Alice over a garage-punk, riffing guitar-based rawness that recalls the Stooges in their heyday. It is in "Nothing's Free" that the Showman demands that Steven sell him his soul: "Sign upon the dotted line, I'll be yours and you'll be mine," he gloats. Referencing Steven's dissatisfaction with his boring life that was expressed in "Sideshow," he assures the boy that hell offers many more opportunities and that, if he signs, he'll be able to do anything he wants to, bound by no moral or authoritative convention or obligation: "Come on little one and dance in the fire—the heat's getting close and the flame's getting higher."

In the third track, "Lost in America," the listener gleans more information about Steven's dissatisfaction with his lot that has made him vulnerable to accepting the dark promises of the Showman. Tipping his hat to Eddie Cochrane's "Summertime Blues," but adding a considerably more dangerous twist to that much earlier and far more innocent teenage lament, the song provides a damning appraisal of American values and morals in the process: "I can't go to school 'cause I ain't got a gun, I ain't got a gun 'cause I ain't got a job, I ain't got a job 'cause I can't go to school, so I'm looking for a girl with a gun and a job and a house." Typically, having delivered lyrics that are both dark and disturbing, Alice then relieves the tension with the lyrical equivalent of a smile and a wink by adding, "with cable." Stylistically, once again the riff-heavy raw energy of the Stooges is invoked, while the primitive but highly effective chorus simply repeats the song title in powerful gang vocal style. Further humor lies in the image of Steven trying to do what every other boy in America aspires to do—learn to play "Stairway to Heaven" on the guitar—while the American reliance on convenience is superbly depicted in the reference to living at the 7-Eleven. Simply, the song serves as an indictment of the worst aspects of American society and makes the moral observation that unless things change, the attractions of the dark side will draw more and more American youth to it.

The strong adherence to the album's concept is maintained in the fourth track, "Bad Place Alone," where Steven, now experiencing first-hand the dark side, meets other inhabitants who have previously taken up the Showman's demonic, death-laced offer. Characters such as "Little Caesar" and "Smokey Joe" boast of their crimes, their deaths ("We're cool, we're cold, we're stiff, we're tagged"), and their underworld prowess, giving Steven a duplicitous assurance that he is on the one hand one of them—their "blood brother"—while at the same time taunting him that he is "all alone."

The subsequent "You're My Temptation" is the point where Alice lays the depth of his faith, and the extent of the album's heavy investment in religiosity, upon the table/altar. Attempting to resist a tide of human lust as an angelic woman working as the devil's instrument tries to seduce him ("Don't move your eyes like that") over a sleazy mid-paced rock groove built on a languid, recurring, descending guitar riff, Alice pleads, "Measure my faith, the devil's awake, he knows you're my temptation." "Mercy please, I'm on my knees," he cries, before finding strength and demanding: "Go away in Heaven's name!" As the song ends the listener hears the Showman chuckling and once again demanding that Steven sign his name to the surrendering of his soul.

Having witnessed the frightening state of those who had succumbed to the Showman before him, Steven makes up his mind about signing the proffered contract in "Stolen Prayer," the track ushered in by ethereal, high swirling synth lines atop a strummed acoustic guitar—a musical depiction of honesty and clarity. Having decided to not follow the Showman's urgings but to instead seek salvation in heaven, Alice declares to his would-be master: "You showed me your paradise and your carnival of souls, but my heart keeps telling me that ain't the place to go." The chorus functions as a dialogue, with Soundgarden lead singer Chris Cornell—cowriter of the song—singing the Showman's lines as he rebuts Steven's fears and doubts and tries once more to convince the boy to abandon his appeal to God and follow his path instead. Enhancing the song-of-worship quality of the track, a backing choir of children's voices joins Alice in parts, and at the end of "Stolen Prayer" Alice/Steven is found "down on my knees."

Cornell also features in the succeeding "Unholy War," a track he wrote alone. The battle lines are now clearly drawn and the song tackles head-on the eons-old, worldwide battle between good and evil—God versus the devil. "I took your cruel abuse, Lord took away my shame," sings Alice to the Showman, before adding that when the war is over and Judgement Day has come, "I'll get my just rewards and you'll have your hell to pay!" Gone are the softer, prayer-enhancing sounds and touches of the preceding track. Instead, with Alice having made his mind up to stand his ground and fight for what he believes in, the musical accompaniment is aggressive here: barnstorming, full-on rock and Alice singing in his snarliest signature voice to underline his passion and commitment to the cause, appearing strong, unshaking, and uncompromising in a fine exhibition of word-painting.

"Lullaby" then ensues, and it begins with the Showman making one final desperate appeal to shake Steven's conviction and surrender his soul. Spoken through a swirling, misty, dream-state maze of echo and reverb with no underlying pulse or beat, once the Showman has finished his pitch, the song proper begins with Alice, over clean, simple, arpeggiated guitar chords, pondering how he has come to this situation despite his upright and proper childhood: "I was the boy who said all of my prayers." Here Alice plays both dramatic roles in the song, Steven and the Showman, using different voices for each and with the latter double-tracked with a hissing, whispered second voice to give a demonic quality to the sound. "Get down—back into hell," implores Steven, accusing his would-be captor of leading him astray with his evil temptations: "You showed me things little boys shouldn't see—you scared me with visions of fire." The song gathers momentum as it proceeds, becoming a fiery rock number with screaming guitars and all the trimmings before dramatically dropping away at the end to repeat the understated, quiet beginning as Alice soul-searches and wonders at how his life progressed to such a low point.

Second to last on *The Last Temptation* is a lush power ballad, "It's Me." While not fitting quite so seamlessly and obviously into the album's narrative, it is clear that the song is being sung from the perspective of a now saved and spiritually cleansed Steven. The probable, unnamed, object of his desire is the woman whose lustful advances he so desperately sought to reject in "You're My Temptation," seeing her as a tool of the devil: "You played your cards, you felt the sorrow, 'cause all that dealer dealt was pain." Just as God had offered to take him in despite his sins, now it is his turn to offer the same deal: "I know you've sinned every sin but I'll still take you in."

Last on the album is the self-evidently titled "Cleansed by Fire," which emphatically and anthemically ties a bow around the strongly delivered evangelical message of the one of Alice Cooper's most conceptual works. After a titanic struggle, Steven has won the battle for his soul: "You lose, I win—you couldn't suck me in." Triumphant, he demands that the Showman go back to hell, because "I'm Heaven bound—go back to where you belong." A church bell rings out poignantly at the end, while the final vocal line, "Go to hell!" provides a nostalgic moment for Alice Cooper fans because almost twenty years earlier, in *Alice Cooper Goes to Hell*, it had been he who was seemingly destined to make that journey. On *The Last Temptation*, such a notion was completely erased.

8

"THE COOP," POST-MILLENNIUM

Brutal Planet, Dragontown, The Eyes of Alice Cooper, Dirty Diamonds, 2000–2005

BRUTAL PLANET, 2000 [US CHARTS #193, UK #38]

After hearing master shock-rocker Alice Cooper's new *Brutal Planet*, it's clear that Marilyn Manson and others of his ilk are pale by comparison. On this monument to Goth-metal headbanging fury, Cooper is the devil's cabana boy. He'll definitely be called irresponsible for this ode to destruction, but he makes people listen—and think.— Dan Aquilante, *New York Post*, June 6, 2000

Brutal Planet is simply dark, simply twisted, simply poignant and simply—Alice Cooper. Alice pokes sarcasm at quite a few things on this new release, including racism, work place burn-out, gluttony, greed, wife abuse and a few more that I haven't quite figured out yet. I really enjoyed this in-your-face release with its off-center view of life in the world of today. I can relate to what Alice says in this recording and appreciate the dark humor he uses.—Snidermann, *Rough Edge*, June 2000

Track Listing

1. Brutal Planet (Cooper/Marlette)
2. Wicked Young Man (Cooper/Marlette)
3. Sanctuary (Cooper/Marlette)

4. Blow Me a Kiss (Cooper/Ezrin/Marlette)
5. Eat Some More (Cooper/Marlette)
6. Pick Up the Bones (Cooper/Marlette)
7. Pessi-Mystic (Cooper/Marlette)
8. Gimme (Cooper/Marlette)
9. It's the Little Things (Cooper/Marlette)
10. Take It Like a Woman (Cooper/Marlette)
11. Cold Machines (Cooper/Marlette)

Those people who assumed that Alice Cooper would change his raison d'être and perhaps tread more lightly in the wake of *The Last Temptation* and the associated revelation that he was a fervent, practising Christian, were proven to be very misguided upon the release of his first album of the new millennium. After a lengthy hiatus from the recording studio—the six years between *The Last Temptation* and *Brutal Planet* is by far the longest gap between albums of his entire career—just what he would come up with might well have been anyone's guess. Produced by Bob Marlette, and notably Bob Ezrin would here make a welcome return to the credits of an Alice Cooper album, this time as executive producer, Cooper's millennial album is the heaviest recorded work he has ever made, in addition to being one of the most poignantly and obviously political. The brutality of the modern world is his target, with its increasing tendency toward terrorism and far-right doctrines, the greed of banks, and the associated lack of regard for humanity and compassion.

The cover of *Brutal Planet* matches the album's title in terms of brooding menace. Metallic in its dominating colors of black, white, and copper, the image is stark and industrial and, despite Alice's face appearing in half profile on the right-hand side, there is no hint of humanity, no skin tone or eye color evident, and the album's title at the bottom is in a stamped mechanical font devoid of human touch. Beneath Alice's one visible eye is a series of five small hieroglyphics in an arc shape, while his raised hand sits between his face and the embossed metallic surface that dominates the rest of the cover.

From the opening seconds of the first song and the album's title track, the musical accompaniment is a metal barrage, an impenetrable wall of industrial steel, and comparisons made by reviewers at the time of the album's release to acts such as Marilyn Manson and Korn are entirely justified. Nevertheless, at all times the vocals stay perfectly audible and not buried in the mix, as happens at times in such extreme metal territory. Describing the Earth in the opening line as a "ball of hate," religiosity once again appears right at the forefront of the work: "Right here we fed the lions Christian flesh and Christian blood—down here is where we hung him upon an ugly cross." Mankind's biggest and most detestable misdemeanors are systematically thrust into the lime-light with other lines making reference to the Holocaust, to cheating the poor, beating children, and starving the hungry. Earth, our "Brutal Planet," is depicted exactly as the song title suggests it should be: ugly, dehumanized, unfeeling, dangerous, and unerringly harsh.

Unequivocally direct lyrics paint a bleak picture of their maladjusted subject in the second song on *Brutal Planet*, "Wicked Young Man." Written in the light of the Columbine High School shootings, Alice takes care to point out that the blame for such evil cannot be leveled at outside influences and at the common youth amusements of popular culture in particular: "It's not the games that I play, the movies I see, the music I dig." Rather, some people are simply bad: "I'm just a wicked young man." As Alice would explain in more depth:

> I started to think about how, on my own *Brutal Planet*, an incident like Columbine High School would probably happen every day! In our real world, we're getting these isolated glimpses of how bad such a world could be. In the song "Wicked Young Man," the subject has got a pocketful of bullets and a blueprint of the school. What I want to do to that guy is to *expose* him, not to condone him or to glorify him. He's not Billy the Kid or Wyatt Earp. He is a guy you want to turn in. [1]

As the title suggests, "Sanctuary" offers a means of escape from the terrors of the Brutal Planet, but it is a false deliverance as the answer proffered is to simply hide away and keep the ugliness out of sight: "Let the world blow away, this is where I will stay, in my sanctuary. Got my mess on the floor, got my lock on my door." Half sung and half spoken, but all in a despairing air over the same impersonal, dehumanizing industrial metal bed that has characterized the album thus far, the song explores the hopelessness of going through the motions and adhering to the societal expectations of obtaining a shirt and tie, a job, insurance, a wife, and "2.3 kids"—the very kind of normalcy that young killers such as Eric Harris and Dylan Klebold so inappropriately attempt to rebel against. "Sanctuary" does not offer the very thing that its title implies.

"Blow Me a Kiss" shifts the focus from the perpetrators of the Columbine shootings, and their ilk, to the innocent victims who lose their lives in such atrocities:

> Trying to be sensitive to the kids that died in Columbine, but at the same time sort of documenting what happened. These kids weren't killed because they were black. They weren't killed because they were gay. They weren't killed because they were scared. They were killed at random. That to me, is totally frightening; there was no rhyme or reason to it. As a writer, I think I need to document that and keep it and make it a historical fact. [2]

Alice articulates with directness and simplicity the very question that is repeatedly asked, en masse, in the wake of such shootings, and he does so from the disturbing perspective of a victim in his or her last moments, looking into the eyes of the executioner(s): "Tell me what you're thinking, tell me why—blow me a kiss then blow me away."

The barbs of accusation that Alice fired in *Brutal Planet* thus far continue unabated in the following track, "Eat Some More," and here he turns his attention to the yawning gap of inequality that exists between the haves and the have-nots: "Sixty million tons of meat spoiling in the stinking heat—train loads full of moldy bread, millions will still go unfed." Built over a huge doom-laden guitar riff that would not have been out of place on an early Black Sabbath album, the track is unrelenting and maintains its sharp focus throughout.

By the sixth track, "Pick Up the Bones," something new about *Brutal Planet* is becoming quite evident to the listener. While Alice Cooper and horror have always been a hand-in-glove fit, the brand of horror has always been trashy and cartoon-like, delivered with humor to soften the impact. On *Brutal Planet*, however, Alice has traded pop-culture entertainment-horror for the real, undiluted, and unmitigated thing, and there is no cushioning, no comforting sly wink. "Pick Up the Bones" is no exception, and with disturbing clarity explores the horrific scenario of the survivor of a massacre picking his way through the remains of his home after an unidentified group of thugs has murdered his entire family: "There were demons with guns who marched through this place, killing everything that breathed, they're an inhuman race. There are holes in the walls, bloody hair on the bricks and the smell of this hell is making me sick." The song is based on footage of the war in Kosovo that was shown on the television news in the United States, of a man collecting the bones of his family:

> He's walking with a pillowcase picking up human bones and putting
> them in the bag. I thought, "What is this?" I turned up the volume,
> and the man was saying, "This is my uncle, and this is my cousin . . ."
> He picks up a ribcage, and puts it in the bag. I was astonished. This
> was the most horrific thing I'd ever seen in my life.[3]

The song's funereal tempo is perfectly matched to the subject matter, and one can well imagine its subject making his way slowly through the smoking ruins of the family home and stopping to retrieve what is left of his loved ones. "Pick Up the Bones" is probably the most disturbing song Alice Cooper has ever recorded.

In the subsequent track, "Pessi-Mystic," Alice sings of the numbing effect that witnessing such vile atrocities as a matter of course during the daily news can have: "Watching CNN and holding my breath—to face the daily news scares me to death." But rather than inspiring people to make a change, the problem can come to simply seem too big, and an overriding pessimism may be the result, ending in impotence and inaction: "Everything is dark so why not accept it? Everything is far more black than white." Repeatedly, Alice screams "Shut up!" throughout the song, as if denial will make the problem go away.

Thus far, religiosity has been markedly absent on the album, but on "Gimme" the subject matter so clearly outlined on *The Last Temptation* is revisited. In Cooper's increasingly longer checklist of human failings, it is greed and a misplaced sense of entitlement that provide the subject matter here, and the unarticulated implication in the context of *Brutal Planet* is that such self-centeredness is what prevents human beings from being concerned about, and attending to, the needs of others less fortunate than themselves: "Don't you deserve to have it all? Kneel down and tell me what you need—fame and money all for you, I can make your every dream come true." A good-versus-evil, God-versus-the-devil war is being waged in the lyrics of "Gimme" and, playing the devil's advocate, Alice offers anything and everything in return for just a small price—presumably, one's soul.

Nine songs in, and for the first time on *Brutal Planet* a touch of Alice Cooper humor surfaces to alleviate the unrelenting heavy tension just a little. In a (at times) tongue-in-cheek plea for tolerance, the frenetic "It's the Little Things" paints a picture of the artist being driven over the edge to ungovernable and inappropriate rage by small, inconsequential events and losing sight of the bigger picture. While the subject matter is not humorous in itself, obviously, the way that Alice tells it is. Professing not to care as he reels off a list of dire actions/assaults upon his person, it is one of the "little things" that he claims would eventually rouse him to violent action: "But if you talk in the movies I'll kill you right there." Elsewhere he self-references: "You push me too far? Welcome to my nightmare—no more Mr. Nice Guy."

The touch of humor lasts for just the one track, as the album's second-to-last song, "Take It Like a Woman," instantly returns the listener to the dire subject matter of the vast majority of the album. Understandably, Cooper fans will immediately align the song to "Only Women Bleed" from *Welcome to My Nightmare*, a work similar in its theme of violence against women and spousal abuse, and similar too in its rock ballad format. However, "Take It Like a Woman" presents more graphic imagery than did that hit ballad of twenty-five years earlier: "He tied you up pulled your hair, and slapped your innocent face— yeah, you were black and blue, he laughed at you." The real tragedy of the song, though, is the cyclical pattern that Alice identifies, one that often sees women escaping from one abusive relationship only to repeat it in their next, because "the world above is still a brutal place and the story will start again." Opting for strings and poignant melody over the industrial metal onslaught of the rest of the album, "Take It Like a Woman" offers aural respite and introduces a moment of stylistic variety that serves the album well.

"Cold Machines" has the final say on *Brutal Planet*. With musical underpinning that draws the listener to reference Marilyn Manson's 1996 "The Beautiful People" of four years earlier—most especially the guitar riff on which the song is built—the "Cold Machines" provides an Orwellian glimpse of a cold, emotionless future devoid of humanity, where "Love's forbidden, so is passion." The *1984* allusions are many, and never has Alice Cooper portrayed such bleakness with a total absence of humor. David Bowie's take on Orwell's work in his 1974 album, *Diamond Dogs*, painted a similar scenario, but here in Cooper's hands twenty-six years later, the brutality and harshness of the industrial metal style that he has so convincingly adopted renders the message even more potent and terrifying for the new millennium.[4] Crying that he doesn't want to end up just a memory, Alice makes it clear that rather than being a glimpse into a possible future, the world he describes is already unfolding around him and us: "Like cold machines, we're marching on and on."

Brutal Planet is, as Alice Cooper himself attested, the artist's heaviest album, but not only in terms of its musical style. The subject matter is unrelentingly bleak and finds Alice at his most socially and politically provocative. Whether this can be held as the reason for Alice's fortunes on the US album charts plummeting—*Brutal Planet* reached only a lowly number 193 stateside, and while achieving a more respectable number 38 on the UK chart, this too represented a decline—is hard to ascertain, but certainly the downward commercial trend from the highs of his 1990s albums must have been of considerable concern.

DRAGONTOWN, 2001 [US CHART, #197 UK#87]

> The point on that one is, "You can even be a nice guy and be in Hell. The road to Hell is littered with nice guys with good intentions."— Alice Cooper, interviewed by Doug Van, *HM*, March 2002

> In the past couple of years Alice Cooper has enjoyed something of a creative, critical and commercially successful renaissance since the release first of *Brutal Planet* and its accompanying world tour, and now more recently with the release of *Dragontown*, which sees Alice return to themes and ideas first explored on its predecessor . . . a sordid world hell bent on self destruction where sex, death and money are the coda for life—a place, where like an anti-hero, Alice is our commentator, guide and ultimately the perpetrator to a vision of the world that's maybe not that far off from reality.—Brian G, "Chasing the Dragon," *Get Rhythm*, November 2001

Track Listing

1. Triggerman (Blake/Cooper/Marlette/Wilson)
2. Deeper (Blake/Cooper/Marlette/Wilson)

 3. Dragontown (Blake/Cooper/Marlette/Wilson)
 4. Sex, Death and Money (Cooper/Marlette)
 5. Fantasy Man (Cooper/Marlette)
 6. Somewhere in the Jungle (Cooper/Marlette)
 7. Disgraceland (Cooper/Marlette)
 8. Sister Sara (Cooper/Marlette)
 9. Every Woman Has a Name (Cooper/Marlette)
10. I Just Wanna Be God (Cooper/Marlette)
11. It's Much Too Late (Cooper/Marlette)
12. The Sentinel (Cooper/Marlette)

The similarity of color scheme with the cover of *Brutal Planet* ensures an instant visual linkage between *Dragontown* and its immediate predecessor. In shades of fiery red copper with black and white, the cover features a portrait of Alice set for battle, his face split by the blade of an ornate medieval sword that he holds before him, his face focused and serious. And such synergy between the two albums is by design, as Alice relates:

> When I finished work on *Brutal Planet* I was really pleased with the way it had turned out, but I sat back and thought the story was not finished—I could think of at least ten or eleven more things I wanted to say to finish it all up, so when I started to write the next album it just sort of turned into part two. So I didn't try to fight it and just let the idea run. I came up with the name *Dragontown*; I wanted it to be the worst part of *Brutal Planet*, like its capital.[5]

The album opens in uncompromising fashion with "Triggerman," a profile of a shady, anonymous figure who wields great destructive power but remains behind the scenes, beyond retribution and retaliation: "I ain't got a name, I don't gotta face—no fingerprints or DNA." As Alice puts it,

> He is a bit like the cigarette smoking man in the X-Files, the cancer man. He is the power behind the throne, he is the guy that pushes all the buttons that nobody ever knows about, no DNA, no identity. He's the guy that makes things happen but in my story he finally meets his match and ends up in *Dragontown*.[6]

The second track, "Deeper," serves as a metaphor in the *Brutal Planet/Dragontown* storyline for a civilization plummeting out of control and down into the depths of moral and social decay in what is described as an elevator that has plunged through the floor and keeps going downward uncontrollably: "We're in a deadly spin, hating this spin we're in—our helpless panic grows, down and down and down we go." The downward-spiraling chord sequence paints the theme, and Alice's melody in the verses does likewise.

The album's title track appears third up and, as mooted by Alice above, the lyrics of "Dragontown" paint a dire picture of the Brutal Planet's most horrific and violent city. The characters are dangerous and lawless, and there are clearly evident links to events and/or characters visited in songs from the preceding album: "There's a wicked young man cooking slowly in the frying pan and our family of bones are back together sleeping all alone," sings Alice, thereby directly and simultaneously referencing both "Wicked Young Man" and "Pick Up the Bones." In addition, he inserts himself into the scenario: "Then there's Alice, dear, and all the little things that got him here."

"Sex, Death and Money" then addresses clearly the album's theme of a world descending beyond the point of no return into moral decay, because in Dragontown, "Sex, death and money, sonny, makes this wicked world go round." Many people in the past had accused Alice Cooper of eroding the moral fabric of society through his work, so, in "Sex, Death and Money" there exists a humorous and ironic turning of the tables when Alice complains to the government: "When I go to the show all I see on the screen is a stream of pure vulgarity." He is laughingly told in response that he is one of a tiny minority and that the values of the vast majority, who seek the exact stimulations that make up the song's title, are what truly matters in Dragontown. The official then adds, laughingly and without caring, "That is why we all are gonna fry!" Hell, it seems, is of no consequence on the Brutal Planet because they are one and the same.

In the subsequent "Fantasy Man," Alice directs his anger against one of the factors that he sees contributing to the declining society we live in—that is, the macho mold of American male who possesses an inherent refusal to change, lest he be seen as weak, compliant, or embracing things feminine: "I don't read books, I don't French cook or stroll around in galleries." Managing to insert a moment of classic Cooper-style humor despite the subject matter, he continues: "I hate opera, I hate Oprah," and whines, "Don't fill my head with poetry." Dismissing men who do the above-mentioned things as mere women's fantasies, and adamant that he won't ever change, Alice accuses those who would like to see him amend his ways thus: "You just want to squeeze my masculinity."

Just as the modern-day city was described analogously in "Welcome to the Jungle" by Guns N' Roses, Dragontown is described similarly in "Somewhere in the Jungle" but depicted as a far more dire and lethal place, where: "Countless heads, ears and eyes, never hear, never cry—tribal chants, tribal war, tribal death, tribal gore." Alluding to the sentiment of previous song, after the genocide of "Somewhere in the Jungle" has been carried out by men unwilling to compromise on the warmongering that they see as a legitimate expression of their masculinity, it is the women who are left to mourn the waste: "the mothers will cry their tears." The song's lyrics use real African genocide as the blueprint for the descriptions of mass, wanton killing, and the musical underpinning of the brutal subject matter remains harsh, impersonal, and aggressively masculine throughout.

Making an unexpected thematic appearance on *Dragontown* is rock 'n' roll icon Elvis Presley, the subject of the wonderfully punning "Disgraceland." Held up as the epitome of a star for whom everything went wrong when he lost his way, destroyed by the excesses and destructive distractions of capitalist celebrity success, Alice is unflinching in describing the public and humiliating demise of his former idol: "He ate his weight in country ham—killed on pills and woke in Disgraceland." Turning a negative spotlight on a figure such as Presley is brave in the extreme for any artist, but as an analogy for what is wrong with American society, the tactic in Cooper's hands is highly effective and successful. Introducing religiosity, Alice tells how Presley describes himself as the King of Rock 'n' Roll when waiting at the Pearly Gates following his death. However, he is summarily turned away by Peter who declares: "Well son, we already got ourselves a king," and thus the King of Rock 'n' Roll is consigned to hell, being no match for the real thing. "Disgraceland" begins in a pure rockabilly style, and Alice takes on the Presley vocal inflections with aplomb. When the firepower of heavy metal instrumentation subsequently kicks in, the feel of the song remains nostalgic and retrospective; however, the loss of innocence of those early rock 'n' roll days is sonically palpable in the now overtly heavyweight parody. Alice has explained his rationale for using Presley in this manner:

> I felt that after thirty years I was tired of hearing things like "he died and went to rock 'n' roll heaven." I went "I don't think so." . . . I'm a big Elvis fan and I got to know him and consider him a friend of mine. He invited me over one night and we talked for a real long time. That would be back in about '72 when he looked real good, he was like the Elvis we all like to remember. When I saw how he ended up, saw that he was bloated and stoned and wasn't really the Elvis I knew. So when he died I don't think he died in a state of grace, he died in a state of disgrace, so I used the play on words between Graceland and "Disgraceland" and it all kind of fitted in and I think he would see the sense of humor in this.[7]

The notion that even highly religious figures who should be beyond temptation are susceptible to following the darkness of Dragontown instead of upholding the light is the subject matter for "Sister Sara," with its description of a nun's spectacular and complete fall from grace. Religious jokes abound in the lyrics in lines such as: "Even cardinal sin tried to feed her habit" and "Oh come all ye faithless." As Alice has done many times before, in "Sister Sara" he sings from the perspective of the devil himself, informing the shamed nun: "You'll be a lovely little demon in my private stock."

On an album in which so much human ugliness is explored and highlighted with graphic description, the ballad "Every Woman Has a Name" emerges as a rare moment of truly touching humanity and tenderness. Gone for the entirety of the song is the coldly impersonal musical shell of industrial metal, replaced by an acoustic guitar sensibility and the usual Cooper ballad accoutrement of lush strings. The signature Alice sneer is nowhere in evidence and, occupying the same pro-women, anti-misogyny territory of "Only Women Bleed," in "Every Woman Has a Name" the artist presents a heartfelt plea for respect and common decency that is every bit as effective as that far more well-known predecessor. The plea is all-encompassing, and includes: "Small town debutantes and queens . . . cocktail waitresses with dreams, every woman has a name." The presence of this song on the heels of the sentiments expressed earlier in "Fantasy Man" and "Somewhere in the

Jungle," and in the face of the violence by men as portrayed in the other songs, makes it clear that in Cooper's view, the worlds of *Dragontown* and *Brutal Planet* would do well to listen far more to the views of women.

The intriguingly titled "I Just Wanna Be God" follows, adding further critique and insight into how a society can descend into the depths that *Dragontown* has plumbed. Specifically, it addresses the notion of humankind's adoption of false idols, and Alice plays the part of exactly the kind of figure he is talking about; a self-made rock star who believes his own bloated myth and regards himself to be the equivalent of—or better than—God: "I invented myself with no one's help—I'm a prototype supreme." A follow-on from the content of "Disgraceland," in which the rock 'n' roll god was denied access to heaven because a "real" king already dwelt there, but here without targeting Elvis Presley specifically, humor surfaces in "I Just Wanna Be God" with a clever pun on rock 'n' roll in the line: "I was born to rock and I was born to rule."

"It's Much Too Late" occupies the penultimate position on *Dragontown*, and in the face of the overwhelming evidence of mankind's moral and societal demise presented in the preceding tracks, the idea that the city has passed the point of redemption comes as no surprise. Further, the song purports that even the ostensibly good people who stood by and allowed their society to crumble, or who became distracted and focused on other things, are complicit in Dragontown's destruction because "The road to hell is littered with nice guys with good intentions." The musical accompaniment is light and Beatles-esque in comparison to the majority of the rest of the songs, with sweet harmonies and harmonious melodies a reminder of a time when the world was in much better moral health. This paints the song's theme further in its musical representation of what has been lost, and appears consonant and touchingly naive when set against the violence of the industrial metal sound of the new millennium.

The end of the album comes in the form of "The Sentinel" and, having established that things have gone too far to be corrected, the end of the album is left to someone who typifies the inevitable bottom-of-the-heap spawn of Dragontown's misery, violence, and neglect—a hardened, heartless terrorist who goes by the song's title and whose tragic goal is simply to end his own life, take as many other people with him into hell as possible, and be immortalized for the deed: "'Cause it's my fate—I operate on hate." It is about Columbine and 9/11 and Rwanda and all other sites of such twenty-first-century horror. And yet—and surely Alice Cooper is the only artist who could possibly pull this off—there is humor to be found in the lyrics: "There's something disturbin' going on in my turban—I'm home, home on de-range." This final track on *Dragontown* is appropriately musically violent, the metal a suitable vehicle for the subject matter, and when it ends suddenly and without any sense of completion or tidiness, it reinforces the fact that there is no happy ending or solution to be had; the world is in dire trouble.

Despite the thematic material being as deep and unrelentingly dark as that of *Brutal Planet*, on *Dragontown* Alice states his case with songs that, on balance, contain more humor and are thereby arguably more consistent with his long-established style. But it is also clear that the post-millennium Alice Cooper is performing with real social conscience and a make-the-world-a-better-place agenda.

THE EYES OF ALICE COOPER, 2003
[US CHARTS #184, UK #112]

The oldest shock rocker in town goes back to his garage roots. . . Whether this makes him an icon with an instinctive feel for the musical zeitgeist or a sad old chancer desperate to stay in with the kids is open to interpretation, but at least this represents a return to what Alice does best . . . it soon becomes clear that this is the best AC album in years.—Paul Travers, *Kerrang!*, September 2003

Now that garage rock is popular again, Cooper's returning to his roots. His new album, *The Eyes of Alice Cooper*, sheds the bloated trappings of his last few albums for a bare-bones approach that sounds like it was recorded in 1971. In fact, he's calling his current outing the "Bare Bones Tour."—Rod Harmon, *Boston Herald*, October 2003

Track Listing

1. What Do You Want from Me? (Cooper/Dover/Reid)
2. Between High School and Old School (Cooper/Dover/Roxie)
3. Man of the Year (Cooper/Dover/Roxie)

4. Novocaine (Cooper/Dover/Roxie)
5. Bye Bye, Baby (Cooper/Dover/Roxie)
6. Be with You Awhile (Cooper/Dover)
7. Detroit City (Cooper/Garric/Roxie)
8. Spirits Rebellious (Cooper/Dover/Roxie)
9. This House Is Haunted (Cooper/Dover/Roxie)
10. Love Should Never Feel Like This (Cooper/Dover/Roxie)
11. The Song That Didn't Rhyme (Cooper/Dover/Roxie)
12. I'm So Angry (Cooper/Dover/Roxie)
13. Backyard Brawl (Cooper/Dover/Roxie)

The front cover of *The Eyes of Alice Cooper* instantly conveys the album's title, as in this striking portrait of the artist it is his piercing, reddish-orange eyes that immediately draw the focus of the viewer's attention. Artificially colored, they are piercingly bright and stand out starkly against the otherwise black-and-white image. With black gloved hands Alice holds a piece of dark cloth over the lower part of his face, leaving his eyes the only visible feature. Staring directly at the viewer with unnerving intensity, his trademark tarantula makeup adds to the horror quality of the portrait. Abstractly inferring another eye, a drawn, incomplete, red circle surrounds the A of his name where it appears in the album title that is written at the top left side of the cover.

Clever and unrestrained humor sets the scene from the start, as in the opening "What Do You Want from Me?" Alice lists the many sacrifices he has made in order to please his partner—yet is still, as the title suggests, left wondering what he must do to achieve that goal. A lesson in effective lyric rhyming, there are jokes galore throughout the song as the list of sacrifices is rattled off to the dissatisfied, unidentified woman. Among the things he has bought for her in the course of his unsuccessful quest are: "Some decals for your fingernails, and your bass master singing trout—and a TV, and a CD and DVD from QVC, and baby, wotcha think of me?" Other gestures of his fealty include giving up his other girlfriends (even the "dirty ones"), burning all of his pornography, and disconnecting his Xbox. The musical underpinning harks back to the Alice Cooper sound of the early 1970s, lacking the sledgehammer qualities of his industrial metal albums and the gloss of his glam metal days but with an uncompromising rough/garage edge to it. It is a welcome return.

Humor is again evident in the title of track two, "Between High School and Old School," which immediately infers a quality of autobiography given the importance of *School's Out* to his establishment as a front-line rock superstar in the 1970s and his status now as old-school rock royalty. "Nobody wants me hanging 'round, unless it's from a tree in the middle of town," complains Alice as he visits once again the career-long theme of being the misunderstood, alienated misfit. Unlike some of the estranged characters he has portrayed in his darkest albums, who express their sense of abandonment and difference through physical, sexual, and emotional violence, here there is a sense of gleeful revelry and an irreverent musical nose-thumbing in the frenetic garage punk style of MC5, the Stooges, and even the New York Dolls: "And I don't care much—no I don't care at all," wails Alice defiantly.

Riddled with irony, the fast-paced, faux self-aggrandizing "Man of the Year" follows and, although still built on a foundation of humor, the message ultimately packs a serious punch by song's end. "I eat a low-fat breakfast, I tie a perfect tie," boasts Alice, and throughout the first three-quarters of the song a picture is painted of an impossibly perfect man, with elements of himself inserted here and there, such as: "The president plays golf with me." But it all turns sour as his life is exposed as a facade that hides deep unhappiness and despair within, and when he places a gun inside his mouth prior to the last verse (complete with the special-effect sound of a gun being cocked), the act provides a jarring juxtaposition to the sentiment that had preceded it. Essentially a too-good-to-be-true exposé of living a false life and not being true to oneself, the humor returns in the final verse when he describes himself once again as unblemished; the perfect corpse at a perfect funeral.

"Novocaine" appears fourth up, and in its raw, stripped-back, and economical delivery and production, the spirit of the original Alice Cooper band is once again revived. Couched in straightforward rock 'n' roll style, "Novocaine" is an appeal to human feeling and emotion, to feeling something other than numbness: "'Cause when you touch me, when you hold me, when you kiss me I don't feel anything."

"Bye Bye, Baby" maintains the pace and retro vibe of the album in a breakup song with a difference. Having been left by his girlfriend, who now prefers New York to their Los Angeles home and who loses no opportunity to bad-mouth him, Alice laments that she "Said I'm the worst you've ever had—I ain't delusional or institutional, but I'm pretty sure I ain't that bad." In a humorously contradictory touch, from the conciliatory mid-song assurance that he is not angry about the situation, by the song's end Alice professes to be "mad as hell!"

A change of pace occurs with the sixth song on *The Eyes of Alice Cooper*, when the touching and very personal ballad "Be with You Awhile" begins. While most Alice Cooper ballads take the power ballad form, here the musical accompaniment remains understated and restrained, allowing lyrics and vocal tonality to convey the simple message of the song, and exhibiting once again the artist's mastery of ballad form. "I just want to be that someone you weren't looking for," sings Alice, displaying in this line and in many others in the song the kind of simple human observation that allows effortless communication to take place between songwriter and listener; throughout, the subject matter remains universal and touchingly familiar.

"Detroit City" picks up the pace of the album once more in a sleazy, shuffle-based, early 1970s-era glam rock celebration of the delights to be found in the America's most notorious rock 'n' roll city. Name-dropping everyone from Iggy Pop to the MC5, to Bob Seger and Ted Nugent and David Bowie's Ziggy Stardust incarnation, the lyrics too are retrospective in their content as the Golden Era scene is recalled: "Feel your heart beat, hit the concrete, dance the mean streets, Detroit City."

Taking its title from the 1908 book by Kahlil Gibran, the ensuing "Spirits Rebellious" finds Alice introducing a religious theme to the album, whereby "There's a living breathing devil trying to tear my soul apart in a cold, cold grave on a dark, dark night." High in energy and fully in the spirit of the garage band ethos of the album heard thus far, a them-versus-us notion permeates throughout, ensuring that the oppositional qualities that have served Alice so well throughout his career are as evident here as anywhere else: "You tell us everything's ok—no way!"

"This House Is Haunted" comes as a complete surprise. Musical Grand Guignol, Alice Cooper–style, the first three-quarters of the track is eerie and atmospheric, slow and floating, with strings and haunting woodwind dominating the musical landscape and supporting the partly sung, partly spoken lyrics that are reminiscent in their delivery style to "Alma Mater" from the *School's Out* album. Rock instrumentation finally enters at two minutes, twenty seconds to play an alternative version of the, by now, well-established theme. However, this sudden intrusion of drums and guitars only lasts for twenty-five seconds before once again giving way to the sparse, eerie, instrumentation of the opening. A story of loss, the song's protagonist is content to withdraw from the world and sit alone at home with the ghost of his deceased lover: "I feel you sit down on the couch right here next to me—then I feel your lips touch mine just like we used to do." More reminiscent of *Welcome to My Nightmare*–era Alice Cooper in terms of its dreamy and dark subject matter, "This House Is Haunted" is a surprising delight in Cooper's later-era catalog.

The unexpected stylistic deviation of "This House Is Haunted" goes as quickly as it came, as the hard-rocking "Love Should Never Feel Like This" follows. With a verse melody that readily brings to the listener's mind the song "Love Potion Number 9," written by Jerry Leiber and Mike Stoller in 1959 and covered by many artists over the next six decades, "Love Should Never Feel Like This" is a hard-hitting falling-in-love song with a twist. Instead of experiencing the oft-quoted birds singing and bells ringing, finding true love in Alice's case has resulted in physical afflictions. "I can't eat, I can't sleep—I feel sick, I'm so weak," he complains, before imploring at the song's conclusion, "What's wrong with me?"

The following track is mischievous and playful and completely contradicts its own title, because "The Song That Didn't Rhyme" rhymes throughout. Everything that can be wrong within a song appears in a list of faults that unfolds throughout the track, but in delivering the information, the rhyming structure of the lyrics is perfect. A song so bad that "Billboard declared it a crime," the slow-paced, somewhat gentle novelty track is as unexpected in its stylistic divergence as "This House is Haunted" has been. Humor remains to the fore throughout, as the list of flaws in the song results in the finger of blame being pointed: "All the record guys got fired—the president retired."

A sentiment expressed in an earlier song on the album, "Bye Bye, Baby," returns as the title of the frenetic second-to-last track of *The Eyes of Alice Cooper*. "I'm So Angry" appears to act as a delayed couplet to that preceding song. Whereas in "Bye Bye, Baby" his lover has run off to New York and left him behind in Los Angeles, in this subsequent song Alice appears to have roused himself to such a state of fury that he seeks revenge: "Running after you is what I gotta do . . . better hide the knife, better run for your life." Painting the theme of the lyrics most effectively, the musical accompaniment to "I'm So Angry" is fast and rough and prickly, with Alice using the gravelliest and most snarling signature voice he can muster.

Just as "I'm So Angry" was true to title, so too the last song of the album lives up to its billing. The ugly, angry, uncompromising sentiment of "Backyard Brawl" is fully realized in both words and music. "Only got six teeth but three of those are sharp enough to bite off your nose," threatens Alice, ensuring that however violent his words and intentions might be, his trademark humor still permeates. Yet another depiction of his character that has for so long been established as an outcast in songs such as "Public Animal #9," here Alice describes himself as "the neighborhood legend who just can't wait."

While doing little to resurrect his fortunes on either the UK or US album charts, *The Eyes of Alice Cooper* is a highly effective album that manages to recapitulate much earlier work in terms of its garage band vibe, while still moving forward. The songwriting is tight and concise, while throwing up surprises such as "The Song That Didn't Rhyme" and this reviewer's favorite, "This House Is Haunted," and the music is refreshingly raw and direct.

DIRTY DIAMONDS, 2005 [US CHART #169, UK#89]

Yes, shine on . . . an aged but unbowed Alice Cooper is still making spirited, vital records. 38 years after his first coupla' singles, still greatly participating in life, still energetic and disarming in conversation.—Martin Popoff, *BW&BK*, August 2005

Alice Cooper's *Dirty Diamonds* stands up to almost anything the revered shock-rocker has ever recorded. The legend has been chopping up dolls onstage since 1969, influencing generations of metal bands.—Mike Greenblatt, *Metal Edge*, January 2006

Track Listing

1. Woman of Mass Distraction (Boston/Cooper/Garric/Johnson/Roxie)
2. Perfect (Cooper/Johnson/Roxie)
3. You Make Me Wanna (Boston/Cooper/Johnson/Roxie)
4. Dirty Diamonds (Boston/Cooper/Garric/Johnson)

5. The Saga of Jesse Jane (Cooper/Roxie)
6. Sunset Babies (All Got Rabies) (Cooper/Johnson/Roxie)
7. Pretty Ballerina (Brown)
8. Run Down the Devil (Cooper/Elizondo/Hudson/Hughes/)
9. Steal That Car (Cooper/Garric/Johnson/Roxie)
10. Six Hours (Cooper/Roxie)
11. Your Own Worst Enemy (Cooper/Roxie)
12. Zombie Dance (Boston/Cooper/Roxie)

Dark and dangerous, Alice Cooper stares from his portrait on the cover of *Dirty Diamonds*, making full eye contact with the viewer as his eyes gleam and sparkle like the prized and precious stones from which the album's title is drawn. Surrounded by inky blackness and with the album's title and artist's name scrawled in blood-red writing that frames his picture, the black of his signature makeup around the eyes makes his gaze all the more piercing and unsettling. It is a powerful, potent image.

As soon as the music begins with track one the career-defining quality of humor is immediately established once again, with the title a great pun on the well-known term "weapon of mass destruction." In the up-tempo, hard-rocking "Woman of Mass Distraction," Alice more than meets his equal: "I never met my match until I met that lady—she hooked me, she cooked me, she practically filleted me." Retaining the straightforward instrumental simplicity of the previous album, the four minutes of the track establish a celebratory heavy rock vibe that makes it abundantly clear that *Dirty Diamonds* is not going to be any sort of step backward in intensity just because its driving force by now happens to be nearer sixty years old than fifty.

The mid-paced, sleazy guitar raunch of the following track, "Perfect," paints a very different picture with its female subject a far cry from the all-powerful woman tour de force introduced in the opening track. The very antithesis of the song's title, here Alice's lover is perfect only in her reflected image in the mirror or within the confines of their bedroom, becoming an accident-prone uncoordinated nightmare outside. Despite this, Alice proclaims his love for her: "She can't sing or dance, she ain't got a chance—but baby, I don't mind." The lyrics paint humorous vignettes of his girlfriend in various social settings, but his

observations of her inadequacies—and the tone in which they are delivered—remain forgiving and empathetic, never wounding or acerbic.

The third track, "You Make Me Wanna," makes it three songs in a
row about love, and the focus here is on the quality of naivety. "Well I
know it don't make much sense but I'm in love with your innocence,"
sings Alice atop a straightforward rock accompaniment. Endearingly
old school and uncomplicated, "You Make Me Wanna" possesses a fine
vocal hook with its falsetto "Woo hoo hoo" call-and-response chorus
and timeless rock 'n' roll qualities.

The album's title track is next and, as suggested by that title, "Dirty
Diamonds" breaks away from the love/sex theme of the opening trio of
tracks to something far darker and in keeping with the album's striking
cover. The scene is set: "You're tied to a chair with a gun at your head—
your face is all smeared with the blood that's been shed." Also referred
to in popular terminology as "blood diamonds" or "conflict diamonds,"
the song references the illegal and exploitative mining activities of a
would-be profiteer who gets caught by an unnamed enemy and faces
torture and death as the result of his greed. Such diamond mining often
takes place within war zones, and thus the song conjures in the listener's mind violent news footage from such locations as Angola, Sierra
Leone, or the Ivory Coast. Set up with a quiet and understated introduction reminiscent of classic Hollywood suspense movies, when the
song proper begins it is fast, violent, and aggressive in keeping with its
subject matter. More dense and instrumentally complex than the previous songs, "Dirty Diamonds" is unrelenting and sounds as dangerous as
its theme, with the vocals growling and edgy and the guitars raw and
uncompromising. In a 180-degree turnaround, while the women appearing in the first three songs are revered in the ways mentioned
above, here in the title track it is the would-be diamond smuggler's
"trophy wife" who is the ultimate villain, betraying him and leaving him
at the mercy of his captors.

Another wordplay occurs in the title of the following song, "The Saga
of Jesse Jane." Clearly taking humorous liberties with the legend of
Jesse James, the fun doesn't stop with the song's title as the lyrics go on
to outline the tale of a cross-dressing cowboy, "In my sister's wedding
gown," who falls foul of a bunch of rednecks in a small Texas town until
"I pulled a pistol from my Wonderbra." Subsequently killing all his
would-be assailants, he is apprehended in a bathroom stall and thrown

in jail. Asking the question: "Are you just an average guy who dresses like a butterfly?" the song critiques gender stereotypes and macho attitudes without ever losing its sense of humor as the Johnny Cash–styled backing easily and appropriately carries the story. Complete with Cash-like, deep vocal stylings and a steel guitar, "The Saga of Jesse Jane" stands out like a sore thumb on *Dirty Diamonds* in much the same way—and perhaps even more so—in the same novelty-song way that "The Song That Didn't Rhyme" did on *The Eyes of Alice Cooper*.

"Sunset Babies (All Got Rabies)" follows "The Saga of Jesse Jane," and banishes the country vibe as quickly as it had come. Sounding like a cross between the Rolling Stones and the Alice Cooper band of the *Killer* era, the song paints a picture of the tough and dangerous young girls who hang around on Sunset Strip and the perils of pursuing them: "Running in packs on a Saturday night—they got their own bark and they got their own bite."

It is rare indeed for Alice Cooper to include on any album a song that he had no part in writing, but Michael Brown's "Pretty Ballerina" is extraordinarily well deserving of its place on *Dirty Diamonds*. Alice's version is surprisingly tender and gentle, the second truly surprising track on the album after "The Saga of Jesse Jane," but most definitely not a novelty or tongue-in-cheek parody like that earlier song was. Sung in an uncharacteristically mellow and unforced tone over music box–styled tinkly arpeggiated guitar strings and soft drums, the song is an exercise in restraint and shows another side to the Cooper vocal palette in its haunting yearning; it is a true and unexpected highlight of *Dirty Diamonds*.

"Run Down the Devil" assuredly brings the album back to rock with its slow-paced, slow-burning, chugging feel, while at the same time reintroducing the artist's Christian beliefs to his work. Characteristically, the message is delivered with a comedic touch: "I want to take him to the Mercury grill—I hope he's ready for the big blast. He'll be my ultimate road kill—I'll kick his future up his past."

On an album in which Alice Cooper takes a clear joy in exploring stylistic diversity, the punk-rockabilly feel of "Steal That Car" comes as less of a surprise than it otherwise might have. Fast, furious, frenetic, and enjoyably one-dimensional, there are nuances of the law-scorning "Public Animal #9" and the auto fixation of "Under My Wheels" to be

found in the track: "I did some time in '99, I'll do some time again—
everybody knows I'm gonna steal that car."

The third-to-last song, "Six Hours," does nothing to arrest the scat-
ter-gun approach to musical style on what has turned out to be one of
Alice Cooper's most intriguing albums. A slow ballad featuring the soul-
ful cry of an electric guitar at its heart, acting out the spirit of the
Beatle's epic, "While My Guitar Gently Weeps" by George Harrison,
the lyrically minimalist song leaves more questions unanswered than it
answers: "There's only six hours, how quickly it goes—in this sacred
place our secret is safe, nobody knows." Just what the shared secret is,
or why only six hours remain, is left a mystery, but there is something
inherently sinister in the heavy and disturbing guitar solo that takes over
from Cooper's voice at the song's conclusion.

Second to last on *Dirty Diamonds* is "Your Own Worst Enemy." If
there is one thing that Cooper fans enjoy immensely, it is hearing their
favorite rock star enjoying himself thoroughly, and this he most certainly does as the album nears its close. A litany of everyday misfortunes,
the listed events—mostly humorous—combine to paint a picture of the
song's title: "Your stocks went south and your girlfriend is gay—your
dog ate your cat and that was your good day." A moderately paced and
simple rock track, the charm lies almost entirely in the lyrics and the
vocal delivery.

Finally comes the very Cooper-esque themed "Zombie Dance," and
on an album light on horror references by the artist's usual standards, it
is a very welcome way to end. Reminiscent for long-term Cooper fans
of atmospheric songs from decades earlier, such as "Black Juju"—enhanced by the mention of Juju bones in the lyrics—and with harmonica
to the fore of the instrumentation just as was the case in the early days
of the Alice Cooper band, "Zombie Dance" brings *Dirty Diamonds* to a
close with tact and restraint rather than with any rock histrionics. Gone
are the comedic touches, and yet it's a highly effective clincher on an
album that has delivered many surprises to the listener. "Night's alive
with music, puts me in a trance—sneak up on the bonfire, watch the
zombies dance," sings Alice, as the song creates landscape and mood,
reminding us yet again of his considerable versatility.

Dirty Diamonds fared somewhat better in the United Kingdom than
had its predecessor, pushing the Alice Cooper name modestly back into
the top 100 albums, yet it continued a poor run in the United States.

Simply, it deserved better, and for anyone looking to discover a relatively unknown gem by the artist, one need look no further than *Dirty Diamonds*.

9

THE RESURRECTION

Along Came a Spider, Welcome 2 My Nightmare,
Paranormal, 2008–2017

Despite critical acclaim for the first four post-millennium albums, Alice Cooper's commercial fortunes had undeniably fallen. If there is one absolute truism regarding the career of Alice Cooper, it is that he is never predictable. Always possessing the ability to surprise his audience, in 2008 he did exactly that once again with his twenty-fifth studio album, *Along Came a Spider*. Rekindling the concept album—something he had proven himself to be a master at in the past—would not only bring more critical acclaim but, crucially, would also go a very long way toward restoring the Alice Cooper name to the forefront of the rock business, ultimately providing a springboard that would bring him right back to the top of the heap with his subsequent release.

ALONG CAME A SPIDER, 2008 [US CHART #53, UK #31]

The rock wins the day, and so does Cooper's lyrics. The man has always had a way to mix campy, creepy and vicious into a catchy chorus. Cooper strings up striking visuals with his lyrics and you begin to forget you singing along with a psychopathic killer. Always a visual artist as much as musical, Cooper's packaging and imagery that accompanies *Along Came a Spider* is equally striking. Several short YouTube clips and a series of posters released over a few weeks unveiled the album more as a horror film rather than an album. *Along Came a Spider* is not the album that will frighten parents, certainly not in 2008. What is scary is just how good Alice Cooper still is thirty years after his riotous rise to the top of the rock heap.—Zane Ewton, *Anti Music*, July 2008

With its twisted lyrics, devastating sonic crunch and vicious hooks, many are calling *Along Comes a Spider* a return to the demented Alice Cooper of old. The new album from the shock-rocker—his 25th—tells the story of a serial killer who, imagining himself as a spider despite an acute case of arachnophobia, wraps his victims in silk during a murderous spree that comes to a halt when the psychopath, unexpectedly, finds love. Only Alice Cooper could spin a rock 'n' roll yarn like that.—Peter Lindblad, *Goldmine*, July 2008

Track Listing

1. Prologue/I Know Where You Live (Cooper/Hampton/Saber)
2. Vengeance Is Mine (Cooper/Hampton/Saber)
3. Wake the Dead (Cooper/Osbourne/Saber)
4. Catch Me If You Can (Cooper/Hampton/Saber)
5. (In Touch with) Your Feminine Side (Cooper/Garric/Johnson/Kelli)
6. Wrapped in Silk (Cooper/Hampton/Saber)
7. Killed by Love (Bacchi/Cooper/Garric/Kelli)
8. I'm Hungry (Cooper/Hampton/Saber)
9. The One That Got Away (Cooper/Kelli/Lane)
10. Salvation (Cooper/Fowler/Hampton/Saber)
11. I Am the Spider/Epilogue (Cooper/Hampton/Saber)

The cover of *Along Came a Spider* gives little hint of what transpires in the music that it houses, but nevertheless carries its own nuances of danger and darkness in the close-up portrait photograph of Alice in (left) side profile. This in itself, is also a departure from all previous cover portraits that had shown him front-on. Here, he looks menacing and unsmiling, while a close perusal of his exposed eye reveals that he is far from passive and is instead looking intently to his extreme left; watching someone or something but without wishing to arouse the attention or awareness of the object of his interest. He is thus portrayed as predatory and furtive. A trademark black line extends downwards from the corner of his mouth, and his signature tarantula eye makeup surrounds his eye, giving way to a deep purple on his eyelid. The skin of his face is a pale cadaver-white, exacerbated by his jet-black hair and the blackness that surrounds him. It is a powerful and spooky image awaiting the contextual information that will be provided in the music.

Just like the scene-setting opening of a movie, the first track, "Prologue/I Know Where You Live," outlines the territory. The opening words are spoken by a woman who announces matter-of-factly: "We found his diary today," before going on to report how meticulously the as-yet unnamed killer had planned his executions. In her final line before the prologue gives way to the song proper, however, she alludes to him overlooking "One thing." Then, following a heavy guitar riff that ushers in "I Know Where You Live," in Alice's opening line the furtive qualities of the album cover image suddenly make perfect sense as he boasts: "I like to watch from my car." The content of the ensuing verses makes it clear that he is stalking his victim day and night, even breaking into her home, going through her things and lying on her bed while she is at work. Alice's voice is as threatening and malicious as it has ever been, the signature sneer well to the fore. Admitting to having killed people in her life that he did not approve of, he ends with an eerie admission, dripping with threat: "I see, I feel, I watch over you."

"Vengeance Is Mine" takes up the story, shifting the perspective to give the listener insights into the mind and motivation of the serial killer. He feels himself to be a victim, and his brutal acts are acts of retribution against those who he believes have persecuted him: "They hated every part of me and expect me to forget it—they tried so hard to bury me but I survived it every time." His mantra is the oft-repeated "What I want, what I need," and during an extended virtuosic guitar solo from guest star Slash, one can easily imagine another life being taken—such is the violence of the solo's nature. There is no sign of the Alice Cooper wit in any of this; it is pure anger, rage, and malice.

"Wake the Dead" seamlessly furthers the plot in a song cycle that is already, just three songs in, proving to be one of the strongest conceptual collections of tracks the artist ever recorded. While the preceding song gave cause to the killer's actions, here we learn who his prime target victims are, and they are primarily women. More than this, the listener gleans that he sees them not as individuals, but instead regards them as being all the same: "Give me a redhead, give me a brunette, send a blonde to me—when I unwind, I'm colorblind, they're all the same to me." It is chilling, and the stark aggression of the metal backing offers no respite to either the lyric content nor the menacing, always threatening, vocal performance. Describing himself as insane, and admitting that he acts without rhyme or reason, there is not an ounce of compassion or regret in evidence in the song as he ponders where and when he will strike next.

"Catch Me If You Can" taunts Alice in the guise of the Spider in the song of the same name. In this, his most brutal and violent role ever, he continues to sing from the first-person perspective as he mocks the authorities who would apprehend him. "You won't have a clue of what is coming next," he jeers. Referring to himself as an "arachnophobic psychopath," he vows to go on and on until forced to stop. Sung atop a drum-dominated metal palette complete with double-kick drum passages, the music too is unrelenting. The childlike melody of the chorus with its repeated "Catch me catch me if you can" lines lends a "nya nya nya nya nya," schoolyard challenge to proceedings, a device most particularly disturbing during the breakdown section three-quarters of the way through the song when Alice's voice sits atop drums only.

The level of creepiness steps up another notch as the Spider attempts to attract a victim in the fifth song, "(In Touch with) Your Feminine Side." Exhorting the young woman who has caught his eye to "Stop running, stop hiding," he first appraises her and then imposes a kind of twisted notion of ownership upon her: "You look cool, you look so sweet . . . it's your world but it's my street." With the different perspectives offered in each song thus far on the album, an increasingly complete picture of the serial killer's personality and modus operandi is being carefully built up, and perhaps the scariest thing about this is that one suspects serial killers do indeed feel exactly like that which Cooper is portraying. The sense of persecution and then entitlement sounds all too familiar in real-life critiques of such criminals.

The narrative has been so well compiled thus far that the sixth song, "Wrapped in Silk," seems an entirely logical, if shudder-inducing, next step. While at times it is hard to be certain of the time frame—parts of the song appear to be pre-murder and parts post-murder, and not in chronological order—the sentiments and descriptions of the action are clear. "When did I smell your scent? I followed you from behind everywhere you went," Alice gloats before describing his victim being wrapped up in silk, just like a spider would do having caught and killed his victim. "Where could you feel the knife?" he asks. "Was it your final thought, the moment I took your life?"

The clarity of the album's narrative dips slightly in the ballad "Killed by Love," with the perspective seemingly twisted between captor and captive, perpetrator and victim, and at times it is unclear which is speaking. "You pushed me way too far," is surely the killer's perspective, directed toward his victim and, by association, wider society, both of whom he blames for his psychopathic state. But when Alice sings "You know you're killing me baby, baby, baby," it is unclear if that is sung from the victim's perspective or, perhaps more likely, whether it is Alice using the term metaphorically about himself after killing her. Regardless, the largely acoustic ballad provides an effective change of pace from the hard rock/metal that has flavored the musical mise-en-scène thus far.

The sweetness and surprising gentleness of "Killed by Love" is quickly dispensed with when the album's eighth track, "I'm Hungry," kicks in and finds the Spider prowling the city streets—"A city full of prey"—at night, looking to once again sate his need: "I gotta bed in my basement fit for two—I got some chloroform and handcuffs just for you." The song's title is repeated over and over in the chorus, the two syllables of "hun-gry" elongated and set to the first two beats of the bar for maximum emphasis, a most effective piece of emotive word setting that sends a chill down the spine.

In "The One That Got Away," Alice aka Spider debates out loud with himself whether he should let his latest victim escape with her life. His thoughts go one way and then the other: "Keep it down, don't talk, I have to think—I could let you walk, I could feed the sink." The listener's thoughts immediately turn to what his victim must have been thinking during this monologue by her captor, and in an album full of chilling moments perhaps the worst of all is imagining her crushing disappointment and terror at the end of the song when he reaches the conclusion that seals her fate: "Hmm, maybe some other time."

Occupying the last-but-one position on the album, "Salvation" delivers a very big surprise to the narrative with the emphatic return of Cooper's religious beliefs. Initially set to acoustic piano and with a soft vocal sound devoid of the growling threat evident throughout the rest of the album, Spider the serial killer appears to experience a divine revelation that relieves him completely of his violent urges. "Someone died for me, washed in blood—He cared enough to pity me," sings Alice in exaltation at Jesus' sacrifice. The message is clear and wholly Christian—that no person is too bad to be denied salvation from God upon true repentance of their sins. Classical strings dominate the mid-section of "Salvation" in a musical representation of depth, gravitas, and legitimacy, and the repeated cries of "salvation" at the song's end atop swirling banks of instrumentation take on a church-like quality. Unlikely though it seems in the face of the overwhelming horrors of the earlier narrative, Spider's killing spree has been brought to a halt in a most unlikely and surprising way.

"I Am the Spider/Epilogue" completes *Along Came a Spider*, and in the song portion of the couplet the Spider opines that serial killers such as he was can be anyone at all within society: "I'm your lover, I'm your brother, I'm your killer, I'm your friend." Gone, however, is the redeemed voice that flavored "Salvation," and back is the sneer and the growl of the killer. For the first time on the album a hint of Cooper humor surfaces; light, certainly, but in the face of the unrelenting horror themes that have dominated the album, it stands out nonetheless. "You're my sinner, you're my dinner," sings Alice in what is surely the first and last example of that particular rhyming pair being uttered in popular music. It is in the "Epilogue," however, that the album's narrative is effectively wrapped up with a bow. Delivered in Alice's spoken voice, and beginning with the discovery of his diary, thereby linking it directly to the "Prologue," we learn that he is in prison and his eight victims have been found, each wrapped in silk and with one leg missing. Grisly details aside, one big shock remains for long-term Cooper fans when he delivers the line: "We've been in this cell for twenty-eight years, Steven." To hear Cooper's most popular alter ego/character in this latest context—returning long, long after he appeared in *Welcome to My Nightmare* and *The Last Temptation*, and particularly in such a gory context, is shocking and powerful. Steven, a serial killer??? Further, it seems the saving of his soul as was implied in "Salvation" was not the end of it, because now denial has set in: "We couldn't have done all those horrible things," he ponders, as a dissonant, swirling bed of strings and low synths ebb and flow beneath.

Along Came a Spider is the album on which Alice Cooper gave full vent to the horror side of his act, more so than ever before and almost completely without the alleviating quality of comedic touches. It is an extraordinarily effective and cohesive piece of work, and a testament to this is the turnaround in commercial fortunes for the album, reaching number fifty-three in the United States and thirty-one in the United Kingdom—by far his best result in many a year.

WELCOME 2 MY NIGHTMARE, 2011 [US CHART #22, UK #7]

I think any time you get Bob Ezrin and I together, we bring out the worst in each other. . . . Our dark senses of humour merge and we come up with a lot of good songs. We just thought, "Okay, what would Alice's nightmare be 30 years on? Would he still be afraid of things under the bed?" No, Alice's nightmares would be disco, technology (Alice would just hate technology), working nine-to-five in a cubicle, that sort of thing. Then we took themes from the previous album and found a way for them to fit this album. For example, at one point the guy is singing over this piano song, and all of a sudden he says, "But I think I heard that song before" and then the "Steven" theme kicks in. If you're an Alice fan, that sends a chill up your spine because all of a sudden you realize you are going to be connected to the original nightmare. It's a scary album, but I think it may be even cleverer than the first one.—Alice Cooper, interviewed by Aaron Von Lupton, *Rue Morgue*, September 2011

On 1975's *Welcome to My Nightmare*, Alice Cooper largely traded in high school parking-lot hard rock for fright-show theater; it had bruising moments, but also self-parodying schmaltz. *Welcome 2 My Nightmare* is its sequel, so we get recurring bad-dream rockers, plus an "Underture" that melds Cooper's melodies into a symphonic montage. The fun comes when he abandons the sequel concept in favor of a New Wave duet with Ke$ha and a decades-tardy anti-disco tune ("Disco Bloodbath Boogie Fever") in which Alice tries to rap. Slapstick was always his strong suit.—Chuck Eddy, *Rolling Stone*, September 2011

Track Listing

1. I Am Made of You (Child/Cooper/Ezrin)
2. Caffeine (Cooper/Ezrin/Henriksen/Nelson)

3. The Nightmare Returns (Cooper/Ezrin)
4. A Runaway Train (Cooper/Dunaway/Ezrin)
5. Last Man on Earth (Cooper/Ezrin/Montgomery/Spreng)
6. The Congregation (Cooper/Ezrin/Henriksen)
7. I'll Bite Your Face Off (Cooper/Ezrin/Henriksen/Smith)
8. Disco Bloodbath Boogie Fever (Cooper/Ezrin/Henriksen)
9. Ghouls Gone Wild (Cooper/Ezrin/Henriksen)
10. Something to Remember Me By (Cooper/Wagner)
11. When Hell Comes Home (Bruce/Cooper/Ezrin)
12. What Baby Wants (Cooper/Ezrin/Henriksen/Ke$ha)
13. I Gotta Get Outta Here (Cooper/Ezrin/Hood)
14. The Underture (Child/Cooper/Ezrin/Fordham/Henriksen/Rubolino/Wagner)

With good reason Alice Cooper fans looked forward greatly to the release of the cleverly titled *Welcome 2 My Nightmare*. After all, the Coop's star was once again on the rise with the critical and commercial success of *A long Came a Spider*, and the news that he would be reuniting with original Alice Cooper band members Michael Bruce, Dennis Dunaway, and Neal Smith created a clearly palpable buzz among fans and critics alike who had all but given up on such a thing ever happening. In addition, it was announced that the chief collaborator for the album would be none other than Bob Ezrin, something which came as great news to the multitude of admirers of the previous highly acclaimed works that they had jointly produced.

That there was to be a large element of nostalgia was a certainty, with the title alone ensuring that. But the album cover too was designed to draw heavily on that groundbreaking solo work of three-and-a-half decades earlier. Once again, Alice is pictured breaking through an inverted triangle, but here, in 2011, the image is more horror inspired. Instead of the polite, top hat–doffing, perfectly attired Alice of 1975, the latter image shows him bursting through the cover with aggression, a snarling, sneering grimace, with his heavily bloodstained white shirt open at the neck and white bow tie long discarded. The letters of his name are written in dripping red blood above him, and the overall mood is a far cry from the much more restrained cover of yesteryear.

"I Am Made of You" opens *Welcome 2 My Nightmare*, and the nostalgia hits hard straight away as Steven's piano figure from the original album is replicated, slightly faster but instantly recognizable as it plays all alone in the exposed introduction. When the rest of the instrumentation joins in, it is to support a lyric that carries strong religious overtones: "In the beginning you were revelation—a river of salvation and now I believe." Describing himself as being initially all alone and in darkness, his transition to the light and the status of one who is saved clearly resonates with Alice Cooper's own life story. Ballad-paced, "I Am Made of You" is a gentle and measured opening to the album, quite different to the scene-setting opener, and title track, of the 1975 album.

If track one evoked a musical memory of the album's predecessor in the Steven piano figure, it is in track two of *Welcome 2 My Nightmare*, "Caffeine," that the lyric theme too is largely recapitulated. Just as Steven was caught in a terrifying neither-awake-nor-asleep state in 1975, here he is afraid to fall asleep because of the Freddy Krueger–like doors that dream state will open: "I won't sleep at night, I won't rest my head—because I realize if I shut my eyes I'm gonna wake up dead." Caffeine, cold showers, and speed are his allies in the quest to remain awake, and thus far he has staved off sleep for a week. The fast tempo and in-your-face heavy rock instrumentation paints the agitated state of an over-indulgence in caffeine very well. Throughout, Alice appears wired, edgy, and scared.

The third track has a message very clearly set out in its title, "The Nightmare Returns." Sure enough the minimalist song, lasting just over a minute and consisting of just four lines of lyrics, builds on the previous song and the thing that Steven fears most—falling asleep—finally takes its inevitable hold, plunging him all-too-knowingly into a new nightmare. Using a child's sing-song voice that mirrors the piano accompaniment and creates a music-box effect that would have been just as at home on *Welcome to My Nightmare*, as he falls asleep he speaks fearfully of what he knows lays ahead: "Ugly faces, awful places, I don't want to go, no." The lyrics are over by the midway point and, once asleep, the nursery-rhyme quality of the music changes to a darker, heavier sonority that borrows in part—as another clearly evident linking device—melodic phrasing from the earlier *Nightmare* album.

Fourth up is "A Runaway Train," and seeing the name Dennis Dunaway listed in the writing credits provides a poignant moment. All three former Alice Cooper group members perform on the track. The faux-rockabilly musical style bears little resemblance to the Alice Cooper band's work of three-and-a-half decades earlier, but in terms of advancing the album's narrative, it works well as the nightmare takes hold. Although Alice/Steven fell asleep in his bed, he now awakens in a boxcar, chained to thirteen condemned criminals: "Speeding toward a flaming wall." He tries to wake but cannot, and after the train crashes he wakes within his dream once more to find that this time he is "sleeping in the graveyard on the wrong side of the dirt." Ascending guitar scale passages in the song's outro lead to a chaotic musical breakdown to end the track in confusion and disarray.

From the surprising departure to rockabilly, *Welcome 2 My Nightmare* takes an even more dramatic shift with the authentic-sounding cabaret style of "Last Man on Earth." Led by the decidedly un-rock 'n' roll lineup of tuba, violin, ganjo, and cocktail drums, the nightmare now has its victim waking to find he is the only person left on Earth. "Got no troubles, got no time, and everything is fine," sings Alice in clear opposition to the truth of the matter, and his "Don't need to care about tomorrow" affirmation sounds lonely and hollow.

Celebrity guest Rob Zombie acts as tour guide in the following song, "The Congregation"—easily the most ROCK, in capital letters—of anything heard on the album thus far, and the comedic touch of Alice Cooper is all over the track. With locations chopping and changing with every song, here Steven is found in hell, a member of the devil's congregation. He's there because he was not allowed access to heaven: "Your application sadly was denied—but let's be clear, we love you here, you're on the other side." Alice's list of fellow hell-dwellers includes lawyers, Wall Street brokers, telemarketers, a defrocked priest, pimps, and, hilariously, mimes. Heavy rock set to an infectious formula, complete with fist-pumping cries of "Hey!," the track is a real highlight and as good as any Alice Cooper song from any of his prodigious output of albums.

Once the rock heights of "The Congregation" have subsided, the wonderfully titled "I'll Bite Your Face Off" would appear to have a hard task ahead of it. Neal Smith's name appears in the songwriting credits, once again pushing the nostalgia button for many fans, and again all three former members of the original band perform on the track. Another full-on and highly energized rock song with the oft-repeated title line providing a fine chorus hook, it does not have the lyrical wit of the preceding track but the sheer power of the performance ensures that it does not pale by comparison, sustaining the quality of *Welcome 2 My Nightmare* through its mid-section. In a return to the sex/lust themes of old, the alluring but deadly female protagonist is a temptress not to be messed with: "She put the whip in the cream, she was a sinner's Queen . . . c'mon and lick my skin."

With the rock credentials of the album most firmly and emphatically re-established, another stylistic departure can evidently be risked, and "Disco Bloodbath Boogie Fever" provides the listener with exactly that. Over sixteenth-note hi-hats—a hallmark of the style—Steven now finds himself inside a disco hell that is about to be shot up by unnamed mass shooters, from whose perspective the song is sung: "Face the wall, count to ten—We mow you down, reload again." The age-old rivalry between rock and disco—popular music fans usually come in one or other form, seldom both—is played out in "Disco Bloodbath Boogie Fever," because at the two-and-a-half-minute mark as the massacre is taking place, the music shifts emphatically from disco to rock, and when the vocals re-enter the assassins are found crowing about their success in wiping out the disco enthusiasts: "We cleaned the house tonight—we did our job alright."

Rock having won the day, "Ghouls Gone Wild" then salutes the early days of rock 'n' roll with its tip of the hat to Eddie Cochrane's "Summertime Blues." Fast, celebratory, and funny, the ghouls in Steven's new nightmare are partying hard: "We're gonna raise some hell yeah— we're gonna rot 'n' roll here." Built on a standard, simplistic rock songwriting formula complete with key change for the last chorus, "Ghouls Gone Wild" is short, sharp, unpretentious, and a fine lesson in effective perfect rhyming: "You're delicious, so suspicious—come on and play, what do you say?"

On an album in which the narrative has been very clearly expressed thus far, the ballad "Something to Remember Me By" sees a significant departure, with the song seemingly standing alone outside the nightmare concept. As Cooper himself explains:

> We recorded a song that we wrote in the late '70s called "Something to Remember Me By." The four biggest hits . . . were the ballads "Only Women Bleed," "You and Me," "I Never Cry" and "How You Gonna See Me Now?" but this might be the prettiest ballad we've ever done.[1]

Certainly, it is a beautifully composed and performed track. "I just wanna give you something to remember me by—I won't be gone forever and our love is for all time," sings Alice in his most unaffected and natural voice, supported by the sublime arrangement prowess of Bob Ezrin with his trademark soaring strings and emotive sonorities. While out of place in terms of the album's nightmare concept, perhaps, Cooper is right in deeming it one of his best-ever ballads.

Things turn horrific and downright ugly in the eleventh track, the forebodingly titled "When Hell Comes Home." A distressing and somewhat graphic tale of domestic abuse, the song's young protagonist and his mother are the victims of a heavy-drinking, abusive monster of a father and husband: "We live in darkness and despair—I'm just so tired of being scared." This is a new component of the nightmare, and Steven's planned solution is to shoot his father between the eyes in order for his mother and him to escape. The subject matter is brutal, the solution is brutal and, appropriately, the musical portrayal of the theme is just as brutal. Alice, his voice at its most sneering, is joined by his three former bandmates once again, and the accompaniment is unrelentingly heavy and aggressive. During the guitar solo the sounds of a violent disagreement are heard in the background, with a snarling male voice screaming out "Steeeven!!!" at its end, before the vocals begin once more.

A deadly seductress appears as the next character in Steven's nightmare. In "What Baby Wants," guest star Ke$ha (her role noted in the liner notes as "The Lady in Red") performs a duet with Alice, in which he tries to warn Steven to stay away from her: "She feeds on flesh and blood and boys like you." But she will not be denied, because "What baby wants, baby gets."

In the second-to-last track of the album, the self-explanatory "I Gotta Get Outta Here," Steven has clearly had enough: "I can't wait to wake up in my very own bed, far away from the madness and my pounding head." In a veritable summation of the album's entire storyline thus far, the lyrics of each verse recount facets of the nightmare, referencing almost all of the previous songs, that Steven has endured and survived. The outro of the song takes a bizarre twist when a gospel choir tries to convince Steven that he is actually dead, asking: "What part of dead don't you get?" Steven argues vehemently with them, but the song ends with Steven despairing that he is sinking downwards.

"The Underture" closes *Welcome 2 My Nightmare*, and is the collaborative songwriting effort of Cooper and no less than six additional musical minds. Combining rock instrumentation with lavish orchestral instrumentation, the piece is a highly skillful amalgamation of multiple themes derived from *Welcome to My Nightmare*, mostly performed true to the originals in terms of melodic, harmonic, and rhythmic properties, but with the addition of linkages created to ensure a seamless medley that can succeed in its own right. A powerful ending, it serves a remarkable reminder of the quality of those original themes, hooks, riffs, and figures that made Alice Cooper's debut solo album such a telling statement all those years earlier.

In all, *Welcome 2 My Nightmare* achieves many things. While obviously, purposefully, harking back to earlier times, it is no mere pale or lightweight nostalgia trip because it succeeds in its own right through the power, quality, and variety of its songs. While the nightmare here is, in actuality, more a case of nightmares plural, and therefore the album lacks the more singular focus and cohesion of the first album, the trade-off is eclecticism and a bigger investment in humor, and these Cooper hallmarks are rendered with aplomb. The reinstatement of the Cooper/Ezrin partnership carries significant weight and attraction, and so does the overdue (to original fans' way of thinking) contributions from Michael Bruce, Neal Smith, and Dennis Dunaway. That *Welcome 2 My Nightmare* fared so well commercially, reaching number twenty-two in the United States and a very impressive number seven in the United Kingdom, is undoubtedly due to this combination of factors, but one shouldn't forget the springboard provided by *Along Came a Spider*, which had already ensured that Alice Cooper's fortunes were once again on the rise.

PARANORMAL, 2017 [US CHART #32, UK#6]

Ol' snake eyes is back with a new album after a six year gap, and the impressive two cd/eighteen song package that is *Paranormal* ensures that it's a return in style. The first cd contains ten new tracks and is enough to keep any fan of The Coop happy, notable also for some top-shelf invited guests including Larry Mullen from U2, Roger Glover from Deep Purple, and Billy Gibbons from ZZ Top. Impressive while this is, the real magic happens on the second cd which begins with something that fans of the original Alice Cooper band have dreamed about for decades: two brand new songs performed by Alice alongside surviving members, Michael Bruce, Dennis Dunaway and Neal Smith. Forty-four years after 1973's *Muscle of Love* album, they are finally reunited. And as if that weren't enough, a further six tracks follow; each one a scorching live-in-concert rendition of an Alice Cooper classic performed by his current touring band of superb musicians. Truly, the fans' six-year wait has been well and truly rewarded with *Paranormal.*

Using the original band just felt normal to me. It didn't feel like anything unusual at all. The band never broke up with any bad blood. Nobody sued anybody, nobody was after anybody's blood. We didn't divorce as much as we separated, and we always stayed in touch with each other.—Alice Cooper, interviewed by Gary Graff, Billboard.com, July 28, 2017

We went in to just do another Alice Cooper album, and it accidentally became a concept. . . . Lyrically every single character has some sort of abnormal, paranormal problem going on and I didn't have a name for the album, so *Paranormal* ended up sounding like the thing that cemented this all together.—Alice Cooper, interviewed by Gary Graff, Billboard.com, July 28, 2017

Alice Cooper's 27th LP is produced by Bob Ezrin, who helmed the shock rocker's best Seventies work, and features cameos by members of U2 and ZZ Top, as well as Cooper's original band. The result is a loose affair true to his legacy as a golf-club-wielding villain with a dark sense of humor.—Kory Grow, Rollingstone.com, August 16, 2017

Disc One

1. Paranormal (Cooper/Denander/Ezrin/Glover)
2. Dead Flies (Cooper/Denander/Ezrin)
3. Fireball (Cooper/Dunaway)
4. Paranoiac Personality (Cooper/Denander/Ezrin/Henrikson)
5. Fallen in Love (Cooper/Denander/Ezrin/Henrikson)
6. Dynamite Road (Cooper/Denander/Ezrin)
7. Private Public Breakdown (Cooper/Ezrin/Gispert)

8. Holy   Water   (Bernauer/Cooper/Demaree/Ezrin/McLaughlin/
   Monyhan/Richards)
9. Rats (Cooper/Ezrin/Henrikson)
10. The Sound of A (Cooper/Dunaway)

Disc Two
New studio recordings with the original Alice Cooper band:

1. Genuine American Girl (Cooper/Ezrin/Smith)
2. You and All of Your Friends (Cooper/Dunaway/Ezrin)

Live in Columbus, Ohio, May 6, 2016, with the current Alice Cooper
band:

1. No More Mr. Nice Guy (Bruce/Cooper)
2. Under My Wheels (Bruce/Dunaway/Ezrin)
3. Billion Dollar Babies (Bruce/Cooper/Vinson)
4. Feed My Frankenstein (Coler/Cooper/Manning/Richardson)
5. Only Women Bleed (Cooper/Wagner)
6. School's Out (Bruce/Buxton/Cooper/Dunaway/Smith)

Paranormal opens with its title track and firmly establishes from the
outset that this is an Alice Cooper album with its glam metal perfection
(notably, it is the most glam metal work on the entire album) and its
supernatural/horror thematic territory. As Alice explained:

> My definition of paranormal is something that is "other than normal"
> or "alongside of normal." You could say my whole career has been
> that. I would look at what was normal and step left of it. That's what
> gets people's attention. They'd listen to our music and see our show
> and say, "That's so strange . . . oh yeah, that's so Alice."[2]

Further, and speaking of the title track specifically, Alice explains in a
track-by-track interview released by his record company on YouTube
that "Paranormal" explores the relationship between a couple who can
never physically be together because he's dead and she is alive. It's
typically creepy and atmospheric stuff, musically depicting the different
worlds of the two protagonists through its duality of dynamics—stark,
hollow, and sparse in its instrumentation one minute, then full-on rock

with all of the glam trimmings the next. "I'm condemned to the long endless night," sings Alice in the opening line as he watches over his lover, unable to do more than send her paranormal signals such as making her telephone ring, leaving his scent on her clothes, or placing a "spider-web kiss on your face." She senses his efforts and his presence, but their physical irreconcilability ensures a tragic element to this very strong album opener.

Immediately conjuring up memories of "Halo of Flies" from four and a half decades earlier through its title, the second song, "Dead Flies," once again keeps things firmly Cooper-esque in both style and subject matter. The album's shortest track at just two minutes and twenty-two seconds, the lyric cleverly addresses the yawing gulf between today's children and their parents: "Your sister's high on angel dust and so's your porno brother. And your phone knows more about you than your daddy or your mother." Meanwhile, the way that the lines are delivered and the manner of their rhyming bring back memories of "Generation Landslide" from *Billion Dollar Babies*. Cooper has confirmed that, for him, "Dead Flies" represents an addendum to that much earlier song, updated to address today's plethora of false prophets and cults and their ever-emptier promises.

The unrelentingly hard rocking "Fireball" is next up, and it's an apocalyptic song of Dennis Dunaway origin on which he, appropriately, also plays bass. The song has a clever twist: the original apocalyptic scenario of an approaching meteor witnessed by the song's central character is at first purported to be just a dream when he wakes in a cold sweat. However, going to the window to take in some fresh air, he once again sees a fireball approaching in the sky. This time, though, it's for real. Whether it is the subject matter, the pairing of Cooper and Dunaway, the vocal styling, or the (intrinsically linked) mastery of Bob Ezrin at the controls, this track is vintage Cooper and wouldn't have been out of place on *Muscle of Love*.

In the fourth track, "Paranoiac Personality," the usually (understandably) decried affliction of paranoia is given a typical Cooper twist and turned on its head. In Cooper's hands the protagonist with the "paranoiac personality" not only admits to his condition, but seemingly both likes and embraces it. Further, he exposes a universal truth with his accusation that "Everybody's got something hiding in the back of their mind." The song leaves the out-and-out rock of "Fireball" behind and instead offers the listener a groove-based and infectious bass-driven experience that is in keeping with the furtive subject matter while also reminiscent of the creepy vibe of "The Black Widow" from the 1975 *Welcome to My Nightmare* album.

"Fallen in Love," according to Alice's track-by-track interview released by his record company, is "a classic 'No More Mr Nice Guy' kind of song." It is also typically witty, with the full title line expanding to "I've fallen in love and I can't get up." Immediately apparent during the writing process that the song was in the style of ZZ Top with its "Tush"-like boogie groove, Billy Gibbons was then recruited to grace the track with his distinctive style. And it works. The second verse brings Cooper's humorous talent for self-referencing to the fore, with every line providing a reference to previous work, from being a "Billion Dollar Baby [from the album of the same name] in a diamond dress," to a "dirty Desperado [song from *Killer*] and a steaming mess," followed by "She Drives Me Nervous " [referencing "You Drive Me Nervous," also from *Killer*] to "a dirty cup of Poison [the hit single from *Trash*] that I can't refuse."

Like a hard rock homage to "The Devil Went Down to Georgia" by the Charlie Daniels Band, the following "Dynamite Road" has a frenetic behind-the-wheel quality that makes it the perfect driving song. The lyrics and tempo conjure in the listener's mind an automobile race against the devil; cars going hell-for-leather down a deserted highway in a race to the death. Alice and his band, in his "tricked-out Cadillac," lose the duel and end up forced off the road and crashing. Alice wakes up at the end of the song as the only survivor, but with typical Cooper black humor, his thoughts turn not to his deceased comrades-in-arms but instead to the demise of his beautiful car: "Man, I loved that car to death." Based on a real location in Arizona, "Dynamite Road" is an instant, breathless, petrol-head classic of a song.

The seventh track on *Paranormal* is "Private Public Breakdown," and describes the public madness of a zealot protagonist who is anything but normal. The twist in this scenario, rarely visited within rock music, is that while he knows he is not normal, rather than being defensive or feeling ostracized because of it, he instead relishes his status of insanity. Over a stomping, fat, 4/4 rock beat, his claims to be "the savior resurrected" who can float "above the ground" seem oddly acceptable, along with his self-deluded faith-healer talents offered to the listener in his parting lines: "And I assure you that, given time, I can cure you."

The misguided but religious-leaning subject matter of "Private Public Breakdown" segues nicely into the next track, "Holy Water." Virtually an Alice Cooper take on "When the Saints Go Marching In," it stakes a claim as the album's most innovative track in the way it merges hard rock, gospel, and faux rap, and with the unlikely but entirely Cooper-esque highlight of a walking cane tapping on the ground throughout the first verse in celebratory rhythmic accompaniment. Alice' faith is laid as bare here as it ever has been in lines such as "Kiss the devil goodbye" and "Raise your eyes to the Lord above." Triumphant and saber-rattling in its religious fervor, the sing-along choir choruses and fanfare banks of brass give the song a congregational flavor.

For an artist who has benefited greatly from being associated with creepy crawlies, with things that go bump in the night, and with multiple horror allusions of many kinds, "Rats" seems like a perfect song title. Creating an instant association with "Road Rats" of *Lace and Whiskey* (1977), the much-maligned rodent here sits easily among the spiders and snakes of Cooper history. Also sitting comfortably for longtime Cooper fans is the knowledge that all three surviving members of the original Alice Cooper band also play on the track. Despite the opening sound effects of hordes of squeaking rats that occupy the track until the instruments kick in—it sounds like a scene from the 1971 horror movie, *Willard*—these rats are all too human, and the word is used analogously to describe the unstable, dangerous dregs of society who deal in "death, terror and hate" and who are "coming for you." This paranoid, frantic, and unrelenting track refuses to allow the listener any comfort, and its central message of "give the rats what they want" is a disturbing commentary on the times we live in.

"The Sound of A" occupies the final position on disc one of *Paranormal*, and its spacey psychedelic vibe offers a fine—if very different—bookend to the glam metal edge of the album's opening title track. A great story accompanies "The Sound Of A"; brought to the *Paranormal* pool of songs by Dennis Dunaway, it was written by Alice no less than fifty years earlier back in 1967. Further, according to Dunaway, it was the first song Alice ever wrote; something the man himself had forgotten.[3] Despite being brought back to life and reworked for 2017 sensibilities, the era in which it was written permeates the track, with its slow build and almost hallucinogenic freak-out qualities toward the end along with Alice's dreamlike vocal sonority. Just what the song is about is less clear, however. "The Sound of A" could be the sound of Alice Cooper; "Meaningless noise is everybody's toys," but there is no clear confirmation of this and thus the lyric is ambiguous enough for listeners to read into it whatever they wish. How very psychedelic. Fifty years in the making is a long gestation for a rock song. But thank goodness it finally made it.

Disc two begins with the Alice Cooper tongue firmly embedded in his cheek. America's most famously notorious singer here claims more than just a girl's name. In "Genuine American Girl" he purports to be the real deal in a funny, yet spiky and perceptive, sendup of beauty-by-facsimile, reducing the all-American girl stereotype to a virtual Stepford wife. But humor abounds, and nowhere more so than in the obvious allusions to silver screen star and pop culture icon, Mae West: "Hey there, big boy. Why don't you come up and see me sometime," sings Alice, and the listener can just *see* him batting his eyelids and puckering up his sneering lips in his best rendition of come-hither allure. In this long-awaited return to the original Cooper band fold—all three surviving members play on this track and the next—it is impossible to not to feel nostalgic, and surely this must have been especially true for Cooper, Dunaway, Bruce, and Smith in the studio during the recording process. If the song itself is fairly perfunctory retro rock 'n' roll, it doesn't matter one jot as the sound of Alice's sneering, teasing, tormenting voice atop the efforts of Cortez High School's finest graduates washes over you.

"You and All of Your Friends" is the twelfth and final new song on the album, the remaining six tracks on disc two being live recordings of classic tracks from Cooper history. One of the strongest songs on the album, "You and All of Your Friends" punches like a heavyweight throughout its fleeting two-and-a-half minutes. Part celebration, part anthem, part warning, and constantly in-your-face, it has no obvious target for its fist-pumping rallying call. It could be a commentary on today's seemingly omnipresent terrorism, another generational protest against what has gone before, or triumphant recognition of the longevity of Alice Cooper and crew who are still doing it with such class after so many decades have passed, during which so many other rock stars and pretenders to the throne have fallen by the wayside: "'Cause we'll be dancing on your graves." Either way, whatever one makes of it, "You and All of Your Friends" ensures that the collection of original songs on *Paranormal* ends in style.

Of the remaining six live tracks, all recorded in May 2016 at a concert in Columbus, Ohio, and each and every one a Cooper classic, one can only sit back and enjoy the power and precision of the fine ensemble of musicians that Alice performs with today. In their hands every one of these masterpiece songs pays testament to the adrenaline rush of witnessing an Alice Cooper live show. Together they comprise a superb and sublime addition to *Paranormal*.

In summation, *Paranormal*, the twenty-seventh album in the Alice Cooper catalog, contains all of the elements that have made him the hugely successful artist that he continues to be. Humor, horror, quirkiness, and a readiness to treat musical styles as playthings are all in evidence through the course of the album, while the nostalgic touch provided by the original band's reunion puts the cream on the top. For anyone looking to develop a deeper understanding of Alice Cooper's work through guided listening, as is the intention of this book series, *Paranormal* is an essential listening experience. Alice himself provides a candidly apt closing description:

> This album is like the sideshow at a circus. It's a little creepy. There's a three-headed monkey and the snake woman, but you're intrigued. That's where Alice lives, and it's been the place to go for 50 years.[4]

POSTSCRIPT

Alice Cooper *supporting* Mötley Crüe on the band's "All Bad Things Must Come to an End" farewell global tour? That never really seemed quite right from the moment you'd heard about it, did it? Shouldn't the pecking order have been the other way around? And yet one must deservedly salute Mötley Crüe for: a) their courage in inviting the performer who'd given birth to the glam metal genre in which they had made their fortune to accompany them on their global farewell tour, and b) the obvious tipping-of-the-hat respect for Alice Cooper shown by that invitation. So, regardless of the dubious order of billing, bring on the show!

And so on May 9, 2015, you joined the hordes of excited and expectant metal fans filing through the turnstiles of Auckland's Vector Arena on a cool, late autumn evening. Resplendent in the uniform of glam metal, images of both Alice Cooper and the Crüe were displayed on numerous T-shirts, badges, leather jackets, and denim jackets throughout the crowd, while the likes of Guns N' Roses, KISS, Skid Row, and others ensured that the wider pack of metal merchants were also represented. Some fans sported clothing or adornments showing allegiance to both Alice Cooper and Mötley Crüe. In addition to yourself, many Cooper fans sported tarantula makeup around the eyes. The only fragment of ambiguity on the scene was the top hats worn without any other obvious attribution. Was it a Cooper fan beneath it, adopting one of Alice's signature adornments, or a Crüe fan paying homage to Mick Mars, who also often wore one as well? But, really, it didn't matter. The occasional bit of playful banter aside, the crowd was not in the least bit combative and most had turned up simply expecting a brilliant show from two American giants, acknowledging the brilliance of both acts.

Local New Zealand metal act Devilskin begin the show and get a warm enough welcome; the politely enthusiastic sort of response that lower tier support acts must surely dream of getting should they get such a break and find themselves supporting rock top-shelf legends. They sweat, they try hard, they're pretty good. But once they leave the stage, the tension among the crowd ramps up considerably. A huge banner featuring a close-up shot of Alice Cooper's eyes with their iconic tarantula makeup, taken from the album cover of *The Eyes of Alice Cooper*, drops down across the front of the stage to cover the changing over of acts. The break is mercifully short, and from the moment the house lights drop and the banner follows suit, the red-and-black pinstriped, cane-wielding Alice and his sublime band are on stage, giving 110 percent to "No More Mr. Nice Guy," and the crowd goes crazy. From that moment onward during the all-too-short, fourteen-song hit-laden set, the energy level never drops once and the ever-changing rock spectacle unfolding before you wows the capacity crowd at the arena. The set list is weighted toward the 1970s, perhaps in a purposeful ploy to leave the 1980s and beyond to his understudies, and this suits original, career-long fans such as yourself just fine. Nevertheless, later songs such as "Feed My Frankenstein," "Dirty Diamonds" and most particularly "Poison" bring the house down. These are clearly the songs that appeal the most to the Mötley Crüe fans, being produced in the same era as the music of their heroes. During "Feed My Frankenstein," Alice—clad in his white, bloodstained operating theater gown–is spectacularly executed by electrocution, signaling the appearance of a gigantic Frankenstein figure that strides across the stage, looming over the musicians and leering at the audience. This is rock theater writ large and your howls of approval, along with those of the rest of the crowd, stand testament to its impact upon the senses. Where else would you ever see such a thing, but at an Alice Cooper concert?

The hits come thick and fast and back-to-back, a salient reminder to you and everyone in the venue of just how much of a legacy the artist has assembled over the five decades of his reign. Hired-gun guitarist Nita Strauss quickly establishes herself as a crowd favorite and prime Cooper sidekick, while choreographed moves and interplay between band members designed to cover the main man's costume changes are carried out with theatrical flair and slick timing. The Alice Cooper arena rock theater machine runs like clockwork. For a fan in his fifties, the late-set trio of "Ballad of Dwight Fry," "Killer," and "I Love the Dead" is worth your price of admission alone, while the (expected) finale/encore of "School's Out" has the entire Vector Arena crowd, Cooper and Crüe fans alike, in something approaching ecstasy. It is party time in Auckland, and in the time-honored ritual of Alice Cooper finales, the balloons and bubbles from the stage are welcomed with open arms by the euphoric crowd.

All too soon it's all over, the Coop has left the stage and the house lights come up again. Weirdly, however, for the legions of mind-blown Cooper fans, the wider show is not over and the stage gets reset for Mötley Crüe. Here and there small gaps in the seated areas appear, as those fans who'd come purely for the "support act" made their way home, more than happy.

When the headliners take to the stage, their fans erupt. As a Cooper fan, you sit back and take in the show with enjoyment but without the same engagement, somewhat detached but still appreciative of hearing some fine glam metal performed live in the flesh by America's finest. But one thing becomes clear, and it's not just sour grapes because Alice was not at the top of the bill. Whereas the Alice Cooper set was wall-to-wall hits, in the Mötley Crüe set there is filler. The hits are spread out strategically. There's "Girls, Girls Girls" . . . there's "Dr Feelgood," and so on, with lesser quality songs interspersed to fill the nineteen-song set. The ballad "Home Sweet Home" is the surprising choice of encore, leaving the crowd a little bemused. And then the biggest glam metal event to hit Auckland—perhaps ever—is truly over. You and the rest of the fans file out, and a buzz surrounds the place. You can't help but hear the post-mortems of other punters chatting as they queue to leave, and the consensus matches your own. Alice Cooper has killed it. Mötley Crüe were good, and what a privilege to see them in New Zealand on their first and last trip to our shores. But the old master, Alice Cooper, won the night. The old showman had reigned supreme.

Even the critics got it right:

> Alice Cooper's always been in on the joke. The Vincent Price of hard rock, he revels in the schlock. And yes, there are all the nightmare

visuals you'd expect, including roadies in skeleton onesies. But behind the vaudeville is driving, straight-ahead rock. He and his five-
piece band—notably precise and tasteful guitar virtuoso Nita
Strauss—play songs that span his career. They open with "No More
Mr. Nice Guy"; the audience knows every word and they're screaming along. Even at 67, Cooper still prowls the stage like a teenager. . . . Although the set draws somewhat from earlier albums, it's his
harder-edged later material that really connects—"Poison," in particular, stirs a loud reaction, even if his vocals falter somewhat. Things
reach a peak during "Feed My Frankenstein," where he dons a
bloodied surgeon's robe and gas mask, disappearing behind an operating table, only to be replaced by a giant, costumed version of Frankenstein's monster. His set wraps up with a raucous sing-along to
"School's Out" while bubble machines fill the stage and giant balloons are passed around the crowd.[1]

It can't be easy following Alice Cooper onto the stage—especially
when an executioner has just pashed his freshly severed head. That's
not all that made the shock rocker a tough act to follow during
Saturday night's opening stint for Motley Crue. . . . It was pure
gothic theatre, with Cooper delivering songs like "Poison" and "Welcome to My Nightmare" alongside shopping trolleys full of dolls
parts and band mates straight out of a horror film. When he closed
with "School's Out," as he stabbed giant balloons with a hand knife
while bubbles blew over his head, it was a reminder that Cooper did
all of this before Marilyn Manson and Slipknot—and he's still doing
it better. . . . Motley Crue's bare boned stage show didn't come close
to matching Cooper's.[2]

Set List

The Underture
Department of Youth
No More Mr. Nice Guy
Under My Wheels
I'm Eighteen
Billion Dollar Babies
Poison
Dirty Diamonds
Welcome to My Nightmare
Feed My Frankenstein

Ballad of Dwight Fry
Killer
I Love the Dead
School's Out

NOTES

INTRODUCTION

1. The two artists find common ground in their love of surrealism, Dada, and art-house film.

2. Alice Cooper, *Alice Cooper: Golf Monster* (New York: Crown Publishers, 2007), 99.

3. Interview with Pitch Black, 2000, http://www.horrorgarage.com/horror/interview-alice-cooper.php.

4. Cooper, *Alice Cooper: Golf Monster*, 240.

5. It's pleasing, for instance, to see Cindy Neal get the recognition she richly deserves for the ahead-of-their-time costumes she created for the band that added so much to their all-important point of difference.

I. NEW FREAKS ON THE BLOCK

1. Dennis Dunaway, *Snakes! Guillotines! Electric Chairs!* (New York: St. Martin's Press, 2015), 79.

2. THE HALCYON YEARS OF THE ALICE COOPER BAND

1. Alice Cooper, *Alice Cooper: Golf Monster* (New York: Crown Publishers, 2007), 82.

2. Cooper, *Alice Cooper: Golf Monster*, 82.

3. Cooper, *Alice Cooper: Golf Monster*, 81.

4. Michael Bruce, *No More Mr Nice Guy: The Inside Story of the Alice Cooper Group* (London: SAF Publishing, 2000), 56.

5. Quoted in Dave Thompson, *Alice Cooper: Welcome to My Nightmare* (London: Omnibus Press, 2012), 95.

6. Lester Bangs, "Killer," *Rolling Stone*, January 6, 1972.

7. Bruce, *No More Mr Nice Guy*, 67.

8. Cooper, *Alice Cooper: Golf Monster*, 95.

9. Cooper, *Alice Cooper: Golf Monster*, 96.

10. Bruce, *No More Mr Nice Guy*, 71.

11. Cooper, *Alice Cooper: Golf Monster*, 99.

12. Cooper, *Alice Cooper: Golf Monster*, 100.

13. Bruce, *No More Mr Nice Guy*, 91.

14. Bruce, *No More Mr Nice Guy*, 91.

15. Cooper, *Alice Cooper: Golf Monster*, 116.

16. Bruce, *No More Mr Nice Guy*, 106.

17. Bruce, *No More Mr Nice Guy*, 104.

18. Bruce, *No More Mr Nice Guy*, 104.

19. Bruce, *No More Mr Nice Guy*, 106.

20. Quoted in Thompson, *Alice Cooper: Welcome to My Nightmare*, 156.

21. Thompson, *Alice Cooper: Welcome to My Nightmare*, 156.

22. Quoted in Thompson, *Alice Cooper: Welcome to My Nightmare*, 158.

23. Kim Fowley, "Alice Cooper: *Muscle of Love*," *Phonograph Record*, January 1974.

24. Thompson, *Alice Cooper: Welcome to My Nightmare*, 161.

25. Bruce, *No More Mr Nice Guy*, 111.

26. Bruce, *No More Mr Nice Guy*, 113.

3. ALICE DREAMS ALONE

1. Charles Shaar Murray, *New Musical Express*, February 22, 1975.

2. Bruce quoted in Ed McCormack, "No More Mr. Horror Show Droog: School's Out for Alice Cooper . . . But Has He Reformed?" *Rolling Stone*, July 31, 1975.

3. Alice Cooper, *Alice Cooper: Golf Monster* (New York: Crown Publishers, 2007), 122.

4. CONFESSIONS FROM THE HEART OF THE MONSTER

1. Dave Thompson, *Alice Cooper: Welcome to My Nightmare* (London: Omnibus Press, 2012), 183.
2. Thompson, *Alice Cooper: Welcome to My Nightmare*, 189.
3. Mitchell Schneider, "Lace and Whiskey Review," *Circus*, July 21, 1977.
4. Thompson, *Alice Cooper: Welcome to My Nightmare*, 189.
5. Quoted in Thompson, *Alice Cooper: Welcome to My Nightmare*, 189.

5. THE DEMISE OF ALICE COOPER

1. Dale Sherman, *The Illustrated Collector's Guide to Alice Cooper* (Ontario: Collector's Guide Publishing, 1999), 140.
2. Dennis Dunaway and Chris Hodenfield, *Snakes! Guillotines! Electric Chairs!: My Adventures in the Alice Cooper Group* (New York: St. Martin's Press, 2015), 73.
3. Dave Thompson, *Alice Cooper: Welcome to My Nightmare* (London: Omnibus Press, 2012), 210.
4. Sherman, *The Illustrated Collector's Guide to Alice Cooper*, 147.
5. Pete Makowski, "I am the Future," *Kerrang!*, April 7, 1983.
6. Thompson, *Alice Cooper: Welcome to My Nightmare*, 225.

6. THE WORM THAT TURNED

1. Alice Cooper, *Alice Cooper: Golf Monster* (New York: Crown Publishers, 2007), 183.
2. Anonymous, "Crawl to be Kind," in *Kerrang!*, October 16, 1986.
3. Quoted in Edgar Klusener, "'I Wanna Be Elected!'—On Tour with Alice Cooper," *Metal Hammer*, March 28, 1988.
4. Quoted in Klusener, "'I Wanna Be Elected!'"
5. Quoted in Dave Dickson, "Shriek of the Mutilated," in *Kerrang!*, October 24, 1987.
6. Quoted in Dickson, "Shriek of the Mutilated."
7. Cooper, *Alice Cooper: Golf Monster*, 206.
8. Anonymous, "Alice Cooper: *Trash*," *Circus*, August 1989.
9. Nicholas Pegg, *The Complete David Bowie* (London: Reynolds & Hearn, 2002), 277.

7. TAKING STOCK AGAIN IN THE 1990s

1. Dave Thompson, *Welcome to My Nightmare: The Alice Cooper Story* (London: Omnibus Press, 2012), 250.

8. "THE COOP," POST-MILLENNIUM

1. Quoted in Joshua Sindell, "Brutally Honest," *Metal Edge*, October 2000.
2. Alice Cooper quoted in Thomas Bond, "Delivery from Evil," *Get Out*, May 18, 2000.
3. Alice Cooper quoted in Sindell, "Brutally Honest."
4. *Diamond Dogs* is also one of Marilyn Manson's favorite albums, and he has often claimed it had a major influence on him.
5. Quoted in Brian G, "Chasing the Dragon," *Get Rhythm*, November 2001.
6. Quoted in Brian G, "Chasing the Dragon."
7. Quoted in Brian G, "Chasing the Dragon."

9. THE RESURRECTION

1. Quoted in Aaron Von Lupton, "Still Creepin' While You're Sleepin'," *Rue Morgue*, September 2011.
2. Quoted in Daniel Kreps, "Alice Cooper Announces New Album 'Paranormal,'" *Rolling Stone*, June 12, 2017.
3. Alice Cooper "Paranormal": Track by Track Interview, "The Sound of A," YouTube, August 5, 2017, https://www.youtube.com/watch?v=tiLTvl4U4lI.
4. Alice Cooper, "Paranormal Track by Track Interview," Blabbermouth.net, August 3, 2017, http://www.blabbermouth.net/news/alice-cooper-paranormal-track-by-track-interview/.

POSTSCRIPT

1. James Cardno, "The Prince of Darkness Rises," Stuff, May 10, 2015, http://www.stuff.co.nz/entertainment/music/gig-reviews/68418295/the-prince-of-darkness-rises.

2. Chris Schultz, "Concert Review: Motley Crue and Alice Cooper," *New Zealand Herald*, May 10, 2015.

SELECTED LISTENING

Pretties for You, released June 30, 1969, Straight Records.
Easy Action, released March 27, 1970, Straight Records.
Love It to Death, released March 8, 1971, Straight Records and Warner Brothers Records.
Killer, released November 27, 1971, Warner Brothers Records.
School's Out, released June 1972, Warner Brothers Records.
Billion Dollar Babies, released February 25, 1973, Warner Brothers Records.
Muscle of Love, released November 20, 1973, Warner Brothers Records.
Welcome to My Nightmare, released March 11, 1975, Atlantic Records.
Alice Cooper Goes to Hell, released June 25, 1976, Warner Brothers Records.
Lace and Whiskey, released April 29, 1977, Warner Brothers Records.
From the Inside, released November 17, 1978, Warner Brothers Records.
Flush the Fashion, released April 28, 1980, Warner Brothers Records.
Special Forces, released September 1, 1981, Warner Brothers Records.
Zipper Catches Skin, released August 25, 1982, Warner Brothers Records.
DaDa, released September 28, 1983, Warner Brothers Records.
Constrictor, released September 22, 1986, MCA Records.
Raise Your Fist and Yell, released September 28, 1987, MCA Records.
Trash, released July 25, 1989, Epic Records.
Hey Stoopid, released July 2, 1991, Epic Records.
The Last Temptation, released July 12, 1994, Epic Records.
Brutal Planet, released June 6, 2000, Spitfire Records.
Dragontown, released September 18, 2001, Spitfire Records.
The Eyes of Alice Cooper, released September 23, 2003, Spitfire Records.
Dirty Diamonds, released July 4, 2005, Spitfire Records.
Along Came a Spider, released July 29, 2008, Steamhammer Records.
Welcome 2 My Nightmare, released September 13, 2011, Universal Music Enterprises.
Paranormal, released July 28, 2017, earMusic/Sony Music.

INDEX

ABOUT THE AUTHOR

Ian Chapman, PhD, is an author, performer, and head of the Performing Arts degree program at the University of Otago, Dunedin, located deep in the South Island of his native New Zealand. *Experiencing Alice Cooper: A Listener's Companion* is his seventh book. He specializes in writing books about theatrical rock, most particularly glam rock of the 1970s, and the wider culture of that colorful decade. Chapman has also written individual articles and book chapters on glam rock—most particularly the work of David Bowie—for many academic and popular publications both in New Zealand and internationally, and has given papers at many international musicology conferences. The development of performance personas, such as those of Alice Cooper and David Bowie especially, are the focus of his ongoing interdisciplinary research, and he puts his findings into practice in both his university teaching and his own on-stage performances, frequently in the guise of his own interdisciplinary performance persona, Dr Glam.

A professional vocalist, drummer, and guitarist for two decades prior to entering academia, Chapman brings a "real-world" perspective to his work within both academic and popular contexts, and enjoys writing most of all when straddling these two often disparate (unnecessarily so, in his view) worlds. His conference presentations always include a live-performance component, and for this reason he is a popular speaker and presenter in both the academic and public arenas.